A Social Experiment in Program Administration

A Social Experiment in Program Administration

The Housing Allowance Administrative Agency Experiment

William L. Hamilton

Abt Books
Cambridge, Massachusetts

Library of Congress Catalog Card Number 79-87501

© Abt Associates Inc., 1979

Printed in the United States of America

ISBN: 0-89011-533-8

To Barbara

Contents

Appendices

Tables and Figures

Acknowledgments

This book reflects the work of many people. The most direct contributions come from Administrative Agency Experiment staff who prepared the experiment's major reports to the Department of Housing and Urban Development, particularly David Budding, Donald Dickson, William Holshouser, Jean MacMillan and Charles Maloy. Chapters 2 through 6 make heavy use of their ideas, analyses and presentations, and indeed the conduct of the research as a whole was strongly influenced by their efforts.

Many additional members of the experiment's staff carried out analyses which were used in preparing the discussion here. These include Frederick Temple, Rex Warland, Charles White, Patrick Madden, Bradford Wild, Marian Wolfe, Michael Trend, Ulrich Ernst, Terry Lane, Judith Feins, Alvin Jacobson, Susan Ferguson, Marda Mayo, Howard Chernick, Jonathon Silberman, and Bradford Smith.

The design and conduct of the Administrative Agency Experiment involved the efforts of people far too numerous to name here, but a few extraordinary contributions must be acknowledged. Walter Stellwagen, director of the experiment in its initial stages, was in large part responsible for designing the research. As the principal technical reviewer in later stages, he contributed greatly to the structure and the quality of the analyses that were performed. Barbara Sampson deserves much credit for managing a most unwieldy project, both as Project Director at one stage of the experiment and subsequently as Area Manager. Additional important contributions to managing the project were made by Franklin Smith, who also served as Project Director for one phase of the experiment, and by Helen Bakeman and Grover Gregory, who served as Deputy Project Directors. Mireille Leger-Ernst contributed throughout the duration of the experiment to its design, to the translation of the design into operating procedures and data collection instruments, and to structuring and maintaining the integrity of an enormous, complicated data base.

Without the support and guidance of personnel in the Department of Housing and Urban Development, the experiment could never have been undertaken or successfully completed. Special recognition is due to the efforts of Jerry Fitts, Terrence Connell, Evelyn Glatt, and Yvonne Treadwell in the Office of Policy Development and Research.

Finally, thanks are due to Rex Warland and Barbara Sampson, who reviewed the manuscript and provided much substantive assistance and moral support, and to Billie Renos, who produced the manuscript with her customary incredible efficiency.

1

Introduction to the Administrative Agency Experiment

The Housing Allowance Administrative Agency Experiment (AAE) was a social experiment that used a nonexperimental research design to study the way that local agencies might administer a housing allowance program. These characteristics—the social experiment, the administrative focus, the nonexperimental design—make the AAE an unusual entry in the policy research ledger.

Social experiments are no longer the novelty they were a decade ago —or even in 1972, when the housing allowance experiments began—but they are still unusual in the federal policy process. Historically social programs have been implemented first and studied later, if at all. The advent of social experimentation has meant that some program ideas have been tested before full-scale implementation, to allow research conclusions to influence the decision about whether or how to implement the program.

There is no clear definition of a social experiment, but the projects bearing that label generally share four characteristics.[1] They are prospective; they examine policy alternatives that might be adopted rather than those already in operation. They are of a substantial size, generally involving more than a thousand beneficiaries. They include program features that respond explicitly to a research agenda, in contrast to the traditional pilot programs which are small-scale versions of the intended programs. Finally the social experiments are characterized by unusually intensive data collection and analysis.

The Administrative Agency Experiment had all these characteristics. The policy under consideration was the housing allowance, in which the government would give low-income families a monthly check to help them obtain adequate housing. This concept was debated in the Congress for several years, and elements of it were subsequently incorporated in the Section 8 rent subsidy program. The AAE, one of three experiments on housing allowances, involved nearly six thousand beneficiary families. Among the program features chosen to meet research objectives were the selection of several kinds of local agencies (public housing authorities, welfare agencies) to administer the program and guidelines that encouraged agencies to differ in their administrative procedures. The intensive data collection effort produced thirty-six separate computerized data files containing more than ninety thousand individual forms and a narrative data base resulting from a year's on-site observation of eight agencies.

The Administrative Agency Experiment differs from most other social experiments in two respects: the research questions focused on program administration, and the research design did not fit the usual experimental mold. Most social experiments have focused on the nature of the benefits (for example, grant levels and the grant computation formula) and the effect of the benefits on the recipients. Administrative questions have seldom been included in the research design; indeed several of the experimental programs have been administered by research contractors to preclude any distorting effect that might arise from administrative variations. For the AAE, in contrast, administrative variation was the heart of the project. The central purpose was to identify alternative means by which local agencies might carry out necessary administrative functions, especially alternatives that might be susceptible to regulation at the national level, and to evaluate the effectiveness and costs of the alternatives.

In pursuit of this research objective the AAE used a nonexperimental design. The eight agencies operating the test program had a relatively free rein (and even considerable encouragement) to devise their own procedures. The general trend in social experimentation, in contrast, has been to use control groups and systematic variation of program features wherever possible and to minimize the sources of uncontrolled variation. Considerable controversy surrounded the decision to adopt a nonexperimental design in the AAE, and the design had in fact both major strengths and substantial weaknesses, as described in subsequent chapters.

The purpose of this book is to provide for the general reader an overview of the Administrative Agency Experiment. It presents a brief description of the background and structure of the experiment and discusses the findings emerging from the main research areas. The reader concerned about the effect of administrative practice on the costs and outcomes of social programs should find at least suggestive information and hypotheses worth testing in the context of housing, welfare and other social programs. The reader interested in the process of social experimentation and related research should gain a general understanding of the topics that were investigated and the methodologies employed. More detail on substance and methodology can be found in the design and analytic reports of the experiment, which provided the raw material for this book and which are referenced throughout.

HISTORY

The housing allowance concept has been debated for more than four decades. Rent certificates were considered but rejected in formulating the Housing Act of 1937, in the Taft Subcommittee hearings on postwar housing policy in 1944, in designing the Housing Act of 1949, and in the 1953 report by the President's Advisory Committee on Government Housing Policies and Programs. The Housing and Urban Development Act of 1965 added two programs—the rent supplement program and the Section 23 leased-housing programs—that moved in the direction of the housing allowance by giving beneficiaries more flexibility in choosing the places they could live and by making the value of the subsidy depend on a family's income.

In 1968 the President's Committee on Urban Housing (Kaiser Committee) argued in favor of the housing allowance and recommended that the government undertake an experiment to determine whether a housing allowance program would be feasible and worthwhile. The recommendations inspired preliminary analytic efforts, and small-scale demonstrations were conducted by the Model Cities agencies in Kansas City, Missouri, and Wilmington, Delaware. The 1970 Housing and Urban Development Act called for the Department of Housing and Urban Development (HUD) to carry out a major investigation of housing allowances; under this rubric HUD initiated the Experimental Housing Allowance Program (EHAP).

The Experimental Housing Allowance Program consisted of three major social experiments. The Demand Experiment was designed to examine the effects of alternative formulations of the housing allowance on the behavior of households offered an opportunity to participate. The Demand Experiment operated in Phoenix, Arizona, and Pittsburgh, Pennsylvania, and involved approximately twelve hundred experimental and five hundred control households in each city for a three-year period. The Supply Experiment was undertaken to study the effects of an allowance program on the housing market. Operating in Green Bay, Wisconsin, and South Bend, Indiana, this experiment was to provide subsidies on an open-enrollment basis and to collect experimental data for five years.[2] As of August 1977 the Supply Experiment was providing subsidies to about eighty-one hundred families. The Administrative Agency Experiment provided allowance payments for two years to as many as nine hundred families in eight locations. Research contractors were selected and began work on the three experiments in 1972; the Administrative Agency Experiment was completed in 1977, and work on the other two is continuing.

Of the three experiments, the Demand Experiment most closely followed the model of prior social experimentation, drawing heavily on the design of the income maintenance experiments. The Supply Experiment flowed naturally from the public debate, in which the possible inflationary effect of the allowance on rents had been a major issue.

The origin of the Administrative Agency Experiment is less clear. It was probably motivated in part by a belief that the Congress might enact a national housing allowance program well before results from the Demand and Supply experiments could be expected. (In fact, President Nixon announced in 1973 his administration's desire to implement such a program, beginning with a pilot program for the elderly. Had the political climate been different, a nonexperimental program might have been in operation by 1974.) An experiment that could start relatively quickly and be operated by public agencies rather than research contractors would offer a valuable base of experience if a national program had to be implemented quickly. The salience of administrative issues may also have been raised by adverse publicity alleging HUD mismanagement of public housing and similar publicity concerning the management of welfare programs.

DESIGN

HUD's basic approach to the experiment was to have a variety of agencies operate test programs of limited scale and duration. The allowance program was the same for all agencies and was the version considered most likely to be implemented. Housing allowances were to be computed under a "housing gap" formula: $P = C^* - 0.25Y$ where P is the monthly value of the allowance payment, C^* is the estimated "typical" cost for acceptable housing in the local market for a household of a given size, and Y is total household income less certain deductions (such as those for medical or work-related expenses). In effect the allowance payment would make up the difference between the amount a family was expected to have to spend for housing and one-fourth of the family income.[3] To qualify for payments, all participants would have to occupy housing that the agencies determined to be "decent, safe, and sanitary." Eligibility for the program was determined mainly on the basis of income and household size; home owners were excluded, as were one-person households and a few other categories such as full-time students and military personnel.

In addition to HUD and the local agencies, a central research contractor, Abt Associates, played a major role in the AAE experiment. The agencies were responsible for implementing the program. The research contractor was responsible for designing basic administrative records to ensure data comparability across locations, for collecting independent data on agency operations and participant experiences, and for analysis. Unlike research contractors in the Demand and Supply experiments, the AAE research contractor had no direct role in designing or conducting program operations.

HUD chose eight public agencies to operate the experimental program, in a selection process that emphasized diversity and competence. The diversity is suggested in table 1-1. HUD selected two agencies in each of four categories: local housing authorities (Salem, Tulsa), state agencies responsible for housing programs (Springfield, Peoria), welfare agencies (Bismarck, Durham), and county or metropolitan governments (San Bernardino, Jacksonville). The agencies were widely scattered geographically. On a population density spectrum they represented all but the most rural and the largest urban areas. They included areas with comparatively large and comparatively small poverty and minority populations and agencies with relatively good and relatively poor housing markets.

Only on the question of the agencies' management competence did HUD reject diversity. Regional HUD offices and other agencies were asked to nominate agencies with a record of management competence, agencies that would probably be able to administer a new program successfully.

Table 1-1.   Characteristics of the Eight AAE Sites

Location of Administrative Agency	Contracting Agency	Census region	Population of program area	Character of Site: Geographic character	Demographic Characteristics				Housing Market		
					Percentage of families below poverty	Percentage of minority	Eligible population (no. households)	Eligible households as percentage of total households	Percentage rental	Percentage lacking plumbing	Rental vacancy rate (%)
Salem, Ore.	Housing Authority of City of Salem	Pacific West	186,658	Metropolitan area	7.9	1.7	5,232	9	37.3	1.5	7.2
Springfield, Mass.	Commonwealth of Massachusetts Department of Community Affairs	New England	472,917	Metropolitan area (4 cities and 15 surrounding towns)	6.6	5.0	17,572	13	41.5	2.7	6.2
Peoria, Ill.	State of Illinois Dept. of Local Government Affairs Office of Housing and Buildings	East North Central	196,865	City of Peoria and Fulton County (rural) and Woodford County (rural)	5.9	6.3	5,235	10	30.9	3.0	4.5c
San Bernardino, Calif.	San Bernardino County Board of Supervisors	Pacific West	547,258	Valley portion of San Bernardino County (includes 10 incorporated cities and towns and an equal number of unincorporated places)	9.8	23.0a	19,745	12	36.4	.9	12.0
Bismarck, N.D.	Social Services Board of North Dakota	West North Central	104,187	Four rural counties (Burleigh, Morton, Stark, and Stutsman) each with one major city	11.8	.8	2,176	9	31.4	5.9b	8.1d
Jacksonville, Fla.	Jacksonville Department of Housing and Urban Development	South Atlantic	545,900	Metropolitan area (includes all of Duval County)	14.0	22.9	17,429	11	32.7	4.4	4.0c
Durham, N.C.	Durham County Department of Social Services	South Atlantic	132,681	Durham County (includes city of Durham as well as rural portion of county)	14.0	37.6	5,620	14	53.0	2.9	6.0
Tulsa, Okla.	Tulsa Housing Authority	West South Central	342,000	Metropolitan area	9.0	12.5	8,734	7	33.0	1.9	13.6

Source: Frederick T. Temple et al., *Third Annual Report of the Administrative Agency Experiment Evaluation* (Cambridge, Mass., Abt Associates, 1976).
aIncludes 16 percent "Persons of Spanish Language or Surname."
bMore recent housing studies of Bismarck indicate that the degree of substandardness in the city's housing is considerably lower than census figures for the full program area suggest.
cVacancy rates for Peoria and Jacksonville are adjusted for standardness (locally defined).
dVacancy rate for the city of Bismarck is 6.1 percent; for the full program area, 8.1 percent.

This criterion caused some debate at the time and has subsequently been criticized in a review of the experiments by the General Accounting Office. The problem is obvious: selecting on perceived competence should produce a bias in favor of "success," that is, a finding that the housing allowance program is administratively feasible. The counter-argument is that a nonexperimental program would probably be phased in slowly; the more competent and ambitious agencies would be the first to implement the program, and the others' chances of success would be enhanced by the experience of the first agencies. In the end two prag-matic concerns strongly influenced the decision to use the competence criterion. First, if there was soon to be a national program, information about successful operations would be more useful than information about failures. And second, learning anything from the experiment would depend on the agencies' producing reliable data. Selecting for competence was seen as the best means of satisfying both concerns.

A second controversial feature of the research design was the deci-sion to allow natural variation in administrative procedures rather than impose a systematic variation design. The research contractor and HUD prepared a set of program administration guidelines that identified the functions of the agencies and specified minimum requirements. For example, agencies had to certify the accuracy of information used to determine participants' eligibility and payment levels, and they were required at a minimum to obtain participants' signed statements attesting to the accuracy of information. Beyond the minimum, agencies were free to adopt almost whatever procedures they chose. Each agency proposed a budget and procedures to HUD in an initial operating plan. Most of these plans were accepted; in a few cases HUD urged an agency to alter procedures, mainly to keep the budgets within an acceptable range.

The natural variation design has some obvious disadvantages rela-tive to the systematic variation design. At worst, important options might not be tested. More realistically agencies might choose procedures in "packages" or in direct response to an environmental characteristic such as the housing market. Either pattern could make it impossible to separate the effects of two or more procedural choices or to separate administrative effects from the influence of the housing market.

There were two strong reasons for allowing natural variation. First, with only eight agencies a systematic variation design would have to be quite selective in the options tested, and there was no adequate theoret-ical or empirical basis for identifying the most important options. Second, HUD wanted some insight into the likely need for federal specifi-cation of local procedures. Would local agencies, left to their own devices, choose the procedures most appropriate to their situations? If the agency's behavior in the choice and development of procedures was to be studied, the research design had to avoid constraining that behavior. Closely related was the belief that a sound systematic variation design would need variations within as well as across agencies but that requiring an agency to carry out two procedures in parallel would be difficult and would lead to biased estimates of administrative costs. Ultimately, then, the nonexperimental design was implemented.

OPERATIONS

Intensive design work on the Administrative Agency Experiment began with the award of the research contract in the spring of 1972. Five years later, in the spring of 1977, the last analytic reports were published. Figure 1-1 outlines the experimental operations during that period.

Figure 1-1.   Timetable of the Administrative Agency Experiment

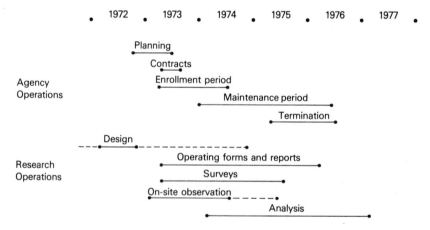

The eight agencies were selected in the summer of 1972, and each was awarded a three-month planning grant to develop an administrative design for operating a housing allowance program. HUD and the agencies signed contracts supporting operations of the experimental programs in the spring and summer of 1973. Once the contract was signed, each agency had approximately seven months in which to accept applications and enroll families for participation. An enrolled family had ninety days in which to demonstrate that it occupied or had acquired an acceptable housing unit. About ten months after signing their contracts, the agencies had begun making allowance payments to all families who qualified. Families could receive up to twenty-four months of allowance payments. When these payments ended, they could receive assistance under other housing programs (generally the Section 23 leased-housing program) if they were eligible and interested. Thus the agencies' responsibilities after the initial enrollment period were limited to providing payments and other required services for recipients and helping place them in other programs after two years of payments.

Although the basic research design for the Administrative Agency Experiment was developed in 1972, the development and modification of data collection instruments continued through 1974. The major data collection period coincided with the first two years of agency operations in 1973 and 1974; routine administrative data generated after that point were generally not included in the analytic data base. Analysis began when partial data became available early in 1974 and continued for about three years.

DATA

The data base resulting from the experiment is extensive. As table 1-2 shows, thirty-six separate data collection instruments were used and stored in computer files, with a combined total of more than ninety-two thousand individual records.

Operating forms were the most numerous. The research contractor designed the forms,[4] both to ensure comparability across agencies and to obtain a few items of information that would probably not have been captured simply for administrative purposes. The operating forms were routinely used by the agencies, for example, each applicant filled out an application form, although agencies supplemented some forms with worksheets or additional items to match their existing record systems. The agencies regularly shipped forms to the research contractor for entry in the computer files.

To complement the operating forms, the research contractor collected data for analytic purposes. The major efforts were a series of three surveys and housing evaluations conducted with a panel of participants. The surveys obtained information on households' background, current financial circumstances, housing history, attitudes toward their current housing and preferences for the future, and experiences in the program. For the housing evaluations the research contractor trained inspectors in

Table 1-2. AAE Data Base

Description	Number in Data Base
Operating Forms	
Application forms	15,399
Certification forms	8,787
Enrollment forms	8,095
Prepayment termination forms	2,330
Initial payment forms	5,756
Postpayment termination forms	3,579
Recertification forms	8,153
Payment change forms	8,958
Housing inspection forms	9,135
Monthly Financial Reports	240
Participant Surveys	
First (at enrollment)	1,272
Second (after 6 months)	878
Third (16 months after enrollment)	589
Housing Evaluations	
First (at enrollment)	1,151
Second (after 6 months)	858
Third (16 months after enrollment)	578
Former Participant Surveys	
Prepayment terminations	369
Postpayment terminations	216
Staff Survey	
First	169
Second	131
Third	105
Staff Background Data Forms	212
Special Study of Elderly Participants	
Survey	1,502
Housing evaluations	493
Special Study in Jacksonville	
Application forms	4,575
Selection forms	2,055
Certification forms	1,337
Enrollment forms	1,288
Initial payment forms	641
Termination forms	647
Inspection forms	771
Service representative forms	1,182
Counseling log forms	120
Inspection quality control	108
Preenrollment terminee survey	237
Enrollee survey	494
Total	92,410

Row groupings (left margin labels):
Provided by Agency — Operating Forms through Monthly Financial Reports.
Collected by Research Contractor — Participant Surveys through Housing evaluations (Special Study of Elderly Participants).
Provided by Agency — Special Study in Jacksonville: Application forms through Inspection forms.
Collected by Research Contractor — Service representative forms through Enrollee survey.

the use of a common evaluation instrument that described the physical condition of the dwelling unit and neighborhood. The survey and the housing evaluation were administered to the same sample of participants.

Although the quantitative data base was large, the size and nature of the nonquantitative data base were more unusual. The research contractor employed eight on-site observers, anthropologists in most cases, for about one year. They observed agency operations from the latter stages of the planning period through the completion of enrollments and transition into the maintenance period. The observers kept logs describing the structure and evolution of agency procedures for each of a designated set of agency functions (such as outreach, housing inspection, and making payments). They kept a narrative chronology of events as the programs developed and produced lengthier memoranda on topics of particular research interest at the individual agencies. The observers also collected agency plans, reports, and memoranda, and materials describing the local situation (for example, documents from local planning agencies) that might be useful in interpreting other data. The observers' accounts were summarized into a series of more structured documents for internal analytic use; this refined data base amounted to about eleven thousand pages.

Intense data collection is characteristic of social experiments, but the nonexperimental design of the AAE required an unusual breadth of information. The central research questions focused on the costs and effectiveness of alternative procedures, but the alternatives were not specified in advance. Careful on-site observation was necessary both to define the policy-relevant procedures and to develop hypotheses about their likely results. Quantitative data collection had to anticipate a wide range of possible hypotheses. Moreover because the research design lacked the experimental features that normally allow confident interpretation of the findings, such confidence had to be based on the availability of detailed data and multiple sources of information about the same outcome.

THE PARTICIPANTS

HUD set a target number of housing allowance recipients for each of the eight agencies. Six agencies were to serve nine hundred recipients each. The other two agencies, which were located in areas with smaller populations, had targets of four hundred (Bismarck) and five hundred

(Durham). The targets reflected upper limits on funding available for allowance payments. Because the agencies' administrative funding was contingent on the number of families served, the agencies treated targets as lower limits as well.[5]

But the target numbers, even though they were largely achieved, give a static picture of the number of families involved in the experiment. The agencies accepted applications only for a few months, but many more people applied than could receive benefits, partly because some households were ineligible and some chose not to participate. Figure 1–2 illustrates the steps that interested families had to take to become allowance recipients.

Apart from ineligibility and voluntary withdrawal, participation was constrained by two features of the AAE that differed from general income-assistance programs such as welfare. First, the number of participants was limited; thus agencies had to select some people and reject others. About a quarter of the applicants initially deemed eligible were not selected for participation. Second, enrollment in the program was only a conditional entitlement to benefits. Enrollees had to meet a housing quality requirement; they had ninety days after enrollment to demonstrate that their current dwelling unit met standards set by the agency or to lease a unit that did meet the standards. About 30 percent of households that enrolled in the program failed to receive allowances.

Enrollees in the housing allowance programs could qualify for benefits in three ways. First, if they were satisfied with their existing dwellings and wanted to stay there, they could request an inspection; if the units passed, the households could receive allowance payments immediately. Enrollees whose units failed the inspection (or who believed they would fail or who were not satisfied with the units) had two options. They could try to obtain the repairs or rehabilitation needed to bring the unit up to agency standards and then become allowance recipients. Alternatively they could find a different dwelling; if it passed inspection, they could become recipients when they moved into the unit.

Most families who qualified for payments had some change in housing: 45 percent moved to different units, and 12 percent obtained repairs to their preprogram units. The remaining 43 percent became allowance recipients in their original dwellings without repair or rehabilitation.

HUD required the agencies to attempt to serve a representative cross section of the local population eligible for the program. As a result, allowance recipients display a broad range of characteristics (figure 1–3). A "typical" participant household would be headed by a white female

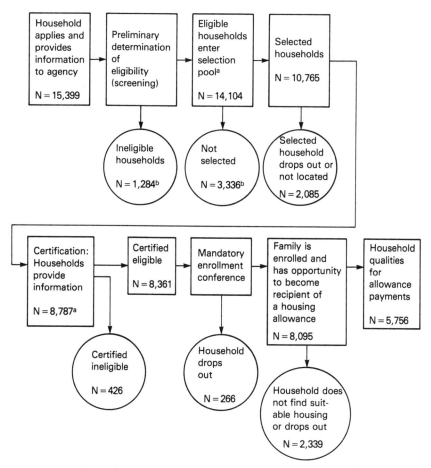

Figure 1-2.   Steps in Initial Participation in the AAE

Source: AAE application, enrollment, and certification forms; Agency selection records

[a]In some cases, mostly in Bismarck, certification took place before selection: a total of 107 households were certified eligible at various sites but were never selected.

[b]Missing cases: Eligibility of applicants, 11; selection, 3.

between the ages twenty-five and forty-four; the household's net income[6] would be between $1,000 and $3,000 per year, and the household would consist of three or four people. The profile in figure 1-3 did not vary dramatically by site. The most striking difference among the sites was

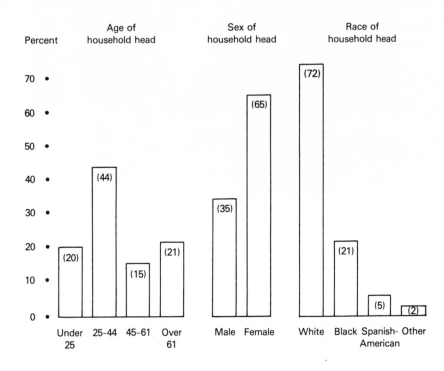

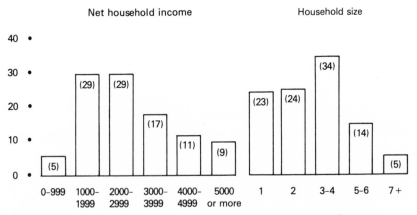

Figure 1–3. Characteristics of Households Receiving Housing Allowances

Source: AAE payment initiation forms

Data base: All households receiving at least one allowance payment (N=5,756)

the proportion of black and Spanish-American participants, which depended on the regional ethnic composition.

Once they qualified for payments, households could receive up to twenty-four months of allowances. Their income and eligibility status had to be reviewed after one year, and some participants contacted the agency to report income or household changes in the interim. Recipients were free to move at any time, but they could continue receiving allowances only if the new units met the program standards. After one year of participation only 10 percent of the initial recipients had voluntarily ceased to participate and another 12 percent had become ineligible for the program. Most households received the full 24 months of allowance payments.

The AAE participants and the agencies' procedures for dealing with them are the subject of the remainder of the book. The next five chapters discuss the five major areas of analysis of the experimental data.[7] Four concern specific administrative functions, in which the analysis attempted to determine the effectiveness and costs of alternative procedures. The fifth focuses on administrative costs, in which the dual objectives were to estimate the cost of administering a housing allowance program and to understand why costs vary. The last chapter presents some reflections on what was done and what might have been done in designing and analyzing the results of the experiment.

NOTES

1. See, for example, the characterization of the negative income tax experiment in Peter H. Rossi and Katherine C. Lyall, *Reforming Public Welfare* (New York: Russell Sage Foundation, 1976).

2. All three experiments involved a commitment to continue HUD assistance to families after the end of the experiment (provided that they continued to be eligible and to desire assistance).

3. A frequently used rule of thumb is that families can be expected to pay about one-fourth of their income for shelter. Residents of public housing cannot be required to pay more than one-quarter of their income for rent.

4. Exceptions to this rule were the inspection forms and some of the operating forms obtained in the special study of Jacksonville.

5. The Annual Contributions Contract specified that each agency would receive a fixed total amount of money for each family qualifying for pay-

ments. Part of the money covered the payment itself, and the remainder was to be used to defray administrative expenses. Agencies initially hired staff according to a plan (and budget) that assumed the full target number of recipients (and their concomitant contribution to administrative funding). Falling seriously short of the planned number of recipients could therefore mean that an agency would not have enough funds to meet its administrative expenses.

6. The amount on which payments were based, which subtracted certain deductions from total income.

7. Two topics touched on only briefly are the special studies of the elderly and of the Jacksonville program. The analysis of the elderly participants can be found in Marian F. Wolfe, William L. Hamilton, and W. G. Trend, *Elderly Participants in the Administrative Agency Experiment* (Cambridge, Mass.: Abt Associates, 1977). The special study of Jacksonville was commissioned because that agency was the only one that fell dramatically short of its target number. A special case study of the initial experience was requested and is presented in William L. Holshouser, Jr., *Report on Selected Aspects of the Jacksonville Housing Allowance Experiment* (Cambridge, Mass.: Abt Associates, 1976). HUD then allowed the agency to conduct a second enrollment period, which is analyzed and compared to the first in Marian F. Wolfe and William L. Hamilton, *Jacksonville: Administering a Housing Allowance Program in a Difficult Environment* (Cambridge, Mass.: Abt Associates, 1977).

2

Outreach and Participation

A social program can serve its intended beneficiaries only if they know it exists. *Outreach* is the process of publicizing a program so eligible people will apply for its benefits. Outreach, as the principal mechanism by which program administrators can influence participation, is a virtually universal component of social programs. Even well-established, widely known programs routinely communicate with other social agencies that might refer clients, and staff members talk to community groups about the program's benefits and regulations. New programs often undertake more active outreach campaigns. Some make direct contact with potentially eligible persons, some take out paid advertisements, most seek news coverage in newspapers and the broadcast media. A broad range of outreach techniques is available to the program administrator. And the concern about outreach sometimes goes beyond the program administrator. In 1974 a federal court in Minnesota ruled that state outreach efforts for the Food Stamps program were inadequate to make benefits available as the legislation intended.

Despite the need for administrative decisions about outreach, research relating participation rates to the nature and extent of outreach is sparse. Studies of participation in public programs have examined differences in participation rates among population subgroups.[1] A few have discussed obstacles to participation, such as ignorance about programs,[2]

Most of the material in this chapter is taken from Jean MacMillan and William L. Hamilton, *Outreach: Generating Applications in the Administrative Agency Experiment* (Cambridge, Mass.: Abt Associates, 1977).

17

lack of interest,[3] or the stigma associated with accepting public assistance.[4] However, none has systematically examined alternative outreach responses to these obstacles. Market research, mass media research, and studies of communication and attitude change deal with issues somewhat analogous to outreach, but they rarely deal with low-income populations and almost never with the consumption of social program benefits. Studies of the diffusion of innovation offer a useful theoretical framework[5] but little empirical application to outreach and participation in social programs.

The data collected in the Administrative Agency Experiment allow more direct analysis of outreach and its effects on participation. The AAE agencies conducted outreach and accepted applications for about eight months. An independent observer, who remained at each agency for the entire period, recorded the nature of outreach campaigns, the rationale for the procedures chosen, and staff perceptions of the effectiveness of their outreach efforts. Paralleling these qualitative observations, over fifteen thousand application forms requesting demographic information and asking applicants where they had first heard of the housing allowance program provide a quantitative data base. Together the qualitative and quantitative data provide a comprehensive picture of outreach and the public's response to outreach. The data allow both cross-sectional and longitudinal analysis, with variation across the eight agencies and over time within each agency.

The analysis was extended by use of a complementary data base, a special survey of 1,417 eligible households in Jacksonville, Florida. Conducted after a period of intensive outreach, the survey sampled respondents who were unaware of the housing allowance program, respondents who knew of it but had not applied for participation, and respondents who had applied. The survey allows deeper analysis of the reasons that outreach generates an unbalanced response from differing population subgroups.

This chapter presents the major findings from the AAE analysis of outreach. The analysis was guided by two central questions: What is the relative effectiveness of alternative outreach procedures in attracting eligible households to apply for participation? To what extent can outreach influence the demographic composition of the applicant pool? The first two sections of this chapter discuss those two questions. The third section draws from the AAE experience a planning framework that shows how a social program's participation goals define the outreach task.

THE OUTREACH OPTIONS

Each AAE agency sought a specified number of families to receive housing allowances. These targets, fixed in negotiations with HUD, were ceilings on the number of participants, but the agencies had strong incentives to meet the full target. A further constraint was that the agencies could accept applications for only seven months. These constraints alone would have made outreach a challenging task. But, in addition, no one knew how many applicants would fail to meet the program's housing requirements and thus fail to qualify for payments. Therefore no one knew how many applicants would be needed to meet the recipient targets.

Although these circumstances were specific to the AAE program, the decisions made in formulating outreach strategies are faced by planners of almost any social program. How intense a campaign should be waged? Should outreach be done through personal contacts or through the mass media?

Outreach Intensity and the Volume of Applications

All agencies but Tulsa originally planned what they considered low-intensity outreach efforts. They feared overapplication, a concern that was reinforced by the *Agency Program Manual*: "Outreach efforts must be designed to avoid raising unrealistic expectations among those who might apply for the program. Prominence should be given to the experimental nature of the program, the eligibility requirements, and the total number of households that can be enrolled."[6] The agencies' low-intensity campaigns were built on news releases, public service announcements, staff interviews on radio and television, speeches before community groups, and flyers and brochures. In this initial phase media were used to inform the public but not to sell the program.

Disappointingly few applicants responded to these campaigns. "The manual said EHAP was supposed to be a low-profile program," one of the program directors later reported, "so we were trying to go low profile. . . . It was a little bit too low." Most agencies were soon working to increase applications rates, sometimes within a month after beginning outreach.

To increase application rates, agency managers had two alternatives: increase the outreach effort with techniques already in use or try different ones. In most cases, as table 2-1 shows, they did both. Agencies

Table 2-1. Outreach Activities in Low- and High-Intensity Periods

Agency	Free News Releases and Public Service Announcements	Distribution of Flyers, Pamphlets, Brochures, and Posters	Contact with Community Groups and Local Organizations	TV and Radio Interviews, Talk Shows	Contact with Local Businesses	Agency-Prepared Paid Media Advertising	Professionally Prepared Paid Media Advertising
Salem	L	L	L	L			H
Springfield	LH	LH	LH		H	H	
Peoria	L	L	LH	L	H		H
San Bernardino	LH	LH	LH				
Bismarck	LH	LH	H	H			
Jacksonville	LH	LH	LH	L		H	
Durham	LH	LH	L	H	H	H	
Tulsa[a]		H	H		H		H

Source: Chronologies of observers at the agencies; monthly progress reports submitted to HUD by agency managers
Key: L=Used in low-intensity period; H=Used in high-intensity period
[a]Tulsa did not have a low-intensity period comparable to other agencies.

increased their contacts with community groups, distributed more brochures, and designed appealing as well as informative news releases.
Durham and Jacksonville used newspaper ads, and Springfield pur-
chased radio and television time. Peoria and Salem hired advertising
agencies to design outreach materials. In general, the agencies intensified
their original strategies and added new techniques, with particular
emphasis on professional design and paid advertising.

These adjustments increased the number of applications most agencies received. Peaks in the number of applications per month generally
coincided with increased outreach. The number of applications at Salem,
for example, increased significantly in June and July, when the professional campaign Operation Outreach was conducted. Applications at
Springfield peaked in September, when the agency began using paid television and radio advertisements. San Bernardino greatly intensified its
original outreach program in June and received its largest monthly
volume of applications that month. Peoria's applications peaked in
August, a month after the agency began using media ads produced by a
professional advertising firm.

The fluctuating intensity of each agency's outreach activity is best
described by its expenditure patterns. Figure 2-1 illustrates the relation
between intensified outreach and the volume of applications, using the
examples of Peoria and Durham. The application curve in Peoria is
similar to the expenditure curve, although the application peaks occur
slightly later than the expenditure peaks. Durham received a relatively
high level of applications at the beginning of the program, despite low
expenditures, but the second application peak occurs one month after the
maximum expenditure month. At all eight agencies the volume of applications clearly parallelled changes in the level of outreach expenditures.
Further, the response to outreach was quick. The examples in figure 2-1
show application peaks lagging one to two months behind expenditure
peaks, but it was more common for the two peaks to occur in the same
month.[7] Modulating the intensity of outreach thus proved a fast and
effective way to influence the number of applications.

By adjusting the intensity of their campaigns and the level of their
outreach expenditures, all but one of the AAE agencies reached at least
90 percent of their recipient goals. The variety of strategies used to
achieve this success suggests that most procedures were effective in producing applications. Multivariate analysis of the factors related to outreach costs supports this conclusion. Expenditures for both personnel
and media-related efforts (such as materials development and advertise-

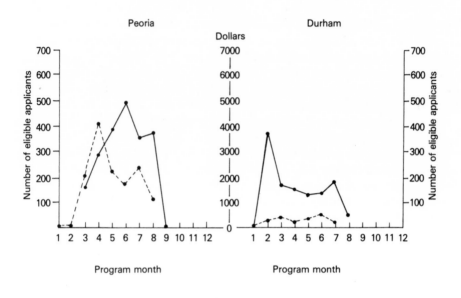

Figure 2-1. Expenditures for Outreach and Eligible Applications per Month in Durham and Peoria

Source: AAE cost reporting and application forms

ments) were positively related to the number of applications.[8] These expenditure categories correspond roughly to the two main outreach strategies the agencies used: personal contacts and media communications.

Personal Outreach Techniques

Agency staff members began publicizing the program by talking to community organizations and individuals. They reasoned that other social service agencies might refer clients to the housing allowance program and that contacting voluntary associations (church groups, unions, senior citizens organizations, and advocacy groups) might encourage members to apply.

Contacts with voluntary associations did not appear to generate many applications. Each applicant filled out a form that included the question "How did you first hear of the program?" Only 2 percent of the applicants said they heard of the program through community contacts. This figure is probably an underestimate, because people who heard of the program from fellow members of a voluntary association might have checked the friends and relatives category on the application form. Anecdotal evidence, however, confirms the conclusion that contact with community groups brought little response.

In contrast, work with other social service agencies generated substantial numbers of applications. One-quarter of all applicants said they were referred by another agency. Referrals accounted for 27 to 35 percent of the applications at six of the eight agencies. The proportion was substantially smaller only at Tulsa and Peoria (14 and 12 percent, respectively). Tulsa was the only agency to place almost all its emphasis on a media campaign. The Peoria agency, in addition to its emphasis on media outreach, had fewer institutional ties than most other agencies because its parent agency was in the state capital seventy miles away.

Almost all AAE agencies had parent housing or welfare agencies. In addition, the new programs frequently hired staff from other social service agencies in the area. These ties encouraged ready communication between agencies and helped create awareness of the AAE programs. The Tulsa, Jacksonville, and Salem agencies, for example, were able to contact families on the waiting lists of the local housing authorities. A staff member in Springfield reported: "Before the program really got started there were people who knew about us, mostly social workers or the housing authority—political kinds of people—and so we were sort of identified already as being another, a different kind of assistance program."

Media Outreach

Media outreach included both paid advertising and free publicity. Radio outreach usually took the form of public service announcements or interviews with agency staff members. Peoria, Salem, and Tulsa, however, used radio messages written by advertising firms. Television outreach consisted primarily of news coverage and appearances on talk shows; only Tulsa used professional advertising on television. Press releases were the most common form of newspaper outreach, but several agencies paid for advertising space. Tulsa used professionally designed newspaper ads. All pamphlets and brochures were designed by agency staff except at Salem and Tulsa, where professional firms produced them.

These varied media approaches consistently attracted a substantial number of applications. Overall 34 percent of the applicants said they had first heard about the program through media. As figure 2–2 shows, more than a quarter of the applications at each agency came in response to media outreach. The Tulsa agency conducted the most extensive media campaign of the eight agencies, and nearly half its applicants said they had first heard about the program from the media.

Peak-month figures—that is, the maximum monthly number of applicants who said they heard of the program from a particular medium—suggest that the techniques do not differ dramatically in their potential drawing power. Pamphlets actually produced the highest monthly application rate recorded.[9] This rate, 2 percent of the eligible population, occurred at Salem during Operation Outreach. Television and newspapers had peak application rates that were not far behind—1.6 percent for television in Tulsa and 1.4 percent for newspapers in Peoria. Only radio, with a peak rate of 0.5 percent, lagged markedly, but it was not used as intensively as the other media. Thus the limited evidence does not show that any one medium is better than all others in attracting applicants. But this finding is not surprising: the diverse use of media to advertise products and services also suggests that no one medium is consistently more effective than others.

Professional design and paid advertising, however, do seem important to the success of media outreach. Tulsa, which relied most heavily on professional assistance, attracted the largest number of applicants from media sources. Peoria, which also used professional design and paid advertising, attracted 40 percent of its applicants through the media. The professionally designed brochure used briefly in Salem was very successful, accounting for 10 percent of all applications at that site.

Word of Mouth: The Echo to Outreach

Outreach, whether through personal contacts or the media, gets the first information about a new program into the community. But as time passes and awareness of the program becomes more widespread, one would expect the direct influence of outreach to diminish. Some applicants might still respond to a media campaign, for example, but an in-

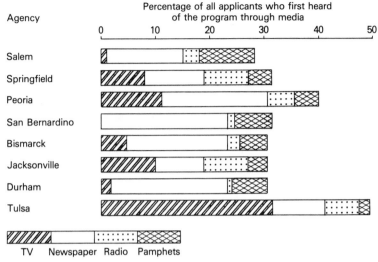

Figure 2-2. Media Applicants

Source: AAE application forms
Data base: Eligible applicants (N = 14,103; missing cases, 1)

creasing number would apply as a result of information received through informal channels—perhaps from people who heard the outreach message directly or from those who had participated in the program.

Word-of-mouth applicants to AAE programs, people who said they first heard of the program from friends or relatives, conform to these expected patterns. Even though the AAE programs were new, word-of-mouth information was the most common source of applicants' knowledge of the program. Thirty-eight percent of all applicants first heard about the program from friends or relatives.

The number of word-of-mouth applications in a given month was closely related to the number of applicants responding directly to outreach that month and the total number of previous applicants.[10] Outreach efforts thus seem to have both an immediate and a long-term echo. In the short term some people apply because someone they know has heard the outreach message. (Some elderly applicants, for example, were motivated to apply, and were often assisted in applying, by sons or daughters who had heard of the program and felt the parents might be eligible.) In the long term applicants to the program themselves become sources of information. Because the cumulative number of applicants inevitably grows, outreach becomes a progressively less important source of information.

Simplifying the Application Process

Some agencies attempted to increase the number of applicants by making the application process easier. They encouraged households to apply by mail or telephone, and they set up special application offices to supplement the central offices.

The circumstances in which mail and telephone application procedures were used do not allow a conclusive assessment, but the anecdotal evidence is favorable. The Bismarck agency accepted mailed applications throughout the application period. Its staff believed the procedure was important for the large and sparsely populated program area. Salem accepted applications by telephone during Operation Outreach. Applications increased substantially, but it is impossible to separate this procedure's effect from the effect of the agency's generally intensified outreach.[11]

Another means used to simplify application was to open neighborhood application centers. San Bernardino, which served the largest program area, opened ten application centers in addition to its main office and its branch office in Ontario. Springfield used eight temporary application centers, and Salem opened seven. Peoria took applications at six special offices that were open for only a few hours a week. Tulsa rented a mobile van and stationed it for brief periods in locations throughout the city.

Opening neighborhood offices to encourage application did not prove very successful. Most offices intended solely as application centers were closed before the end of the application period because they were not being used.[12] Agencies found that those interested in the program tended to come to the main office.

Modifying application procedures was certainly less useful than modulating the intensity of outreach as a means of influencing the volume of applications. The latter technique allowed all but one of the AAE agencies to meet the target number of allowance recipients within the allotted time. The agencies were somewhat less successful, however, in attracting the kinds of applicants they wanted.

ATTRACTING SPECIAL GROUPS

Some population groups seem to respond more quickly than others to the news of a new social program. Each of the eight agencies tried to attract applications from a representative cross section of the eligible population. None succeeded completely. Some groups, such as the elderly, consistently applied at lower rates than others, almost irrespective of the outreach strategies used. This section discusses the application patterns and the effectiveness of outreach in modifying the patterns.

Differences in Application

The AAE analysis categorizes all eligible applicants into three groups, which differ substantially in their application patterns: (1) *the elderly*, all households in which the head of household is sixty-five years or older;[13] (2) *the working poor*, nonelderly households whose income does not include any welfare, unemployment insurance, or other grant income; (3) *the welfare population*, all nonelderly households reporting welfare or any other grant income.

An estimated 67 percent of the eligible welfare households in the AAE program areas applied,[14] compared with 11 percent of the working poor and 6 percent of the elderly households. These differences in application rates occurred because some groups were more aware of the program than others and because some were more interested than others in applying once they learned about it.[15]

To explore the reasons for differing application rates, a special survey was conducted in Jacksonville. The Jacksonville agency was the only one that fell substantially short of its target number of allowance recipients in the original enrollment period. HUD allowed the agency to reopen enrollment, and during the second enrollment period the agency mounted an intensive outreach campaign. The survey was conducted as the intensive campaign was ending, that is, after the program had been in existence for about a year and immediately following an intensive publicity effort. The survey was based on a random sample of housing units in relatively low income parts of the city (households that would have been ineligible to participate were excluded after a few screening questions). Respondents were asked whether they had applied to it and a number of questions pertaining to their sources of information and their application decision.[16]

The Jacksonville survey suggests that both lack of knowledge and lack of interest were important in the low application by the elderly. Figure 2-3[17] shows that members of elderly households in Jacksonville were less likely to be aware of the program and less likely to apply once they learned about it.

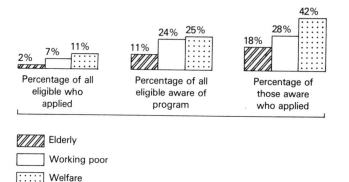

Figure 2-3. Application Rates for Elderly, Working Poor, and Welfare Recipients

Source: AAE application forms, census public use sample, census second count, Jacksonville outreach survey.

Data base: Jacksonville special survey respondents (N=1,381; missing cases, 36)

Differences between working-poor and welfare households resulted almost entirely from differences of interest in, not knowledge of, the program. Households in these two groups were almost equally likely to learn about the program, but 42 percent of welfare households who knew of the program applied to it. Only 28 percent of working-poor households applied.[18] These findings suggest that recruiting working-poor households is mainly a matter of persuading them to apply. Attracting the elderly, however, requires special efforts to reach as well as to persuade them.

The comparative reluctance of the working poor and the elderly to apply may be due to several causes. First, these households are not part of the traditional constituency of assistance programs, and they may only slowly become aware that they are eligible for this program. Second, nonwelfare households may be unwilling to participate because of a welfare stigma attached to any public assistance program.[19] A number of program participants, when interviewed in depth, mentioned their initial reluctance to apply. Some ultimately rationalized that the experimental program was "not like welfare."[20]

Although elderly, working-poor, and welfare households show distinct application patterns, this grouping of applicants might not be inherently relevant to policy. For example, the agencies' participation targets did not distinguish between working-poor and welfare households. These three categories can be related to other groups of potential interest, however, as shown in figure 2-4. Among the AAE applicants, the working poor tended to be male-headed households in the higher eligible income categories. Welfare households had a relatively small proportion of male heads and a high proportion of minority-headed households. Elderly households had the smallest average size.[21]

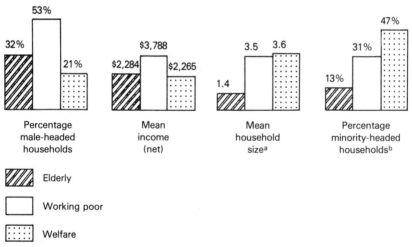

Figure 2-4. Characteristics of Elderly, Working-Poor, and Welfare Applicants

Source: AAE application forms
Data base: Eligible applicants (N = 13,982; missing cases, 122)
[a]Program eligibility rules essentially exclude single-person households, except for the elderly.
[b]Excludes two sites with less than 5 percent minority applicants.

The application patterns of elderly, working-poor, and welfare households can thus be used to anticipate the application behavior of other groups. For example, the low application rate of the working poor suggests that representative participation by households at the upper end of the eligible income range would not occur without special outreach efforts. The AAE agencies did have trouble meeting their recipient targets for higher-income households, and some attempted special outreach efforts to attract that group.

Agency Efforts to Attract Special Groups

An outreach strategy can be aimed at everyone who might be eligible for the program, or it can be targeted to attract particular subgroups. The AAE agencies tried to recruit a representative cross section of the eligible population. If all groups were equally likely to hear about the program and to want to apply, the agencies' logical approach would have been to use a nontargeted outreach campaign.

Most agencies did start with a nontargeted approach, although there was some concern about the possible difficulty of attracting applicants in the eligible upper-income categories. Agencies therefore planned to direct outreach toward the entire eligible population and avoid a welfare image. Tulsa targeted its outreach specifically toward moderate-income households.

It became clear in the first months of outreach that the applicants were not meeting the demographic profiles the agencies had projected. In particular, elderly households and male-headed, higher-income households were applying in much lower numbers than planned. Most agencies took steps to increase applications from the groups that were underapplying.

The agencies could try either to reach more households in the underrepresented groups or to persuade more of those who had heard to apply. Targeted outreach campaigns commonly employed both tactics. San Bernardino's campaign for elderly applicants illustrates the attempt to reach an underrepresented group. The agency mailed flyers directly to elderly households, and staff members armed with application forms stationed themselves in supermarkets, discount stores, and regional shopping centers frequented by elderly persons. During this month-long campaign, elderly applicants increased from 65 to 109. The number of applications from welfare and working-poor households decreased (see figure 2–5). Tulsa attempted to persuade moderate-income, working-poor households to apply by making the content and presentation of its professional media campaign appealing. The advertisements avoided a low-income, welfare image and did not mention the program's connec-

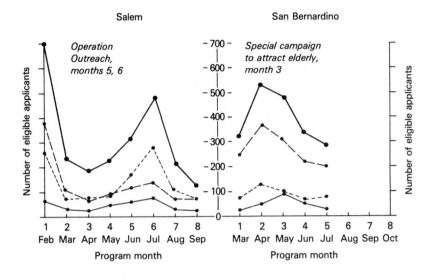

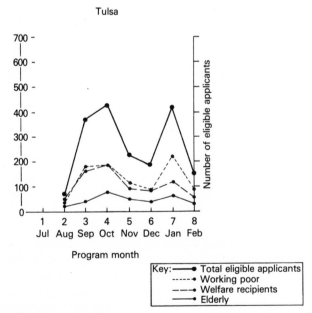

Figure 2-5. Successful Targeting Efforts

Source: AAE application forms

Data base: Eligible applicants (N=2,425 in Salem; missing cases, 9; N=1,903 in San Bernardino; missing cases, 23; N=1,843 in Tulsa; missing cases, 7)

tion with the housing authority. Tulsa's targeted outreach was quite successful in attracting the working poor throughout the application period.

Salem was able to increase the number of applications from working-poor households without increasing applications from welfare households. Salem's Operation Outreach campaign was designed by a professional advertising firm and included paid radio and newspaper advertising, posters, and brochures with reply cards. The brochure did not mention the program's connection with the Salem Housing Authority; it emphasized the "experimental" and "exclusive" nature of the program, and the advertised income limit was deliberately high. During Operation Outreach, applications from higher-income households increased substantially, and the number of working-poor applicants began to exceed the number of welfare households (see figure 2–5). San Bernardino and Salem were the only agencies able to alter the mix of applicants they received.[22] Other agencies were able to increase the total volume of applications but not to obtain more applications from one group without getting more (unneeded) applications from the other groups as well.

The Effectiveness of Targeting Techniques

Salem and Tulsa's successful use of professionally designed media campaigns to attract specific groups suggests that media outreach is the most effective way to attract working-poor applicants. Other AAE experience supports this hypothesis.

Although referrals from social service agencies and media communications were both good sources of applicants, the applicants from the two sources were quite different, as figure 2–6 shows. Referrals were much more likely to be welfare recipients than were applicants generated by media campaigns; 69 percent of the referrals were welfare recipients, but only 20 percent were working-poor households. Media applicants, with about as many working–poor as welfare households, were more representative of the eligible population. However, welfare households were overrepresented even among media applicants. Elderly households did not respond strongly to either referral or media outreach. The elderly are apparently outside the social service network. Further, less of the information communicated through the media reaches the elderly than other groups,[23] although media outreach was still the most important source of elderly applicants. However, managers at some agencies were convinced that contacts with organizations of elderly people helped produce applications. San Bernardino's successful targeting to the elderly

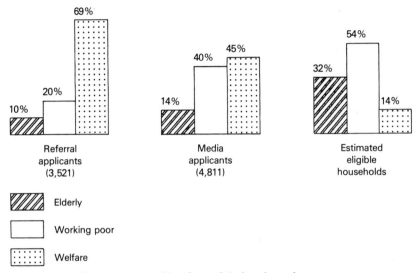

Figure 2-6. Characteristics of Media and Referral Applicants

Source: AAE application forms; census public use sample and census second count

Data base: Eligible applicants; (N=13,981; missing cases, 123); eligible population estimated from census data

involved media with a personal touch: staff members gave brochures directly to elderly individuals.

   Although word of mouth is not a direct outreach technique, applicants who heard about the program this way were demographically similar to the applicants who heard more directly, as shown in table 2-2. Those who knew about the program and were interested in it seemed to talk about it with friends who had similar characteristics.

Table 2-2. Demographic Characteristics of Applicants Hearing through Word of Mouth and Other Sources

Demographic Characteristics	Percentage of Applicants Hearing through Word of Mouth (N=5,277)	Percentage of Applicants Hearing from All Other Sources (N=8,704)
Elderly	10	13
Working poor	36	32
Welfare recipients	54	55

Source: AAE application forms

Data base: Eligible AAE applicants (missing cases, 123)

The Cost of Attracting Special Groups

The agencies that spent the most money on outreach came closest to attracting applicants who were a representative cross section of all eligible households.[24] This suggests that it is more expensive to attract applicants from the underrepresented groups—the elderly and working poor—than from the welfare population. The findings presented earlier provide some explanation for higher outreach costs: if elderly and working-poor applicants are less likely to hear of the program and more reluctant to apply than the welfare population, it will be necessary to expose more individuals to more information in order to generate equivalent numbers of applications.

A more detailed analysis of outreach costs suggests that professional advertising led to the increased costs in the campaigns that produced the most representative applicant profiles. The numbers of applications from all three groups are positively related to labor hours and cumulative nonlabor expenditures on outreach.[25] Applications from the working poor, however, are also positively affected by professional media expenditures. This finding supports other evidence that professional campaigns are more effective than other means for obtaining a cross section of eligible households, and they are especially effective for attracting the working poor. Apparently the professional campaigns can either inform the elderly and working-poor populations selectively about the program or selectively increase their interest in applying.

The persistent biases in application patterns, together with the cost of influencing those patterns, mean that planners of a new social program may face a trade-off between balanced participation and higher administrative costs. In a housing allowance program requiring applicants to have or find suitable housing before qualifying for payments, the planner's task is further complicated by imbalances in the ability of different groups to meet the housing requirements. The following section brings these factors together in a look at the problems of AAE agencies in planning outreach.

FORMULATING OUTREACH GOALS

The outreach task is defined by three major factors: the participation goals of the program, the number of applicants needed to meet the goals, and the size of the eligible population from which the applicants must come.

Attrition rates determine how many applicants will be needed to meet recipient goals. The AAE experience shows that many applicants who are offered the chance to enroll do not become recipients. Some elect not to enroll, and some enroll but fail to meet the housing quality requirements.[26]

Figure 2-7 illustrates that some households[27] participated fully in the AAE, while others went only part of the way and dropped out. The number of applicants the agencies needed therefore exceeded the target number of recipients, and the size and composition of the eligible population determines the difficulty of obtaining that required number of applicants. This section reviews the AAE experience with application, attrition rates, and outreach costs.

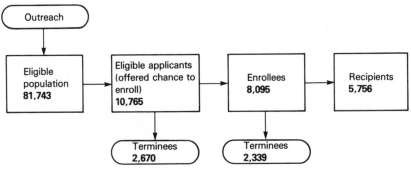

Figure 2-7. Becoming a Recipient in the AAE

Source: AAE application, enrollment, and payment initiation forms; census public use sample and census second count

Overall Recipient Targets

The AAE agencies had two types of participation targets: a target for the overall number of recipients and targets for participation by certain subgroups. Because a national program might have goals for the number of recipients but not for subgroup participation, the two types of targets will be treated separately here.[28]

The AAE's target number of recipients and the attrition rates for applicants can be used to calculate the minimum number of applicants the agencies needed to meet their targets. As table 2-3 shows, seven agencies needed between 1.3 and 2.2 applicants per recipient. The AAE required a median of 1.7 applicants for each recipient.

Table 2-3. Applicants Needed to Meet Recipient Targets

Agency	Applicants Needed per Recipient	Target Number of Recipients	Total Number of Applications Needed to Meet Target Number of Recipients[a]
Salem	1.8	900	1,620
Springfield	1.6	900	1,440
Peoria	1.9	900	1,710
San Bernardino	1.6	900	1,440
Bismarck	1.3	400	520
Jacksonville	4.7	900	4,230
Durham	2.2	500	1,100
Tulsa	1.5	900	1,350
Median	1.7		

Source: AAE application and payment initiation forms
[a]Calculations based on final ratio of selected applicants to recipients at each agency, not on agency planning figures.

Jacksonville, where nearly 5 applicants were needed for every recipient, was an important exception.[29] A tight and segregated housing market, relatively stringent enforcement of housing quality requirements, and reluctance among housing suppliers to accept the program resulted in a much higher than average dropout rate. Therefore, although it would be reasonable to use a ratio of 1.7 applicants per recipient in general planning, the first enrollment period in Jacksonville shows that many more applications could be required in special situations.[30] The difficulty of the outreach task is also influenced by the number of eligible households in the local population. Table 2-4 shows the estimated size of the eligible population in each of the program areas and the application rates necessary to generate the required number of applicants. The number of applicants that the agencies needed ranged from 7 to 33 percent of the estimated number of eligible households.[31] Except for Jacksonville, however, the agencies obtained more applications than needed to meet their target number of recipients.

Participation Targets for Special Groups

Adding participation objectives for special groups can make planning and implementing outreach more difficult. Attrition rates are likely to differ for various groups. If a desired group has a high attrition rate, more applicants will be needed to meet the recipient goal. And if the de-

Table 2-4. Application Rates

Agency	Size of Eligible Population	Application Rate[a] Needed to Generate Enough Applicants to Meet Target Number of Recipients (%)	Actual Application Rate[b] (%)	Average Monthly Application Rate[c] (%)	Lowest Monthly Application Rate[d] (%)
Salem	5,232	31	47	6	2
Springfield	17,572	8	13	2	2
Peoria	5,235	33	39	7	5
San Bernardino	19,745	7	10	2	2
Bismarck	2,176	24	26	4	3
Jacksonville	17,429	24	10	1	1
Durham	5,620	20	22	3	2
Tulsa	8,734	15	21	3	2
Median		22	22	3	2

Source: AAE application forms, census public use sample, census second count
[a]This rate is expressed as a percentage of estimated eligible households.
[b]Total eligible applicants as a percentage of estimated eligible households. The numbers for Salem and Peoria appear very high. The census may underestimate the number of eligible households, but there is no reason they should be biased by site. Salem and Peoria would still show higher application rates than the other six sites if all the population figures were increased.
[c]Total eligible applications averaged across the months in which twenty or more were received.
[d]Excludes the first and last months that applications were accepted because they may not have been full months.

sired group is a small fraction of all applicants, the agency may have to reject many applications from other groups to get enough of the desired group.

The AAE experience summarized in table 2-5 demonstrates the effect of group participation targets. Elderly applicants, for example, had a lower attrition rate than the nonelderly. Two of every three selected elderly applicants became recipients, but only one of two selected nonelderly applicants did. However, the elderly constituted a small proportion of all applicants; as table 2-5 shows, only one of 8.5 AAE applicants was elderly. Combining attrition and application rates for the elderly shows that approximately 13 total applicants were needed to get one elderly recipient, while only about 2 total applicants were needed for every nonelderly recipient.[32]

Table 2-5.   Applications Needed per Recipient for Population Subgroups

Group Characteristics	Subgroup Applicants per Subgroup Recipient[a]	Total Applicants per Subgroup Applicant[b]
Age of household head		
Elderly (65+)	1.5	8.5
Nonelderly	1.9	1.1
Sex of household head		
Male	1.9	3.0
Female	1.9	1.5
Race/ethnicity of household head		
White	1.7	—[c]
Nonwhite	2.4	—
Household size		
1	1.5	6.2
2	1.9	4.0
3–4	1.9	2.8
5 or more	2.1	4.5
Total household income		
$0–1,999	2.1	4.2
$2,000–3,999	1.7	2.3
$4,000–5,999	1.9	4.2
$6,000 and over	2.1	11.9

Source: AAE applications forms, Payment initiation forms
[a]Ratio of selected applicants to recipients in the subgroup combining all eight sites.
[b]Ratio of total applicants to applicants in the subgroup, combining all eight sites.
[c]Because the proportion of minority households varies dramatically by geographic region, summary figures here would be misleading.

Subgroup targets may make outreach much more difficult, or they may have little effect on the difficulty of outreach. Their influence depends on the size of the target and the difficulty of getting recipients from the designated group. Suppose, for example, that an agency had an overall recipient target of 1,000. If there were no special subgroup target, a planner might expect to need the AAE median of 1.7 applicants per recipient, or 1,700 applicants. If the agency wanted at least half its recipients to be elderly, the task would be much more difficult. The AAE application and attrition rates indicate that more than 6,000 applicants would be needed to obtain 500 elderly recipients.[33] On the other hand, a requirement that at least half the recipients be nonelderly would require less work. The agency would have to attract only the same 1,700 applicants it needed in the absence of group targets.

The same procedure can be used to estimate the number of applications the AAE would have needed to obtain a recipient group broadly representative of the eligible population. The major differences in application patterns were among the elderly, welfare recipients, and the working poor. For the recipients to match the distribution in the eligible population among these categories, the agencies would have needed between 2.5 and 10.8 applications per recipient, with a median of 4.8.[34]

Setting participation goals that are significantly higher than the subgroup's proportion of the eligible population tends to make the outreach effort more difficult. AAE agencies attempted to meet recipient profiles that they had estimated to be representative of the eligible population. In many cases inaccurate agency estimates increased the difficulty of meeting the profiles.

Targets for special groups can affect the overall number of recipients the program serves. For example, to achieve group targets approximating the proportions of elderly, welfare, and working poor in the eligible population might require 4.8 total applicants per recipient (the AAE median). If applications are expected from 20 to 25 percent of the eligible households in the first year, the target number of recipients cannot reasonably be any higher than 4 to 5 percent of the eligible population.

Budgeting for Outreach

Outreach expenditures varied widely among the eight AAE agencies (the cost variation is discussed in more detail in chapter 6). Only part of the variation can be explained analytically, indicating that there is still much to learn about the relation between outreach expenditures and applications. Nonetheless, the expenditure patterns in the AAE provide a useful starting point for planning similar programs.

The data provide several estimates of outreach costs per applicant. Median agency outreach cost in the AAE was $6.15 of direct expenditures per eligible applicant.[35] Adding such indirect costs as management and facilities yields a total cost of $13.28 per eligible applicant.[36] The average direct cost per eligible applicant was $5.01, and the marginal direct cost of an additional applicant was estimated at $5.74.[37] In the absence of better data, a program planner might assume $5 to $6 in direct costs, or $11 to $14 in total costs, per applicant.

Three factors determined the wide variation of outreach costs observed in the AAE. First, the difficulty of the outreach tasks differed substantially: larger applicant populations tended to result in lower costs per applicant. Second, outreach expenditures were related not only to the number of applications received but also to the applicants' characteristics. The agencies that attracted more representative applicant groups —that is, higher proportions of the normally underrepresented groups —tended to have higher expenditures. Third, all agencies received some free publicity, such as news coverage and broadcast time for public service announcements. The available data do not allow a valuation of this publicity, but clearly it also varied considerably from agency to agency.

Despite the variations in outreach cost per applicant, the median figures are useful as summaries of the factors involved in the outreach task. Assume that the average cost of attracting an eligible applicant to a new program is $13. If there were no housing standards or similar requirements, as in the case of a simple income transfer program, for example, one might expect the attrition rate to be similar to that of AAE applicants who were offered enrollment but did not accept (about 25 percent).[38] The planner could then expect to spend about $17 in outreach for each household that participated in the program. Participation targets for subgroups would raise the cost. If the participation target for elderly were equivalent to their proportion in the eligible population, then AAE patterns show that outreach expenditures would have to be about $46 per participant.[39] The AAE housing requirements caused additional attrition; factoring in that attrition raises the expected outreach expenditure per allowance recipient to $22 without a subgroup target and to $62 to achieve representative participation.

IMPLICATIONS FOR FURTHER RESEARCH

The analysis of outreach in the Administrative Agency Experiment provides much information useful for implementing a housing allowance program. Moreover, it offers insights that may be broadly applicable to the introduction of new social programs. People may not respond to a housing assistance program as they would to programs offering, for example, general financial assistance or job training or legal help. But the AAE agencies did offer a new social program to a low-income population, a program that responded to general financial needs and had no features that would obviously exclude most low-income groups.[40] Because there has been no previous large-scale research on the effect of outreach on participation in new programs, it is important to seek in the AAE, if not conclusions applicable to other programs, then at least the intuition that can serve as the foundation for future research.

Applications to a New Program

The most striking feature of the application patterns in the AAE was the consistent difference in application rates of the elderly, working-poor, and welfare populations. Compared with their proportions in the eligible community, elderly and working-poor households were under-represented and welfare households were overrepresented among applicants to all eight agencies. This pattern is consistent with participation patterns observed in the Food Stamps program after several years of operations.[41]

One implication of this finding is that program planners should not expect applications from a balanced cross section of the eligible population, even if operating agencies strive to obtain a representative group of applicants, as the AAE agencies did.[42] The planner can ensure a representative beneficiary profile by requiring agencies to fill quotas for particular groups. But quotas will probably require rejecting applicants from the groups with high application rates and will increase the total number of applications needed. Given the AAE application and attrition patterns, achieving a representative profile of beneficiaries would have taken nearly three times the number of applications needed if participants were chosen on a first-come, first-serve basis.

The consistency in differences between low-income elderly, working-poor, and welfare populations suggests that the groups may have distinctive characteristics that influence their response to new social programs and perhaps their participation in established programs. The AAE provides glimpses of such characteristics, but more research is needed to understand the reasons for group differences in participation.

The elderly, for example, were less likely than the nonelderly to be aware of the program, and even those elderly who were aware were less likely to apply. Several factors may influence this pattern. The elderly did not appear to lack formal sources of information (their exposure to media was about the same as that of the nonelderly), but their informal communications networks may be weaker or less effective. The elderly may be more reluctant to apply because older people are less likely to accept new programs, or their reluctance may be due to a stronger value orientation against accepting public assistance. These topics are worthy of further research, especially as the elderly become an increasingly larger segment of the population assisted by federal programs.

The differing application rates of the nonelderly working-poor and welfare populations likewise merit further investigation. As the Jacksonville survey indicated, welfare households were somewhat better informed about the program and substantially more likely to apply to it than the working poor. The greater awareness of welfare households might result simply from greater interest; the survey indicated no significant difference between the sources of information for welfare and working-poor groups. On the other hand, the welfare population's contacts with service agencies or their informal communications networks could bring them word of a new program more quickly than the working poor receive it. (The Jacksonville survey was conducted about a year after the initial announcement of the housing allowance program, and the difference between working-poor and welfare households might have been greater earlier.)

The differential application rates among the working-poor and welfare households who were aware of the program raise anew the hypothesis that a stigma is attached to participation in public programs. Like previous research, however, the AAE offers only anecdotal evidence to support the hypothesis; stigma has yet to be adequately measured and placed in a clear perspective among the factors influencing program participation. A further question is whether the importance of stigma changes as a program becomes more established. Case studies of AAE participants showed that some people who were reluctant to accept "handouts" were able to overcome their hesitation because the program was new and "not welfare" and sometimes because it was an experiment in which their role was one of "helping the government."

The AAE analysis suggests that the dynamic of outreach and application patterns is likely to change as a program matures. Even at the beginning of program operations, many people applied after hearing about the program from friends or relatives. The characteristics of the word-of-mouth applicants mirrored those of applicants from other sources, consistent with the idea that news of an innovation spreads easily within interlocking cliques of individuals with similar social status.[43] As the total number of applicants grew, the number of word-of-mouth applicants increased correspondingly. This finding implies that patterns of subgroup participation in a social program may be self-perpetuating. It may further suggest that the potential influence of outreach diminishes with time, as progressively higher proportions of the applicants respond to information about their peers' personal experiences. The AAE thus provides a first view of the longitudinal process by which the low-income population responds to the introduction of a social program, but it is only a partial view; a full understanding of the process can come only from further and longer-term research.

The Utility of Outreach

Research is often useful in documenting what is common sense to the practitioner. In this vein the AAE analysis shows that outreach produces applications to a new program. Increases and decreases in the intensity of outreach efforts, as measured by agency expenditures, led quickly to increases and decreases in the number of applications. Noteworthy for program planners at the national level is that the finding held for all eight agencies, across a substantial variety of locally designed outreach approaches. This finding implies that the general intensity of outreach can be effectively controlled through the budgetary process; more complicated regulation of procedures is not required.

Such budgetary control should be based on a clear understanding of the factors likely to influence outreach costs per applicant, which requires research that goes beyond the AAE. The AAE analysis indicates that costs per applicant are sensitive to the local situation; for example, costs per applicant decrease as the size of the eligible population increases. But the number of observations is too small for precise estimation of outreach costs, and the limited time frame provides no information about the change in costs that might be expected as a program matures.

The nonexperimental design of the AAE allowed the observation of agency-designed outreach and hence the conclusion that outreach can reasonably be designed and implemented at the local level. At the same time, because the agencies' campaigns varied on multiple dimensions —intensity, the communications channels used, information content, orientation to population subgroups—the relative effectiveness or cost-effectiveness of alternative techniques cannot be completely determined. Thus while it is clear that substantial numbers of applicants responded to almost all the major information channels used (referrals, television, radio, newspaper, pamphlets), it is not clear which factors determined the number of households responding to particular techniques. The effectiveness of alternative techniques could be a fruitful area for research based on systematic variation of a few key outreach dimensions.

The most striking evidence of differential effectiveness was that media outreach was more effective than the referral network in attracting the underrepresented population groups, the elderly, and working poor. But even when targeted specifically to the elderly or working poor, media outreach rarely produced application rates equal to those of the welfare population. If outreach is to be an effective means of attracting elderly or working-poor participants, further research is needed to determine the outreach formats and information content that convince people to apply. The two-stage analytic framework used in the AAE analysis—separating the individual's awareness of the program from the decision to apply for participation—seems to provide a strong underpinning for such research.

NOTES

1. See, for example, Stephen D. Kennedy, T. Krishna Kumar, and Glen Weisbrod, *Draft Report on Participation Under a Housing Gap Form of Housing Allowance* (Cambridge, Mass.: Abt Associates, 1977); Maurice MacDonald, "Why Don't More Eligible Use Food Stamps?" Institute for Research on Poverty: Discussion Paper (Madison, Wis.: University of Wisconsin, July 1975); Barbara Boland, "Participation in the Aid to Families with Dependent Children Program (AFDC)" (Washington, D.C.: Urban Institute, 1973).

2. Oliver Moles, Robert F. Hess, and Daniel Fascione, "Who Knows Where to Get Public Assistance?" *Welfare in Review*, September–October 1968.

3. Joseph Eaton, "Reaching the Hard to Reach in Israel," *Social Work*, 29, no. 1 (January 1970): 96; Neil Gilbert, *Clients or Constituents* (San Francisco, Ca.: Jossey-Bass, 1970); Neil Gilbert and Harry Specht, *Dimensions of Social Welfare Policy* (Englewood Cliffs, N.J.: Prentice-Hall, 1974).

4. Joel F. Handler, "Federal-State Interests in Welfare Administration," in *Studies in Public Welfare*, paper no. 5 (part 2), Subcommittee on Fiscal Policy, Joint Economic Committee of the U.S. Congress, March 12, 1973; Daniel P. Moynihan, *The Politics of a Guaranteed Income* (New York: Random House, 1973); Martin C. Rein, "A Model of Income Support Programs: Experience with Public Assistance and Implications for a Direct Cash Assistance Program" (Cambridge, Mass.: Abt Associates, 1974); Gilbert Y. Steiner, *The State of Welfare* (Washington, D.C.: Brookings Institution, 1971); Burton A. Weisbrod, "On the Stigma Effect and the Demand for Welfare Programs: A Theoretical Note," Institute for Research on Poverty: *Discussion Papers* (Madison, Wis.: University of Wisconsin, 1970).

5. Everett M. Rogers, "New Product Adoption and Diffusion," *Consumer Research*, 2 (March 1976): 290–301; E. M. Rogers, *Diffusion of Innovations* (Glencoe, Ill.: Free Press, 1962).

6. *Agency Program Manual* (Cambridge, Mass.: Abt Associates, 1972).

7. A lagged model was tested in a multivariate (regression) analysis of applications and expenditures. The results showed no definite lag pattern.

8. See MacMillan and Hamilton, *Outreach*, appendix D, section IV.

9. The monthly application rate is computed as the number of applicants at an agency in one month who said they first heard of the program through a particular medium, divided by the total estimated eligible population at the site.

10. In regression analysis both terms were highly significant, yielding an R^2 of 0.75. See appendix A.

11. In its second enrollment period the Jacksonville agency also used a phone-in procedure and had a far higher application rate than in the first period. But again, it is impossible to apportion the effect among such possible causes as increased outreach, the economic recession, and the telephone application procedure.

12. Branch offices that were necessary for other administrative purposes because of the geographic or population distribution, such as the offices in rural counties of the Peoria and Bismarck program areas, received significant numbers of applications.

13. Program eligibility rules defined the elderly as all persons sixty-two or older. The elderly are defined as sixty-five or older for this discussion to allow comparison with census categories.

14. This number seems extremely high, and differences between the census definition of welfare income and the one used by the AAE agencies may have inflated the apparent application rate for welfare households. The overall figure is not unreasonable compared with application rates for other programs, however. For example, it has been estimated that 37.5 percent of the eligible population was being served by Food Stamps in 1974 (MacDonald, "Why Don't More Use Food Stamps?"). It has also been estimated that 60 percent of Food Stamp households also receive benefits from other public assistance programs (U.S., Congress, Joint Economic Committee, Subcommittee on Fiscal Policy, "National Survey of Food Stamp and Food Distribution Program Recipients: A Summary of Findings on Income Sources and Amounts and Incidence of Multiple Benefits," in *Studies in Public Welfare*, December 1974).

15. This two-part theory is discussed in more detail in MacMillan and Hamilton, *Outreach*, appendix C.

16. For a full analysis of the survey research, see MacMillan and Hamilton, *Outreach*, appendix C.

17. The bivariate distributions in figure 2–3 were confirmed in a multivariate (logit) analysis holding constant other demographic and related household characteristics. See appendix B.

18. These results are consistent with the Demand Experiment's findings. When randomly selected heads of eligible households were approached in their

homes and offered the opportunity to enroll, 48 percent of the elderly, 67 percent of the working poor, and 82 percent of welfare households accepted the offer.

19. Psychic costs of participation in welfare programs are discussed in Handler, "Federal-State Interests"; Moynihan, *Politics of a Guaranteed Income;* Rein, "Model of Income Support Programs"; Steiner, *State of Welfare;* and Weisbrod, "Stigma Effect."

20. See the case discussions in Frederick T. Temple et al., *Third Annual Report of the Administrative Agency Experiment Evaluation* (Cambridge, Mass.: Abt Associates, 1976), pp. 94–116.

21. To be eligible for assistance in the program, heads of one-person households had to be elderly or handicapped; this requirement lowers the average size of the elderly household.

22. Tulsa did not alter the mix of applications but had no need to. The targeted campaign succeeded from the beginning in attracting higher-income applicants.

23. Elderly respondents to the Jacksonville survey had about the same exposure to the media as other groups, but were less aware of the program.

24. A measure of congruence between applicant and eligible populations is closely related to agency expenditures per member of the eligible population. The simple correlation between these two measures is 0.85; excluding Tulsa, the correlation is 0.94.

25. This analysis is presented in MacMillan and Hamilton, *Outreach,* appendix D, section IV.

26. In the AAE, families were enrolled after meeting eligibility requirements for income and other household characteristics. After enrollment, they had to meet a housing quality requirement before they were fully eligible for allowance payments. To meet the requirement, an enrollee had to occupy or secure a lease and plan to move to a unit that was inspected and in accordance with agency standards.

27. In the figure and throughout the chapter, those applicants selected for possible enrollment provide the base for computations.

28. A "full entitlement" program, in which any eligible household could participate, might not even have a target number of recipients. In such programs, however, administrative budgets for local agencies are often based on the expected number of beneficiaries. Such an arrangement requires the same kind of planning. The AAE is more typical of "limited slot" programs that can serve only a portion of the eligible population.

29. During the second enrollment period at the Jacksonville agency, in which the agency did meet its recipient goals, the applicant-recipient ratio was reduced but still higher than at other AAE sites.

30. An alternative to increasing the number of applications is reducing the proportion of applicants who fail to become recipients. This chapter concentrates on agency outreach strategies and application; the effect of agency strategies on termination rates is discussed in chapter 3.

31. Estimates of the eligible population prepared for this analysis use 1970 census data. The agencies' estimates were in most cases substantially higher, twice as high in some cases. Assuming that the analytic estimates are more accurate, the agencies' figures provided them with a misleading picture of outreach as an easy task. This problem is examined in depth in MacMillan and Hamilton, *Outreach,* appendix B.

32. Total applicants per recipient can be approximated by multiplying entries in the two columns of table 2-5.

33. For 500 elderly recipients, the agency would need 750 elderly applicants (1.5×500). With one of every 8.5 applicants being elderly, 6,375 (750×8.5) total applicants would yield 750 elderly applicants. This calculation assumes constant application and attrition rates, an assumption valid only up to a point. As the number of applicants in any group approaches the total number of eligible households in that group, fewer people would apply and the composition of the applicant population would therefore change. Of course, an agency with such a goal might target its outreach strategy to attract a higher proportion of the elderly, but the AAE experience suggests that this would yield only a marginal reduction in the total number of applicants needed.

   Note also that the subgroup participation target in this instance would deny many nonelderly applicants the opportunity to participate. Of the 6,375 total applicants, there would be 5,625 nonelderly applicants. If all were offered the opportunity, one would expect 2,960 to become recipients. But because a maximum of 500 nonelderly recipients would be accepted, more than 2,000 applicants who might have become recipients would be rejected.

34. See MacMillan and Hamilton, *Outreach,* appendix B, attachment V, pp. B-73–B-76.

35. This cost has been adjusted for wage variations among the sites. All cost figures presented in these chapters reflect expenditures in 1973–1974; they are not adjusted for inflation.

36. An indirect cost rate of 116 percent of direct costs is used here. See chapter 6 for discussion of indirect costs.

37. Average cost and marginal cost figures exclude Tulsa. See MacMillan and Hamilton, *Outreach,* appendix D.

38. This probably overstates the attrition most programs would expect, because there was some attrition introduced by the delay between application and selection and some by informing applicants of the housing requirements.

39. Since the application rate was lower for the elderly than the working poor or welfare populations, this is equivalent to specifying a representative distribution of participants among the three groups. The computation assumes no differential attrition at this stage. It also assumes no targeted outreach.

40. The major exceptions are home owners and (nonelderly) one-person households, who were not eligible for allowance benefits.

41. MacDonald, "Why Don't More Use Food Stamps?"

42. The same message is salient for researchers who have been concerned about the research design implications of the self-selection of participants in non-experimental programs. See for example, Robert F. Boruch, "On Common Contentions about Randomized Field Experiments," in *Evaluation Studies Review Annual*, ed. Gene V. Glass, vol. 1 (Beverly Hills, Ca.: Sage Publications, 1970), pp. 158–194.

43. Rogers, "New Product Adoption and Diffusion."

3

Supportive Services
to Program Participants

A housing allowance program attempts to improve housing conditions of low-income people by giving them money. But there is some question whether money is enough. Some families may need additional help to use the money effectively—finding decent housing, dealing with discrimination in the housing market or the complications of lease negotiation, teaching household budgeting and maintenance, perhaps even helping with problems not directly related to housing.

A major objective of the Administrative Agency Experiment was to gain some insight into the utility of supportive services in a housing allowance program. The literature on housing allowances, replete with arguments that services were necessary, nonetheless offered no consensus on what kind of services, or how much. The AAE agencies were therefore given a minimum requirement for supportive services and the option to provide as many services beyond the minimum as they wished. At the minimum the agencies had to tell potential participants about their rights and obligations under the program, to give them some information about finding acceptable housing in the local market, and to arrange for legal assistance in any equal housing opportunity cases that might arise. In practice the agencies' services ran the gamut from the bare minimum to intensive advocacy efforts to improve the general position of low-income people in the housing market.

Most of the material in this chapter is taken from William L. Holshouser, Jr., *Supportive Services in the Administrative Agency Experiment* (Cambridge, Mass.: Abt Associates, 1977).

The research goal was to determine whether the variations in supportive services made any difference to participants' experiences. The difficulty of achieving this objective is evident in the record of past evaluative research in this area. Counseling and related services are components of many social programs, including welfare, education, health, and manpower programs as well as housing programs.[1] Yet there has been virtually no research offering strong evidence that such services have had positive effects. Most research has been inconclusive; it has neither demonstrated positive effects nor proved their absence.[2] Significant, positive effects have rarely been established,[3] and some studies have found negative effects.[4]

It is, of course, possible that supportive services rarely have any effect. But there are characteristics of both the services and the prior research that have tended to limit the findings. The literature offers little theory about how counseling might be expected to influence human behavior. Contributing to the lack of theoretical constructs are the diversity of counseling activities (even the practical, "how to" literature provides no consistent definition of counseling) and the often diffuse objectives of such services. Because counseling is often offered as an adjunct to some other service, such as financial assistance or job training, an implicit hypothesis is that counseling may not have a direct effect but may enhance the value of the primary service. In addition to these characteristics, which by themselves would make conclusive research difficult, the research designs have not been powerful. Few studies have involved large data bases or pre- and posttreatment observations, and even fewer have had the control or comparison groups necessary to identify the outcomes that would have occurred in the absence of counseling.

Although the AAE design posed important limitations, it offered several advantages over many prior research designs. Perhaps most important was that supportive services were focused primarily on a single objective: helping enrolled households meet the program's housing quality requirement and thereby qualify for allowance payments. As chapter 1 indicated, eligibility for benefits in the AAE was determined in two stages. If a family's income made them eligible and if other household eligibility criteria were met (nonelderly, one-person households were excluded, for example, as were households headed by full-time students), the family was enrolled in the program. Before they could receive payments, enrollees then had to find housing that met agency standards or demonstrate that they already occupied such housing. Most of the concern in the literature and most of the AAE agencies' attention was directed to the second stage, particularly toward the problem of those who had to move to better dwelling units to meet program standards.

Agency records on the 8,095 families who enrolled, of whom 5,756 ultimately received allowance payments, make up one of the two major data bases for this analysis. The second is the reports of the on-site observers, who watched and categorized agency procedures for their first year of operations. These two main sources are supplemented in particular analyses by three additional data sets: a survey of a sample of enrollees conducted shortly after they enrolled and reinterviews six months and sixteen months later;[5] agency records of expenditures and allocations of staff time for supportive services; and detailed records kept by the Springfield agency of the supportive services provided to individual enrollees.

Together, these data bases allow a comprehensive analysis of the effect of supportive services on the likelihood that enrollees would become recipients. But the limitations of the AAE design are important. Most striking is the absence of a control group. Because all agencies were required to offer at least a minimum level of service, the analysis can test only the effect of variations above the minimum; one cannot say what would have happened if no services had been provided. The other major limitation concerns the possible effects of services beyond helping enrollees qualify for payments. Although the major hypotheses receive cursory examination here, the AAE design does not allow them to be tested conclusively.

After a broad examination of the factors influencing the process by which an enrollee becomes an allowance recipient, this chapter concentrates primarily on the questions whether and under what circumstances supportive services helped. The more limited evidence on issues such as the utility of services for improving housing quality or residential location is also presented briefly.

BARRIERS TO PARTICIPATION
IN A HOUSING ALLOWANCE PROGRAM

To receive a housing allowance in the AAE, many households had to find housing units that would meet the agency's quality standards. Some writers have asserted that nearly all low- and moderate-income households would encounter serious problems in finding standard housing. Hartman and Keating say, "It is inconceivable that low-income tenants armed only with housing allowances can succeed in the housing market, given the current state of landlord-tenant legal relationships throughout most of the country."[6] They predict that unless changes are made in landlord-tenant law and extensive services provided to recipients, a housing allowance program will result in widespread inflation and little improvement in housing quality.

The AAE data make such sweeping assertions seem unduly pessimistic. Almost three-quarters of the enrollees became recipients in units meeting agency housing quality standards.[7] But this achievement rate does not mean that enrollees did not have trouble finding adequate housing. Many had trouble because of tight housing markets, poor local housing stock (relative to agency housing standards), and racial discrimination.

Attempts to Move or Stay

An important factor in determining an enrolled household's likelihood of qualifying for payments was whether the household chose or was required to move to another unit. If a family was satisfied with the unit it occupied at enrollment *and* that unit met the agency's standards *and* the landlord was willing to sign a lease, then the family normally began receiving payments within two or three weeks after enrollment. If any of these conditions was not met, however, the enrollee had two ways to qualify for payments. The family might arrange with the landlord to have the unit repaired, although the short duration of the AAE made it unreasonable to expect more than limited repairs by landlords. Alternatively the enrollee could locate, lease, and move to an acceptable new unit. Finding an acceptable unit within ninety days sometimes required considerable skill, and many enrollees were unable to do it. As figure 3–1 illustrates, enrollees who planned to move were less likely to become recipients than those who planned to remain where they were or who were undecided.[8] About 84 percent of those planning to stay became recipients,[9] while only 62 percent of the households planning to move became recipients. The success rate for those who planned to move varied considerably by location, from 83 percent in Tulsa to 52 percent in Peoria and 28 percent in Jacksonville.

The enrollees' stated plans to move or stay were relatively accurate predictions of their actual behavior. Of those who became recipients, 87 percent followed their plans.[10] Although it may not seem surprising that many people did what they said they would do, behavioral research in this area does not often find a strong relationship between the intentions

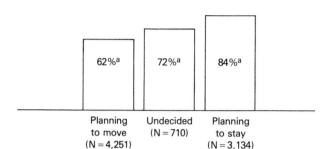

Figure 3-1.   Effect of Moving Plans on the Proportion of Enrollees Becoming Recipients

Source: AAE enrollment and payment initiation forms
[a]Percentage of enrollees becoming recipients

that individuals express and the actions they carry out.[11] This finding may thus imply that the housing allowance program, through the subsidy or the services offered, enabled more than the "normal" proportion of people to achieve their desires.[12] For managers of a housing allowance program, the finding means that enrollees' statements are relatively accurate in identifying the people likely to be looking for housing and that services could be efficiently targeted to this group.

Market Tightness

A widely voiced concern is that housing allowances will not work well, at least in the short run, in tight housing markets.[13] Malcolm E. Peabody, Jr., one of the early advocates of the housing allowance experiments within HUD, believes that housing allowances "cannot be used in tight markets where vacancy rates are less than 5 to 6 percent without some parallel program to expand production. Otherwise there will be an imbalance of supply and demand and rents will be driven up without improving overall housing quality."[14] Others believe that even a small-scale program could not work well if decent units are in short supply. Hartman and Keating, Robert Weaver, and a report from the U.S. Comptroller General's office all cite the high incidence of substandard housing among recipients of welfare shelter grants and military basic allowances for quarters, a problem that is especially prevalent in tighter markets, as grounds for fearing that a housing allowance program would fail.[15]

The AAE includes four cities that had relatively tight housing markets, with vacancy rates estimated to be between 4 and 6 percent during the time most enrollees were searching for housing, and four cities with looser markets.[16] Analysis shows that market tightness was in fact an important determinant of enrollees' success in becoming recipients. About 60 percent of the households operating in the tighter markets became recipients, compared with about 85 percent in looser markets. Not surprisingly, market tightness was most important for enrollees who attempted to move.

Available Housing Compared with Agency Standards

Housing quality requirements define conditions under which enrollees will or will not qualify for payments. If one agency defines and enforces housing quality requirements that exclude a large proportion of the low-cost housing stock and another agency's standard would admit most local units,[17] enrollees in the more stringent program might be expected to have a lower rate of success in becoming recipients. The lower success rate might result because few enrollees would already be living in acceptable housing, and the many attempting to move would find it difficult to find acceptable housing.

This prediction proved accurate in the AAE. Enrollees at sites with more stringent standards succeeded less frequently than those at other sites.[18] Table 3-1 compares the percentages of enrollees who became recipients under different degrees of agency stringency and market tightness. Success rates varied from a low of 57 percent in sites with tighter markets and higher stringency to a high of 86 percent in sites with lower stringency and looser markets.[19]

The quality of enrollees' housing influenced the effect of the agency quality requirements.[20] Where the quality of the original housing was

Table 3-1. Enrollee Success Rates by Stringency of the Agency Housing Standard and Market Tightness

| | Agency Requirements | |
Market	Less stringent	More stringent
Looser	86%	84%
Tighter	65%	57%

Source: AAE application, enrollment, and payment initiation forms; housing evaluation forms; agency inspection forms; and site background data
Data base: Enrollees (N=8,095)

Table 3-2. Enrollee Success Rates for Households
Attempting to Stay, by Unit Quality and Stringency of Agency Requirements

Unit Quality[a] (Adjusted Rent)	Agency Requirements	
	Less stringent	More stringent
Lower	81%	74%
Higher	87%	83%

Source: AAE enrollment and payment initiation forms; site background data
Data base: All enrollees planning to stay in original unit (N=3,117; missing cases, 40)
[a]Lower unit quality is indicated by actual gross rents at enrollment of less than 70 percent of the amount estimated to be the typical cost of housing that would meet the agency's standard (for a household of that size in that market). Higher unit quality is indicated by a gross rent of 70 percent or more of the estimate.

Table 3-3. Proportion of Enrollees Planning to Move
by Unit Quality and Stringency of Agency Requirements

Unit Quality (Adjusted Rent)	Agency Requirements	
	More stringent	Less stringent
Lower	58%	50%
Higher	46%	43%

Source: AAE enrollment forms, site background data
Data base: All enrollees (N=8,095)

good and the agency standard was not stringent, the success rate for enrollees who wanted to stay in their units was high. Table 3-2 shows the outcomes for enrollees who planned to stay in their preprogram units. Of those in better housing at agencies with less stringent requirements, 87 percent became recipients; the rate for those in poorer housing and facing more stringent requirements was 74 percent.

Enrollees' housing also had an indirect effect on their chances of becoming recipients. Those in poor housing were more likely to plan to move to new units either because they were dissatisfied with their current homes or because they felt the units would not meet the standards.[21] As table 3-3 shows, the proportion of enrollees planning to move was highest among those in poor housing at sites where agencies imposed more stringent standards. Because enrollees who planned to move became recipients less frequently than those planning to stay, this combination of poor housing conditions and high agency standards reduced enrollees' chances of becoming recipients.[22]

Discrimination

Another criticism of housing allowance programs is that households subject to discrimination may find it more difficult to rent acceptable housing in desirable neighborhoods. For example, historic patterns of racial segregation might mean that disproportionate numbers of black enrollees live in substandard housing. To qualify for payments, they would have to move. But segregation might make it difficult for blacks to rent better housing, even with the additional subsidy money. If they could not rent adequate housing, they would have to drop out of the program.[23]

The only ethnic groups represented in significant numbers in the AAE were whites (non-Spanish), blacks, and Spanish Americans.[24] The program's results did not apparently differ greatly for whites, Spanish Americans, or the small number of households from such ethnic groups as American Indians and orientals. Blacks had more difficulties than other groups, especially in sites with tight markets. Overall 53 percent of the black enrollees became recipients, compared with 77 percent of the whites. As table 3-4 shows, black enrollees planned to move more often than whites. These figures reflect to some extent the extraordinary problems encountered by black enrollees in Jacksonville.[25] But the patterns persist, though in less extreme degree, if Jacksonville is dropped from the analysis. Blacks tended to start out in lower-quality housing (presumably because of lower incomes and market discrimination) and therefore more commonly had to move to qualify for payments. When moving plans and other household demographic characteristics are taken into account, the black success rate is still lower and impossible to explain without reference to racial discrimination.[26]

Table 3-4. Moving Plans and Success Rates
for Black and White Enrollees (in Percents)

	Black	White
Tight market sites		
Planning to move	73	49
Becoming recipients	47	68
Loose market sites		
Planning to move	73	41
Becoming recipients	82	86

Source: AAE application, enrollment, and payment initiation forms, and site background data
Data base: All enrollees (N = 8,095)

Other Factors Influencing Enrollee Success

Several other factors affected enrollees' chances of becoming recipients, but they were less influential than those already discussed. Large families became recipients less frequently than small families, perhaps because of market discrimination or a scarcity of large units. Female-headed households and those receiving welfare income might also have experienced market discrimination, but they did not become recipients at significantly lower-than-average rates. The elderly tended to be more successful than the nonelderly, largely because they were more often able to stay in their original units. None of these factors caused large enough differences in enrollee success rates that a program administrator would be likely to seek corrective action.[27]

Three factors stand out as major obstacles to enrollees' becoming recipients. Those planning to move were less successful than those planning to stay in their preprogram units, especially in tight housing markets. The stringent housing quality requirements of some agencies and the poor quality of local housing stock combined to make the enrollees' task especially difficult. And black enrollees became recipients less frequently than whites, almost certainly reflecting patterns of housing market discrimination.

Were these patterns to exist unabated in an ongoing housing allowance program, they would limit the kinds of people the program could serve and the types of benefits that they could expect from it. Because much improvement in housing quality results from an enrollee's initial move to acceptable housing,[28] the problems experienced by movers—if unsolved—would limit the housing quality improvement the program could bring about. Agencies operating in tight housing markets or attempting to enforce a stringent quality standard might find it difficult to serve much of the eligible population. Market segregation might limit the benefits received by black households to inequitably low levels. Some have proposed that a housing allowance program provides services that help ameliorate these potential problems, and the AAE experience tends to show that services do work. The evidence on service effectiveness is presented in the next section.

THE EFFECTIVENESS OF SERVICES IN ALLEVIATING BARRIERS TO PARTICIPATION

Agencies offered two types of services: formal and responsive. Formal services were generally standardized and presented to enrollees shortly after their enrollment. Agencies provided responsive services to individual enrollees as particular problems arose.[29] Although all agencies offered both formal and responsive services, their emphases differed. Some agencies concentrated on formal information and training and seldom intervened in enrollees' search efforts. Some gave less front-end information but provided extensive resources or direct help to households encountering problems. Still others offered a high level of both types of services. Table 3–5 shows the agencies' relative emphasis on formal and responsive services.

Table 3–5. Agencies' Emphasis on Formal and Responsive Services

Site	Emphasis on Formal Services	Emphasis on Responsive Services
Salem	High	Low
Springfield	High	High
Peoria	Low	Low
San Bernardino	High	Low
Bismarck	High	Low
Jacksonville	a	Low
Durham	Low	High
Tulsa	High	High

Source: On-site observer logs

[a]Jacksonville planned and offered an extensive program of formal workshops. Unlike any other sites, however, this formal content was offered in voluntary, not mandatory, sessions. Only about a quarter of the agency's enrollees attended. Jacksonville's emphasis on formal services was therefore high in intent but low in practice.

Formal Services

Variations in the level of formal services do not seem to have affected enrollees' chances of becoming recipients. In loose housing markets even the lowest level of services was adequate. Enrollee success rates in these markets were consistently high, no matter what services the agencies offered. In loose markets a low level of formal services appears to result in no loss in effectiveness, and it offers an opportunity to hold down administrative costs.

It is more difficult to assess the value of formal services in tighter markets. Because no tight-market agency offered a low level of responsive services with a high level of formal services, the available data do not allow a determination of the importance of formal services alone under such conditions. Fortunately Springfield offers a partial solution to this problem. The Springfield agency kept careful records of enrollees' attendance at formal sessions and their use of responsive services.

Springfield enrollees who attended only the mandatory formal sessions succeeded at a significantly lower rate than those who also attended voluntary training sessions or used individual responsive services.[30] Among households that planned to move, 52 percent of those who received only formal services succeeded in becoming recipients, while 80 percent of those who received additional services succeeded. These findings suggest that formal services alone, even if provided at a high level, are insufficient to ensure a high enrollee success rate in tighter markets.

The Durham agency also operated in a tighter housing market. It provided minimal formal services to enrollees but offered extensive responsive services. The proportion of enrollees who became recipients in Durham was essentially the same as in Springfield, where both formal and responsive services were offered at high levels.

These examples suggest that it is feasible to hold formal services to low levels, even in tight markets. The AAE data are too limited to consider the findings conclusive but the potential savings of such a policy recommend it for further research.

Responsive Services

Because formal services had so little visible effect in the experiment, analysis of service effectiveness was largely confined to the responsive services. In tighter housing markets higher levels of responsive services were associated with higher levels of enrollee success. Table 3–6 shows the proportion of enrollees who became recipients under conditions defined by moving intentions, market tightness, race, and service level.[31] The percentage of enrollees becoming recipients varied from a low of 26 percent (for blacks who wanted to move in tighter market sites with few services) to a high of 89 percent (for whites in looser markets who wanted to stay).

Only one of the looser-market sites (Tulsa) offered a high level of responsive services. The others (Salem, San Bernardino, and Bismarck) offered primarily formal services. The similarity in success rates of the four agencies may imply that the high level of services in Tulsa was unnecessary to help enrollees become recipients.

The results observed in the tighter-market sites are more striking. Two agencies (Springfield and Durham) offered a high level of respon-

Table 3-6.
Proportion of Enrollees Becoming Recipients Under Various Service and Housing Market Conditions by Race

Market Conditions	Level of Services	Moving Plans				Total
		Move		Stay		
		Black	White	Black	White	
Tighter	High (Springfield, Durham)	65% (290)	63% (336)	77% (223)	77% (470)	70% (1,319)
	Low (Peoria, Jacksonville)	26% (219)	54% (389)	53% (92)	76% (552)	51% (1,252)
Looser	High (Tulsa)	82% (132)	84% (211)	84% (38)	88% (479)	86% (860)
	Low (Salem, San Bernardino, Bismarck)	78% (67)	81% (779)	85% (40)	89% (1,063)	85% (1,949)
Total		47% (708)	69% (1,715)	71% (393)	84% (2,564)	71% (5,380)

Source: AAE Application, Enrollment, and Payments Initiation Forms; Site Background Data; Services Logs and Process Documentation
Data Base: Enrollees (N=7,719; missing cases, 376). Most missing cases are other ethnic groups or those who were undecided about their plans to move.

sive services, and the other two (Peoria and Jacksonville) offered much lower levels. These variations in service level are clearly associated with variations in enrollee success rate: 70 percent of the enrollees in tight-market sites with high levels of services became recipients, but only 51 percent succeeded where service levels were lower.[32]

Services made a difference for households planning to move in tight housing markets. Their effect was significant for whites but crucial for blacks. High levels of responsive services improved the success rate for whites by 9 percentage points; for blacks the improvement was 39 percentage points.

The level of services made less difference for households that wanted to stay in their original units, even in tight markets. However, 77 percent of black households in this category became recipients at higher-service sites, compared with 53 percent where services were lower.

With market tightness and moving plans held constant, services appeared to help female-headed households more than male-headed households and those with welfare income more than those without it. The patterns were weak, however, and not as clear as the effects found for black enrollees. Service levels did not appear to help the elderly more or less than the nonelderly or large households more or less than smaller ones.

These findings are consistent with observational data and participant responses to survey questions. Both show that the high-service, tighter–market agencies responded to the special problems of households at a disadvantage in the housing market. Springfield, for example, emphasized equal opportunity training and aggressive use of legal services. Durham interceded with landlords, helped enrollees negotiate leases, and followed problem cases closely. Both programs apparently worked.

Responsive services to enrollees therefore seem compensatory. Enrollees in tight housing markets, enrollees planning to move, and black enrollees had difficulty becoming recipients; it was precisely these groups that responsive services helped most. Services did not completely equalize success rates. Enrollees in loose markets did somewhat better than enrollees in tighter markets, even with high responsive services. In tight markets enrollees planning to move were still less likely to become recipients than those planning to stay in their preprogram units. But services reduced those differences, and the dramatic disparity between outcomes for black and white enrollees in low-service sites was almost nonexistent in the high-service sites.

Cost Implications

The findings suggest that high levels of formal services may not be necessary in looser-market sites, and perhaps not even in tighter-market sites. The evidence also indicates that low levels of responsive services are adequate for looser-market sites but that more intensive services have definite advantages in tighter-market sites.

These conclusions might have important consequences for the administrative costs of a housing allowance program. Services to enrollees accounted for about 37 percent of all the direct administrative costs of bringing families into the AAE program. Variation in these costs can therefore have an important effect on total administrative costs. Table 3–7 shows that service costs vary substantially by intensity and method.[33] The table shows the estimated cost per enrollee[34] of varying the intensity of formal and responsive services and varying the way formal services are provided.[35]

Table 3–7. Estimated Labor Cost per Participant, by Level and Method of Services Offered

Emphasis on Formal Services	Emphasis on Responsive Services	Method of Formal Service Delivery		
		Group	Individual	Group plus individual
Low	Low	$16.41	$31.86	$45.15
	High	29.33	44.78	58.08
High	Low	35.12	50.57	63.87
	High	48.04	63.49	76.79

Source: AAE cost reporting forms, on-site observer logs
Note: Figures include indirect costs at the median AAE rate.

Within any given format of delivering formal services, the difference between lowest and highest levels of service was about $32 per enrollee. If, for instance, formal services were delivered in group sessions, costs ranged from $16 for low emphasis on both formal and responsive services to $48 for a high emphasis on both. The cost difference between a low and high emphasis on formal services was about $19, and the difference between low and high responsive services was estimated at $13.

The relatively large incremental cost of a high emphasis on formal service is particularly important given the indications that such services may not be necessary. Further research would be desirable to determine conclusively whether such services affect the achievement of program objectives, especially objectives other than helping enrollees become recipients.[36]

The $13 increment in administrative costs for a high level of responsive services may be considered acceptable in tight markets just because it will improve some groups' chances of participating in the program. In addition, the expenditures may reduce the money and administrative effort devoted to dealing with applicants who never become recipients.

Responsive services appear to be one of the major administrative devices to reduce attrition costs, the costs of carrying out such administrative functions as outreach, certification of eligibility, and enrollment for families who ultimately fail to become recipients. These costs can be substantial. AAE attrition costs amounted to 36 percent of all expenditures for bringing families into the program.[37]

Responsive services can reduce attrition costs by helping more enrolled families to qualify for allowance payments. In fact, under some circumstances reduced attrition costs may offset the higher cost of responsive services, yielding a lower average administrative cost per family.

A simulation model, developed for estimating administrative costs under varying assumptions about the program,[38] was used to determine the possible effects of responsive services. The simulation estimated the average direct cost for bringing a family into the program in the situations defined in figure 3-2. Attrition rates for each cell of the figure are estimated on the basis of average rates for black and white AAE households planning to move or stay in tight and loose housing markets. Those estimated rates are in turn used as the attrition parameter values in the simulation model.[39]

As the figure shows, the tightness of the housing market has a substantial effect on attrition rates and consequently on average costs per recipient. When enrollee characteristics and supportive service levels are held constant, the estimated attrition rate in tight markets is 24 percentage points higher than in loose markets. Because of this high rate, direct intake costs in tight markets are estimated at $14 per recipient above the average and $28 above the cost in loose markets.

Enrollee characteristics, specifically, race and plans to move to a new unit, have a striking effect in tight markets but not nearly as great an effect in loose markets. For the enrollee group with a high proportion of black households and households planning to move, the estimated cost

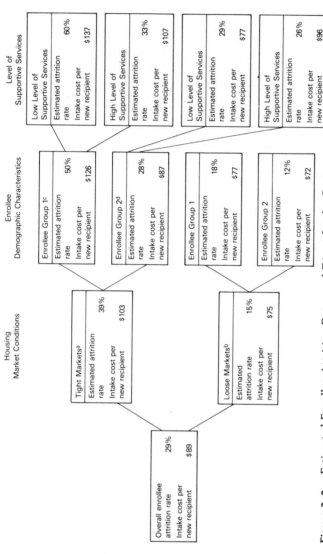

Figure 3–2. Estimated Enrollee Attrition Rates and Direct Intake Costs

Source: AAE operating forms; AAE cost simulation model; reports of on-site observers
[a]Tight market sites are Springfield, Peoria, Jacksonville, and Durham.
[b]Loose market sites are Salem, San Bernardino, Bismarck, and Tulsa.
[c]Modeled after the Jacksonville enrollee population; includes 66 percent black enrollees, or whom 92 percent plan to move and 8 percent plan to stay; includes 34 percent white enrollees, of whom 33 percent plan to move and 67 percent plan to stay.
[d]Modeled after the Bismarck enrollee population; includes 100 percent white enrollees, of whom 29 percent plan to move and 71 percent plan to stay.
Note: Enrollee attrition rate = (enrollees − recipients) ÷ enrollees

per recipient is $39 higher than the estimate for the group with more white households and households planning to stay in their preprogram units. In loose markets the cost gap between the two groups is only $5 per recipient. High levels of responsive services affected attrition mainly in tight housing markets, and then principally for black households and households planning to move. This finding is reflected in the attrition rates shown in figure 3-2. For the enrollee group including a high proportion of black households and households planning to move, the low-service attrition rate is 27 percentage points higher than the high-service rate. In the other enrollee group the difference in attrition rates is only 3 percentage points.

The most interesting effect of services appears in costs per recipient. High levels of responsive services are more expensive—$17 more per enrollee in this simulation.[40] Where these services have little bearing on attrition, high levels merely increase the intake cost per recipient, but where the influence on attrition is greatest, more expensive service procedures may actually reduce the average intake cost per recipient. For the group with high proportions of black households and households planning to move, therefore, the estimated cost per recipient is $30 lower with high levels of responsive services ($107 compared with $137 per recipient).

These figures on attrition costs and per-recipient costs cannot be taken as precise estimates, but they illustrate the main findings from the analysis of responsive services. Responsive services have a tangible effect on program outcomes, enhancing some people's opportunity to participate. Moreover, the effect appears to be compensatory. That is, services provide the most help to the groups with the largest problem: black households and households attempting to find new housing in tight markets.

THE EFFECT OF SERVICES ON OTHER PROGRAM OUTCOMES

The discussion so far has focused on the effectiveness of services in helping enrollees qualify for housing allowance payments. However, other program outcomes might be influenced by services. Training recipients to distinguish standard from substandard housing might help them select better units. Comparative information on neighborhoods, an aggressive open-housing program, or active agency involvement in the housing search might influence participants' choices of location. Services that anticipated or responded to problems encountered by recipients might reduce the number of households leaving the program because of eviction, nonpayment of rent, poor maintenance, and dissatisfaction with the unit or the neighborhood.[41]

This section reviews the limited AAE data relevant to these other concerns. It examines relations between services and change in the quality of housing units occupied by participants, locational changes by recipients, and premature terminations by households that qualified for payments.

Change in Housing Quality

Housing quality requirements were the source of the agencies' greatest influence over the quality of units occupied by AAE recipients. HUD intended these requirements to prevent subsidy money from going to units of unacceptably low quality, but left to each agency the task of defining and applying its own set of standards. They were meant to establish a "floor" below which unit quality could not fall.[42]

An agency might influence the housing conditions of its recipients in other ways. Evaluations of the Kansas City demonstration program suggested, for example, that participants might profit from information on identifying standard units.[43] Most AAE agencies offered such information. Several also identified neighborhoods in which enrollees might find acceptable units at reasonable rents or counseled enrollees in selecting units that met their particular circumstances and preferences. A few agencies helped enrollees locate units and negotiate repairs with landlords.

These services do not seem to have influenced the quality of housing that participants chose, although data limitations do not permit a firm conclusion. Table 3–8 uses two rough indicators of housing quality: the number of deficiencies reported from a selected set and the "standardized rent," the ratio of actual rent to a payment standard. By either measure the changes in housing quality of participants at agencies offering high responsive services differs little from the low-service case.

Survey data on the use of services likewise fail to show any substantial effect. A sample of households that moved and became allowance recipients was asked whether they had received any of four kinds of service, as reported in table 3–9. Housing quality changes were essentially independent of the reported use of services.

Table 3-8.   Services and Improvement in Housing Quality

	High Responsive Service Agencies			Low Responsive Service Agencies		
	At enrollment	At first payment	N	At enrollment	At first payment	N
Mean number of common deficiencies reported[a]	1.4	0.5	(138)	1.4	0.6	(110)
Mean standardized rent[b]	0.78	1.14	(875)	0.74	1.13	(1381)

Source: AAE enrollment and payment initiation forms; first and second participant surveys; first- and second-wave housing evaluation forms

Data base: For mean number of deficiencies, recipients who moved and were members of the joint survey/HEF sample (N = 348); for standardized rent, all recipients who moved excluding those reporting no cash rent at enrollment or first payment (N = 2,256)

[a]Based on the number of selected deficiencies reported for each unit. The selected deficiencies were the presence of leaks or rodents (as reported by participants) and the presence of structural hazards, safety hazards, heating deficiencies, plumbing deficiencies, or other deficiencies causing independent inspections to consider the unit unfit.

[b]The ratio of gross rent (R) to the locally estimated cost of housing meeting the agency's quality standard for a household of the given size (C^*); thus standardized rent $= R/C^*$. A value of one or more suggests that a participant's housing meets or exceeds agency standards.

Although services did not seem to influence the quality of housing that participants selected, they did have an important indirect effect. The groups that were most aided by responsive services, black households and households trying to move in tight markets, tended to occupy relatively low-quality units at the time they enrolled. These groups experienced the greatest gains in housing quality. By helping these households move and qualify for payments, then, services raised the overall average improvement in housing quality.

By providing a high level of responsive services, an agency may increase its ability to enforce relatively high housing quality standards and still avoid a high enrollee attrition rate. It is reasonable that this should be the case. Higher housing quality requirements force more households to choose between moving and dropping out (holding constant the condition of local housing stock). Services make it more likely that they will be able to move successfully.

Illustrative evidence on this point comes from a comparison of Jacksonville, Durham, and Peoria. In its first enrollment period Jacksonville combined relatively stringent housing quality requirements with a minimal services program.[44] The condition of the city's low-income

Table 3-9.   Reported Use of Agency Services and Change in Housing Quality

| | Mean Number of Selected Deficiencies | | | | | |
| | Households reporting use of service | | | Households reporting no use of service | | |
Service	At enrollment	At first payment	N	At enrollment	At first payment	N
Housing list	1.4	0.4	135	1.5	0.6	167
Staff called about units	1.6	0.3	50	1.4	0.6	251
Staff took enrollee to see units	1.4	0.5	28	1.4	0.5	275
Staff looked at units for enrollee	1.5	0.5	37	1.4	0.5	263

Source: First- and second-wave housing evaluation forms; second participant survey (Question 77 asked, "What did the housing allowance agency do to help you find a house or apartment? Did they (1) show you a list of places available, (2) make telephone calls to landlords or real estate agents for you, (3) take you around to look at houses and apartments, (4) look at places for you?")
Data base: Recipient members of joint survey/HEF sample who reported searching for new units after enrollment (N=306; missing cases are primarily "don't know" responses)

housing stock was poor relative to the housing quality standards, and the market for low-income units in standard condition was tight, especially for blacks. Peoria had a similarly limited services program but lower quality requirements. Durham had a high level of responsive services and also a rather stringent set of housing quality requirements. The resulting enrollee success rates are shown in table 3-10.

Comparisons based on single sites are perilous; many other factors were at work in each city in addition to those mentioned here. Nevertheless, it seems reasonable to conclude that the difference in outcomes in Peoria and Jacksonville is partly attributable to the stringency of quality requirements. Most striking is the difference in the rates at which black enrollees became recipients: success rates were 23 percentage points higher in Peoria than in Jacksonville for black enrollees who planned to move, and 34 percentage points higher for blacks who planned to stay. Durham, by contrast, attained a higher success rate than Peoria while maintaining a much higher set of housing quality requirements. It is likely that Durham's higher level of services helped the agency maintain both its standards and a relatively high and equitable success rate.[45]

Table 3-10. Enrollee Success Rates for Varying Levels of Inspection Stringency and Services, by Race and Plans to Move or Stay (Jacksonville, Peoria, and Durham, Black and White Only)

| | Percentage Becoming Recipients | | | |
| | Black | | White | |
Site Conditions	Planned movers	Planned stayers	Planned movers	Planned stayers
Low services, High quality standard (Jacksonville)	20	42	48	63
Low services, Medium quality standard (Peoria)	43	76	56	81
High services, High quality standard (Durham)	65	83	65	76

Source: AAE application, enrollment, and payment initiation forms; service categorizations from cost and utilization analyses in this report; inspection categorizations based on analysis of agreement between agency inspection forms and evaluation contractor inspections.
Data base: Enrollees in Jacksonville, Durham, and Peoria [Black and White only (N = 2,789)].
Note: Only enrollees from the Peoria city office are included because those at the branch offices faced different market conditions.

Residential Mobility

One might also expect that services would influence the number of people who would move and the location patterns resulting from their moves. The potential importance of services in providing minority and low-income households with improved access to the full range of housing in a program area is emphasized in the literature.[46] Some writers have expressed the fear that these households could not gain such access on their own. Others have predicted that these groups would be able to move away from the worst units and neighborhoods, but that this shift might accelerate the decay and abandonment of many areas. A series of multivariate (log-linear) analyses was performed to examine the factors determining the plan to move, search for new housing, and actual move behavior of households who ultimately became allowance recipients.[47] These analyses tested and extended models suggested in previous research, in which expressed satisfaction with housing circumstances is seen as a major determinant of plans or intentions of moving, and plans are a strong predictor of actual moving behavior.[48]

The AAE analyses resulted in the general model illustrated in simplified fashion in figure 3-3. Expressed satisfaction with the housing unit and with the neighborhood proved important predictors of moving plans. The effect differed for black and white households, however. Black households who were dissatisfied with their units generally planned to move regardless of their feelings about their neighborhoods; neighborhood dissatisfaction predicted an intention to move only among those who were satisfied with their units. Among white households, dissatisfaction with either the unit or the neighborhood might lead to a plan to move, and households reporting dissatisfaction on both counts were extremely likely to plan to move. Individuals' statements of their plans to move (reported to the agencies at the time they enrolled in the program) proved very good predictors of their own subsequent reports that they had searched for housing and agency records of whether they actually moved.

Supportive services were not found closely related to either plans to move or actual move behavior among those who became allowance recipients.[49] However, the fact that housing quality (as measured by standardized rent) as well as satisfaction influenced moving plans may indicate that the housing quality requirement has some effect on mobility. Since people living in poor housing may have been satisfied with it while realizing (or believing) that it would not meet the program's quality requirements, these people may have planned to move mainly to qualify for allowance payments.[50]

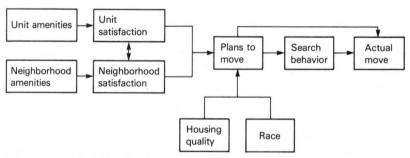

Figure 3-3.   Model for Predicting Move Behavior

Changes in Location Patterns

Households that moved tended to select better neighborhoods as well as better housing. A socioeconomic index (SEI) was computed for each census tract in which participants lived at enrollment and at first payment to estimate the extent of neighborhood improvements.[51] A census tract with an SEI score of 1.00 would be considered average in socioeconomic status for its area; lower scores indicate lower status, and scores above 1.00 denote above-average status. At enrollment households that moved lived in tracts with a mean SEI of 0.75 (0.87 for whites, 0.45 for blacks). At first payment the mean had risen to 0.86 (1.00 for whites, 0.61 for blacks). Because responsive services helped some households that might have dropped out to move, one might conclude that services contributed indirectly to the overall improvement in neighborhood quality.

Some evidence also suggests that services had a direct effect on neighborhood quality. When SEI changes at sites with higher and lower levels of responsive services are compared, those with higher service levels show a greater improvement in SEI. The pattern is statistically significant but not very strong.[52]

The main effect of services on location appears to be facilitating moves outside the neighborhood. Participants who reported receiving assistance in identifying or examining housing units moved outside their original census tracts more often than those who did not receive help (table 3–11). And on the average, participants who changed census tracts moved to locations of higher socioeconomic standing than the tracts they left.[53] Among participants who did move outside their census tracts, however, improvements in socioeconomic status were about equivalent whether they had received services or not.

This finding is consistent with observers' accounts that the agencies did not attempt to guide participants to particular neighborhoods. Had they attempted to do so, services might have been linked to stronger or more systematic patterns of neighborhood change.[54]

Population Redistribution

The possibility that services facilitate longer-distance moves raises the question of how they contribute to changes in population distribution generated by the program. The nature and extent of population redistribution that might result from a housing allowance program have been

Table 3-11.   Influence of Services on Distance Moved

	Percentage Moving Outside Their Census Tract Among Those Who			
	Received service		Did not receive service	
Service	%	N	%	N
Provide housing list	66	191[a]	49	235[a]
Call about units	84	58	53	365
Take to units	78	37	55	389
Look at units	88	40	54	384

Source: AAE enrollment and payment initiation forms; second participant survey; 1970 census

Data base: All recipients whose enrollment and first payment census tracts could be identified, who searched for a new housing unit, and who were part of the random sample of participants receiving a second participant survey. Searchers are recipients responding positively to question 39a, which asked whether anyone in the household looked for a new unit since enrollment (N=429; missing cases include "don't know" responses).

[a]Includes recipients staying in their preprogram units, moving within their original census tract, and moving outside the tract.

widely debated. Kansas City program recipients tended to behave much like nonprogram households. Most participants in that program were black, and most of those households that moved went to areas that were somewhat better but were still black or transitional neighborhoods.[55]

Can services improve access for minority and low-income families to all areas in which suitable units might be found? Would the resulting population shifts weaken inner-city neighborhoods and accelerate abandonment of the poorest units in the poorest neighborhoods? The AAE lacks a control group and therefore cannot distinguish between patterns within its recipient population and those affecting the entire eligible population.[56] There is some AAE evidence on this issue, however. Patterns of locational change in the AAE were similar to those reported in Kansas City. White movers tended to move to many parts of the program areas; black movers usually remained within black or transitional areas. Blacks did move to somewhat more integrated neighborhoods, but they rarely broke free of traditional patterns. This was true even in Springfield, the one agency that strongly emphasized open-housing information and other services intended to overcome obstacles to enrollees' freedom of locational choice.

In two AAE sites with high levels of responsive service, Durham and Tulsa, staff took considerable responsibility for locating and negotiating for units when participants had difficulty doing so themselves. Those agencies thus had considerable opportunity to influence the locational choices of their participants, and often they did. They did not, however, apply specific policies on locational choice. They did not urge black enrollees to move outside traditionally black areas, nor did they attempt to discourage them from such moves. The evidence indicates that with a high level of responsive services, an agency is probably capable of influencing locations chosen by participants. Without a specific policy on locational changes, however, the AAE experience does not indicate that services would advance or retard any particular redistributive patterns.

Much the same is true about the question of whether moves by participants would further weaken decaying neighborhoods. Although a substantial minority lived in suburban areas at enrollment, most AAE movers came from the central city. This pattern tended to persist. Most moves took place within central cities rather than from central cities to suburbs; all AAE moves resulted in only a 1 percent net increase in the number of suburban recipient households. Nevertheless, recipients did tend to move out of the poorest areas into others that were somewhat better.

These experimental results appear merely to reflect trends in the general population. It is impossible to say that the results were due to either the subsidy or the services offered. It is only reasonable to assume that services can have had some effect if an agency decides to make that a goal of its service program. But one cannot say that services actually did have any effect in the AAE beyond the possible facilitation of moves to new neighborhoods.

Services to Allowance Recipients

Once enrollees became recipients, the agencies usually offered them much the same types of responsive services they had offered to enrollees, but at a lower level. This reduction was justified largely because relatively few recipient households attempted to move. Whereas 45 percent of all recipients moved between enrollment and first payment, only 17 percent moved during their first year of payments. For those households that did move, staff were available to remind them of program requirements, provide search assistance, help with transportation, and render assistance in negotiations. For those who did not move, the main requirement for services arose in landlord-tenant relations; the agencies helped in a variety of problems such as evictions, rent arrearages, and disputes over maintenance, repairs, damages, and the recovery of security deposits.

Because services to recipients were not focused on a single event, like the qualification for payments, it is more difficult to measure their results. The most commonly anticipated benefits were reduced rate of termination from the program, more effective searching for new housing, and better maintenance of the housing that recipients occupied.

Termination Rates. One of the most discussed results of the early Kansas City demonstration project was that 32 percent of all households that qualified for payments eventually dropped out of the program and returned to poorer housing in the program area.[57] Some commentators suggested that counseling might have improved the program's performance.

The AAE showed a strikingly different pattern. Although about one-fifth of the participants had dropped out by the end of the first year, most of those terminations took place because the households moved from the program area or became ineligible on income grounds. Over the full 24-month payment period fewer than 10 percent of all recipients terminated because of circumstances the agencies might have been able to modify.

The very small numbers involved make detailed analysis infeasible. The AAE provided services not offered in Kansas City, urging enrollees to consider the services that would be available to them in various neighborhoods,[58] for example, and helping in landlord-tenant disputes. Some of these services might have facilitated continued participation, and they may help account for the different outcomes observed in Kansas City and in the AAE. But such evidence is circumstantial at best.

Although recipients in some sites had more landlord-tenant problems than recipients in others,[59] termination rates resulting from these problems were about the same. Data suggest that more services were generally offered in sites where more problems occurred. That is, recipients asked for agency help more often, and the agencies responded. This may support a hypothesis that services were effective in helping overcome such problems, but again the numbers are too small to permit firm conclusions.

AAE services to recipients were almost entirely responsive and limited.[60] Because these services were not associated with high termination rates or important variations in those rates, it seems reasonable to conclude that a low level of responsive services to recipients is a feasible option for a housing allowance program.

Subsequent Moves.   A higher level of responsive services was helpful to households that moved between enrollment and first payment, and it might also be useful in subsequent moves by program participants. Recipient households might choose to move, or they might be forced to move because of evictions or nonrenewal of leases. The recipients would then be subject to the same lease and housing quality requirements as enrollees. Services useful to enrollees should be useful to recipients who move.

AAE data are inconclusive on this relation, however. The percentage of households terminating within one year after first payment because they were living in or had moved to ineligible housing ranged from a low of 3 percent in Tulsa to a high of 12 percent in Jacksonville. The rate in Jacksonville, where recipients encountered an unusual number of problems with evictions and utility rate increases, was much higher than that for any other site. It was probably not closely related to the services offered by the agency. If Jacksonville is excluded from the analysis, there is almost no difference between higher-service and lower-service sites in the percentages terminating for this reason.[61] However, the numbers are so small that firm conclusions are not possible.

Maintenance.   The maintenance of housing units by tenants and landlords has been a major issue in subsidized housing programs. AAE agency staff normally left routine maintenance questions to the participant and the landlord, as in a private rental agreement. The program and agency retained some responsibility for making sure that recipients continued to live in units of acceptable quality, however. Poor maintenance over time could lead to a loss in any housing quality improvement that had been generated by the program or to a reduction in the supply of eligible units, either because they had become unable to pass inspection or because suppliers had decided not to rent them to program participants.

Some AAE agencies used the annual recertification of income and household size as the occasion for a home visit—a visit that was partly used to observe the unit's current condition. Other agencies made spot-check inspections of recipients' units. Agency staff reported that these measures were useful in helping them identify and deal with maintenance problems. But the AAE was of too short duration to permit any conclusions about the long-term relation between unit maintenance, reinspections of units, and services. As with most outcomes examined in this section, there is little evidence to suggest that agency variations in service procedures had significantly differing effects for the participants.

IMPLICATIONS FOR FURTHER RESEARCH

The most striking and interesting result of the analysis of supportive services in the Administrative Agency Experiment is the finding that services work—that is, that supportive services make a demonstrable, quantitative difference in the chances that an enrolled family will actually receive program benefits. The finding has obvious operational importance for a housing allowance program. But what makes it particularly intriguing is that previous research has rarely demonstrated a statistically significant effect of counseling, especially when counseling is an adjunct to a financial assistance program. The finding thus has implications for research in other program areas as well as implications for operating a rent subsidy program.

Operational Implications

The categorization of services as either formal or responsive was not originally intended but emerged after lengthy examination of the on-site observers' reports and a number of trial analyses. Initially the most useful classification scheme seemed to be one that specified the content of services offered (information about available housing, assistance in negotiations with landlords) or the format of service (whether audiovisual aids were used to communicate information). Another analytic tack focused on the philosophy of agency service policies, identifying laissez faire, casework, and enabling approaches.[62] But none of these categorizations proved as stable in their application to agency behavior or as powerful in analysis as the simpler distinction between services that were responses to the needs of individual families' problems and those that were not. Further research into the utility of specific services and approaches is certainly required, but the AAE analysis at least suggests that flexible responses to individual situations are needed if services are to be effective.

The findings also imply that this discretionary approach is useful only in some environments. Only in tight housing markets did responsive services make an appreciable difference in enrollees' chances of qualifying for payments, and even there services had no effect for white households not planning to move. The effect was apparent for black households, households planning to move, and especially for black households planning to move. This conditional effectiveness implies a need for control of the situations in which a responsive services policy is adopted, even though implementation of the policy, where it is adopted, may be best left to the discretion of the caseworker.

The importance of control is emphasized by the cost analyses. Providing responsive services is more expensive than not providing them —an estimated $13 more per enrollee. In a loose housing market, with a population including relatively few minority families or families moving to new dwelling units, the effect of providing responsive services would be to add about 10 percent to the per-recipient administrative cost of bringing families into the program. But in a tight housing market with a large proportion of the high-risk groups, providing responsive services may actually reduce average intake costs, perhaps by as much as 20 percent.

Research Implications

Because supportive services in the AAE were provided in the specialized context of the rental housing market and the housing requirements of a housing allowance program, the analytic findings have limited applicability to other fields and other kinds of social programs. The most interesting implications of the AAE seem to concern the ways in which future research on counseling and related services might be conducted.

For example, the AAE suggests some characteristics of models that might be explored in research on counseling. First, attention to the interactions among program variables, participant variables, and contextual variables may be critical to finding effects. (If the AAE analysis had used a simple comparison of enrollees in programs offering responsive services and enrollees in programs without such services, the difference in success rates would have barely been visible and certainly not considered important.) Second, supportive services may be usefully defined in terms of their quantity and responsiveness rather than their specific content.

The AAE also suggests that an assessment of the value of supportive services may have to consider indirect effects. Although the analysis could demonstrate no direct influence of services on quality of the dwelling units individuals chose, services did raise the average level of housing quality by improving the odds for people planning to move (that is, for the people most likely to improve their housing conditions). The administrative cost findings provide a more dramatic example, one that might apply to many programs in which counseling is a mechanism for reducing dropout rates.

Finally, the AAE analysis illustrates both the strength and the limitations of nonexperimental designs for research in areas such as supportive services. The central findings would have been more conclusive if they had emerged from a true experiment with, for example, random assignment of participants at each agency into "high responsive services" and "low responsive services" groups. But it is unlikely that an appropriate experimental design could have been developed on the basis of the information available at the beginning of the AAE, even if other obstacles to such a design had not existed. There were simply too many competing hypotheses. Moreover, selecting from those hypotheses would probably have led to a definition of treatment groups in terms of the content, format, or specific mix of services offered, which would probably have resulted in a null finding.

A design providing substantial capacity for exploratory research seems essential to analytic situations with many unknowns, and unknowns may characterize the setting for research on supportive services in other contexts than the AAE. For all its limitations, the nonexperimental design in the AAE did offer enough flexibility to allow alternative post hoc formulations of the treatment variable. It provided a rich observational data base to develop and "reality test" these alternative formulations. It developed a large quantitative data base to test the complicated conceptual structure that ultimately emerged. Ideally such research is only the first step, paving the way for more precise analyses under more controlled designs. In the area of counseling and supportive services, however, even such first steps may make important contributions to the effectiveness of administrative policy in social programs.

NOTES

1. Because the bulk of the supportive services provided in the AAE amounted to the provision of information and advice, counseling is a reasonably appropriate descriptor of the services. Indeed *counseling* was the term originally used in the AAE. *Supportive services* was adopted to include some of the noncounseling activities (provision of day care or transportation) and because HUD felt a political need to distinguish the housing allow-

ance program and its services from HEW's general income support programs and the counseling offered in that context.

2. See, for example, U.S. General Accounting Office, *Social Services: Do They Help Welfare Recipients Achieve Self-Support or Reduced Dependency?* (Washington, D.C.: U.S. Government Printing Office, 1973).

3. A rare example is described in David P. Campbell, *The Results of Counseling: Twenty-Five Years Later* (Philadelphia, Pa.: Saunders, 1965). This study showed that a group of counseled students in the 1930s made a better adjustment to college and had better grades than a control group of non-counseled students. (The twenty-five-year follow-up, however, showed no significant differences between the groups.)

4. Jeanne Lowe, "Housing and Urban Change: Where Does Social Work Fit In?" *Social Service Review* 78, no. 2 (September 1972).

5. The reinterviews were conducted only with households that qualified for payments.

6. Chester Hartman and Dennis Keating, "The Housing Allowance Delusion," in *Social Policy* 4, no. 4 (January–February 1974): 31–37.

7. Each agency had some procedure to screen out housing that did not meet its standard. No such procedure can be expected to operate perfectly, and chapter 4 estimates the extent of the imperfections in the AAE. Nonetheless this analysis generally assumes that families that became recipients did so in acceptable housing; the analysis does not attempt to distinguish or exclude any subset of recipients on housing-related criteria.

8. Plans to move were used as a proxy measure for whether a household attempted a move in order to qualify for payments. The proxy measure was necessary because no other data on whether households attempted to move are available for those who failed to become recipients. Where plans could be compared with actual behavior—for households that became recipients—they matched very closely.

9. The proportion for seven agencies ranged from 79 to 92 percent; Jacksonville was lower, at 57 percent.

10. Although there are no data allowing a similar analysis of households that terminated, one would expect the correspondence to be lower in that group. Some enrollees who planned to stay probably found that their units would not meet the quality standard and were unwilling or unable to move. Some who planned to move probably decided not to do so and terminated because their current units would not meet the standard. In Jacksonville, the only site operating two enrollment periods, data from the second period support the notion that enrollees' plans were less accurate in predicting the behavior of terminees. Still they were quite accurate overall. (Except as noted, data

from the second enrollment period in Jacksonville are not used in the analyses presented here.)

11. See for example Howard Schuman and Michael P. Johnson, "Attitudes and Behavior," in *Annual Review of Sociology*, vol. 2, 1976.

12. Although the design of the AAE does not allow a test of this hypothesis, the Demand Experiment provides some supporting evidence. For example, there is some indication that people who do not previously meet housing quality requirements will choose to join the program when they decide to move, using the subsidy to rent better (or at least more expensive) housing than they would otherwise have obtained. See James E. Wallace, *Preliminary Findings from the Housing Allowance Demand Experiment* (Cambridge, Mass.: Abt Associates, 1978).

13. The short run here might be about six years, the length of time Muth estimates an urban housing market requires to make a 90 percent adjustment after being put out of equilibrium. See Richard Muth, *Cities and Housing* (Chicago: University of Chicago Press, 1969). On the demand side, Mayo has estimated the time that would be taken to close the gap between "actual" and "equilibrium" (with subsidy) housing expenditures for households under a percentage-of-rent housing allowance. He estimates 75 percent adjustment after five to six years, and 90 percent after eight to ten years. See Stephen K. Mayo, *Housing Expenditures and Quality, Part 1: Report on Housing Expenditures under a Percent of Rent Housing Allowance* (Cambridge, Mass.: Abt Associates, 1977).

14. Malcolm E. Peabody, Jr., "Housing Allowances," *New Republic*, March 9, 1974, p. 23.

15. Hartman and Keating, "Housing Allowance Delusion," p. 32; Weaver, Robert C., "Housing Allowances," *Land Economics*, vol. 51, no. 3, August 1975, p. 248; "Observations on Housing Allowances and the Experimental Housing Allowance Programs" (Washington, D.C.: Comptroller General of the United States, 1974).

16. "Tighter" and "looser" markets were defined on the basis of overall vacancy rates in combination with other site-specific information on standardness and quality of available housing, the submarkets in which enrollees were active, and so forth. The concept and measurement of market tightness is important both in this report and in housing literature generally. "Tighter" markets generally had vacancy rates of about 4–6 percent, and "looser" markets had rates of about 8–13 percent.

17. Either course may be perfectly appropriate. If a high proportion of the local stock is substandard, an agency would be required to bar it from the program. If the local stock is generally sound, however, the agency would probably be largely concerned with identifying and excluding the unsatisfactory units.

18. The measure of stringency of agency housing quality requirements is derived from a comparison of deficiencies found on comparable items on agency inspection forms and forms completed by independent inspectors.

19. Multivariate analysis including these factors confirms the relationships. See appendix C for key tables and Holshouser et al., *Supportive Services*, appendix B.

20. Housing quality is defined as the ratio of actual rent to the estimated local cost of renting a unit (of appropriate size for the household) that would meet program standards. This measure is highly consistent with other, more direct measures of unit quality.

21. Multivariate analysis suggests that satisfaction and housing quality were the two most important determinants of moving plans. Evidence from a sample of enrollees in the second enrollment period in Jacksonville indicates that the plan to move was based on a judgment about whether the unit would meet the standard as well as household satisfaction. See Marian F. Wolfe and William L. Hamilton, *Jacksonville: Administering a Housing Allowance Program in a Difficult Environment* (Cambridge, Mass.: Abt Associates, 1977), appendix E.

22. See also appendix C, table C-2.

23. Those possible problems are mentioned by many, including: Jane Shaw, "Do Housing Allowances Work?" *House and Home* (January 1974), p. 8; Cushing N. Dolbeare, "The Housing Stalemate," *Dissent* (Fall 1974); and representatives of the National Tenants' Association, the Mortgage Bankers' Association, and the Rural Housing Alliance (with regard to residents of rural areas rather than racial minorities) in testimony on the Nixon administration's 1973 housing bill. See *Administration's 1973 Housing Proposals: Hearings before the Senate Committee on Banking, Housing, and Urban Affairs*, 1973. The actual occurrence of such problems in one AAE site is reported in William L. Holshouser, Jr., *Report on Selected Aspects of the Jacksonville Housing Allowance Experiment* (Cambridge, Mass.: Abt Associates, 1976) and Wolfe and Hamilton, *Jacksonville*.

24. Most Spanish American households were Chicano participants in San Bernardino. However, there were a number of households of Puerto Rican background elsewhere, especially in Springfield.

25. See Holshouser, *Selected Aspects*, especially chapters 8, 11, 12; and Wolfe and Hamilton, *Jacksonville*.

26. See Holshouser, et al. *Supportive Services*, appendix B.

27. Two other program features were also related to enrollee success: the subsidy the household was entitled to receive (those slated for larger payments were more successful) and a program rule requiring that allowance recipients not occupy housing subsidized by other programs (those already living in subsidized housing became recipients less frequently).

28. See Frederick T. Temple et al., *Third Annual Report of the Administrative Agency Experiment Evaluation* (Cambridge, Mass.: Abt Associates, 1976).

29. A more detailed discussion of the actual content of these broad service types is presented later in this chapter.

30. See also the log-linear analysis tables in appendix D (table D-2); for a full presentation of the log-linear analysis, see Holshouser et al., *Supportive Services*, appendix D.

31. See also the log-linear analysis in appendix D, tables D-2 through D-8.

32. Although the extraordinarily low success rate for enrollees in Jacksonville influences these figures, multivariate analyses excluding Jacksonville yield the same general result.

33. Figures reported in table 3–7 are based on a regression analysis of agencies' expenditures for supportive services during their first year of operations. For a full presentation of the analysis, see Holshouser et al., *Supportive Services*, appendix F, especially section V.

34. The costs shown are based only on labor costs, which were 82 percent of AAE costs. (The percentage would have been higher if the cost of equipment and materials had been treated as a capital cost instead of a current expense. Treatment as a current expense was necessary because of the short duration of the AAE.) Thus these costs understate the full cost of services. Indirect costs have been estimated at 122 percent of direct costs (the median rate for the enrollment period in the AAE), and they are included in the figures shown.

35. Responsive services were almost entirely individualized, so they involve no important variation in format.

36. In particular, one may view formal services as means of training enrollees to act effectively as independent agents in the housing market. Such training could conceivably reduce the need for services in subsequent moves under the program and could be considered a benefit in its own right.

37. See chapter 6 for a more complete discussion of attrition costs.

38. The simulation model is described in chapter 6.

39. For a complete presentation of this analysis, see *Administrative Costs of Alternative Procedures: A Compendium of Analyses of Direct Costs in the Administrative Agency Experiment* (Cambridge, Mass.: Abt Associates, 1977), pp. 1–24.

40. The $13 figure quoted earlier was estimated from agency expenditure levels, uncorrected for wage variations, and so forth; the simulation model attempts to eliminate such sources of variation and therefore yields slightly different figures.

41. Recipients were free to move to other units, providing they met housing quality requirements, were within the program area, were not subsidized under another program, and were rented under an approved lease. Faced with a circumstance such as eviction, resulting in a need to locate a new residence quickly, households might choose to move to noncomplying units even though they lost their subsidy. It is reasonable to hypothesize that appropriate services might help some households remain in the program under those circumstances.

42. A more complete discussion of the application of housing quality criteria in the AAE is presented in chapter 4.

43. See Roland Cage, Bill Jurkiewicz, and Ammi Kohn, *Interim Evaluation Report of the Kansas City, Missouri Housing Allowance Project* (Kansas City, Mo.: Midwest Council of Model Cities, 1971), p. 21.

44. The agency actually planned an extensive formal services program. Unlike other sites, however, most of the information was offered on a voluntary basis and only about a quarter of the enrollees took advantage of it. The agency did not emphasize responsive services.

45. The overall condition of housing stock, measured by census variables, was comparably low in Durham and Peoria, somewhat worse in Jacksonville.

46. Dowell Myers, "Housing Allowances, Submarket Relationships and the Filtering Process," *Urban Affairs Quarterly*, no. 2 (December 1975): 215–240; Robert C. Weaver, "Housing Allowances," in *Land Economics* 5, no. 3 (August 1975): 247–254.

47. Holshouser et al., *Supportive Services*, appendix C.

48. See especially Alden Speare, Jr., "Residential Satisfaction as an Intervening Variable in Residential Mobility," *Demography* 11, no. 2 (May 1974); and R. L. Bach and J. Smith, "Community Satisfaction, Expectations of Moving, and Migration," *Demography* 4 (May 1977): 147–167.

49. Recall the earlier finding that services increase the probability of becoming a recipient for households planning to move in tight housing markets. This analysis suggests that the major effect of services may have been to help those planning a move to find housing that would meet program requirements rather than simply to help them carry out the intention to move. Because no data are available on whether people who did not become recipients actually moved, this suggestion cannot be investigated.

    Agencies (and staff within agencies) varied in the degree to which they encouraged participants to move. This encouragement was not related to the extent of services offered, and hence any effect it might have is not captured in this analysis.

50. Findings from the Demand Experiment suggest that a housing allowance does have a small positive effect on residential mobility, independent of any role played by supportive services. See Jean MacMillan, *Draft Report on Mobility in the Housing Allowance Demand Experiment* (Cambridge, Mass.: Abt Associates, 1978).

51. The SEI contrasts tract levels of income, education, and white-collar employment with those of the program area as a whole. Bismarck was excluded from the analysis of locational change because the program area is not tracted by the census and thus did not have data comparable to that from other sites.

52. A difference-of-means test yields a t-statistic of 1.726, barely significant at the 0.05 level in a one-tailed test. See Holshouser et al., *Supportive Services*, appendix E.

53. The mean score on the socioeconomic index at first payment was 0.859 for participants who stayed in their preprogram units and 0.763 for those who moved but did not change census tracts. Those who changed census tracts went from locations with a mean score of 0.751 to locations with a mean of 0.920.

54. In Tulsa, for example, staff members provided substantial assistance in identifying available units. Participants' locational choices tended to follow the patterns of staff members' knowledge of particular areas and landlords. This fact suggests that if agency services were intentionally structured to guide participants to or away from particular areas, they might have great effect.

55. See Antony Phipps, "Locational Choice in Kansas City, Missouri, Housing Allowance Demonstration" (Kansas City, Mo.: Missouri Chamber of Commerce, 1973), pp. 83–84, 95. See also Weaver, and Myers, "Housing Allowances."

56. The Housing Allowance Demand Experiment is studying these issues more systematically and should provide more conclusive findings.

57. Scott Jacobs, "The Housing Allowance Program in Kansas City Turns into a Notable Failure," *Planning* (October 1973): 10–13.

58. Apparently many Kansas City families moved from neighborhoods in which many supportive services were provided by families and other institutions. They then found that in their new, more middle-class neighborhoods, such services were either unavailable or cost much more (for example, day care for children of working mothers). Some elected to move back, even though it meant dropping out of the program. See Jane Shaw, "Do Housing Allowances Work?" *House and Home* (January 1974): 8.

59. Based largely on on-site observer reports. Another piece of evidence comes from logs of telephone contacts kept by staff during a period of about a

month, after enrollment and search had ended. Service-related calls range from a low of 1.3 per participant per year in San Bernardino to a high of 11–12 in Springfield, Jacksonville, and Durham.

60. One agency offered a number of workshops for recipients, and another attempted to do the same. The workshops dealt largely with matters not directly related to housing, and there is no evidence that they had much impact on termination rates, though they may have benefited recipients in other ways.

61. If Jacksonville is grouped with lower-service sites, the difference between the two groups is larger. Jacksonville was clearly a lower-service site in its overall approach, but it also tended to receive more than the average number of requests for help because of the difficulties recipients faced. The agency usually tried to respond to these requests, but they did so less aggressively than many other agencies. Given the difficulty of grouping Jacksonville, it seems better not to base any findings on such an analysis.

62. Holshouser et al., *Supportive Services,* appendix A.

4

IMPLEMENTING A HOUSING QUALITY REQUIREMENT

A housing allowance program is distinguished from other cash transfer programs by its intention that the subsidy be used for housing. Several features of the allowance program tested in the Administrative Agency Experiment promoted this intention. Some agencies required participants to provide evidence that they had paid their rent as a condition for receiving their monthly allowance payment. The amount of the payment itself was determined in part by the estimated cost of decent housing in each locality. Each agency defined a housing quality standard, and families were required to live in housing meeting that standard in order to qualify for payments.[1] The housing quality requirement—more specifically, the procedures for implementing the requirement—was one of the major foci of AAE research.

The housing quality requirement became a major administrative issue largely because it was one of the few administrative elements of the program that did not have clear parallels in other assistance programs. The closest analogy lay in the Section 23 leased-housing program, in which local housing authorities would lease existing housing from the owners and allow low-income families to occupy the housing at a subsidized rent level. In that program, as in the housing allowance, the agency had to ensure that the subsidized housing met a minimum quality level, described in legislation as "decent, safe, and sanitary." But the Sec-

Most of the material in this chapter is taken from David W. Budding, *Inspection: Implementing Housing Quality Requirements in the Administrative Agency Experiment* (Cambridge, Mass.: Abt Associates, 1977).

tion 23 program operated on a small scale. Thus agencies could select candidate units and inspect them according to an agency-determined schedule; and informal prescreening of the units could ensure that most would be of acceptable quality. The housing allowance program was to involve large numbers of participants, who would select housing at unpredictable times and with little knowledge or expertise in the application of housing standards, and who would need to have the selected dwelling units inspected very quickly.

Neither program experience nor the research literature could give much confidence to the planners of an allowance program. Indeed the literature suggested that both program operators and researchers would face a difficult task.

First there was a lack of consensus about what should constitute standard housing. State and local housing codes vary widely from region to region, and considerable inconsistency can be found in standards established by federal agencies, even within the Department of Housing and Urban Development.[2] Research has not established clear models of the effects of more stringent or less stringent standards, either for consumers or suppliers of housing. The literature provides little more than speculation concerning the effect of standards on low-income consumers in particular; the small body of literature that goes beyond speculation provides more questions than answers, as exemplified in a comment by Hartman et al.:

> In its present form, code enforcement, when pursued aggressively and mechanically, can harm residents economically and socially, and can have detrimental effects on the low-rent housing stock. Conversely, and ironically, failure to enforce codes can also result in greater injury to low-income occupants and to the housing stock.[3]

The housing allowance program represented a more complicated situation—a housing requirement combined with a subsidy—whose behavioral results were even less predictable.[4]

Second, the literature reveals the difficulty of enforcing housing standards. Gaps in enforcement are often attributed to corruption or other motivational problems among the inspectors required to enforce housing codes.[5] But housing conditions are hard to measure accurately, and two attempts to judge the quality of the same unit are quite likely to produce two different answers. Table 4-1 shows the results of Census Bureau studies of alternative means of collecting data for census housing evaluations. The bureau concluded that all procedures produced substantial unexplained variance between paired ratings, even where each rating represented a consensus judgment by two experts.

Table 4-1. Coefficients of Correlation between Ratings on Structural Condition for Four Census Surveys

Survey	Correlation Coefficient[a]
Evaluation study of 1960 census	
Enumerator vs. expert	0.49
Six-city evaluation of condition, 1961; consensus of two experts vs. consensus of two other experts	
Stratum I[b]	0.66
Stratum II	0.84
Fort Smith, Arkansas, study, 1962, expert vs. expert	0.52
Louisville, Kentucky study, 1965:	
Experiment A, enumerator vs. enumerator	0.58
Experiment C, expert vs. expert	0.52

Source: U.S. Department of Commerce, *Measuring the Quality of Housing,* 1967
[a]Ratings were dichotomous, "sound" vs. "deteriorating" or "dilapidated."
[b]Stratum I consisted of the tracts with the poorest housing—all tracts with a level of dilapidation of at least 15 percent in Atlanta, New York City, and San Francisco. Stratum II consisted of all tracts with at least twelve dilapidated units but less than 15 percent. (Stratum III, which consisted of all tracts with less than twelve dilapidated units, was not included in this study.)

The major question addressed in the AAE analysis, similar to that of the census studies, concerned alternative means of collecting data on dwelling units. Some agencies used professional inspectors, some had generalist members of their staff inspect units, and some relied on information that participants provided about the units. Data used to assess the effectiveness of these procedures included:

Independent evaluations of a sample of dwelling units. The sample comprised about twelve hundred units occupied by households at the time they enrolled in the program and the units occupied six months and sixteen months later by those of the sample households who became allowance recipients. The evaluation used the same form at all sites, and evaluators at all sites received identical training.

Agency inspection forms. Each agency defined its own housing standard, and designed the forms it believed necessary to obtain data for enforcing the standard. The forms vary substantially from agency to agency, even where the standards cover the same unit characteristics. Agencies were instructed to keep records of their inspections, but the consistency with which they did so varied, posing some problems for matching agency records and the independent evaluations.

The cost of the alternative modes of housing inspection was also a major issue for analysis. Data for these analyses came from agency records (especially from routine reports of the time allocation of each staff member) and from a simulation model that projected costs on the basis of the time required to perform particular tasks.

In addition to the housing inspection issue, analysis focused on the procedures by which agencies determined whether units met program standards and on the effect of those procedures on the standards themselves. This analysis relied almost entirely on observational data provided by the eight on-site observers, who maintained logs describing agency operations in enforcing the quality requirement.

The results of these analyses are presented in the first three sections of this chapter. The fourth section presents a tentative analysis of the effect of variations in the stringency of the housing quality standard on participants' housing conditions. Because the AAE was not designed to provide conclusive information on this issue, the analysis is necessarily tentative, but it provides interesting evidence that housing standards and their implementation procedures have at least an indirect effect on program outcomes for participants.

INSPECTION: COLLECTING INFORMATION ON DWELLING UNITS

The main administrative activity in enforcing housing quality standards is the collection of information about dwelling units. In municipal building code enforcement and similar contexts trained professionals perform this activity, carrying out a physical inspection of each unit and recording a judgment about its compliance with the standards.

The professional inspector is thus a logical choice for enforcing the standards of a housing allowance program. But some program planners were concerned that a full professional inspection would be excessively costly. In early design meetings for the Experimental Housing Allowance Program, "expert" judgments of the cost of performing an inspection varied from $30 to several hundred dollars. It was thought that a low-income family might need two, three, or more inspections before finding acceptable housing. If many inspections were required per family, at a high average cost, it might be necessary to find some mechanism other than the minimum quality standard to ensure that program participants occupied decent housing.[6]

Two features of the Experimental Housing Allowance Program resulted from this concern about administrative costs. The Demand Experiment examined alternatives to minimum standards, including a requirement that households spend a specified minimum amount for rent and a payment formula in which the subsidy is a fixed percentage of the rent. The Administrative Agency Experiment used only the minimum standards technique, but agencies were encouraged to find less costly alternatives to the full professional inspection.

The agencies developed two alternatives. The first, a minor modification of the traditional practice, substituted less well trained, less experienced, and presumably less costly "generalist" staff members for the trained professional inspector. The second was a more radical departure: agencies decided whether dwelling units were standard or substandard on the basis of information that participants provided, thus avoiding any direct agency expenditures for physically inspecting units.

The questions for the AAE research were whether these alternative procedures were effective means of enforcing the program's housing requirements and to what extent they offered cost savings. This section addresses the effectiveness question; cost implications are analyzed in the following section.

Methodology

Analyzing the effectiveness of the three inspection procedures posed several challenges. Ideally one would like to know the features of each unit that make it standard or substandard and then compare these known characteristics with the data the agency obtained about the unit. Effectiveness could then be measured in terms of the percentage of substandard units or features correctly described in the agencies' data. The major obstacles to this ideal analysis were the differences in definitions of standard housing used by the eight agencies, the differences between agency inspection forms and the housing evaluation form used by the evaluation contractor to independently assess a sample of houses, and the generally low interrater reliability of housing quality measurement procedures.

The approach taken was to try to determine whether the alternative inspection procedures entail different degrees of risk that a substandard unit would be unwittingly subsidized. The first step was to develop a measure that could be used at all eight sites to describe housing units that were probably substandard. A unit was defined as marginal if it had one or more of twelve deficiencies frequently included in measures of substandardness and measured unambiguously on the Housing Evaluation Form (HEF). A unit with two or more other deficiencies was likewise classified as marginal. Most of the analysis was based on housing units identified as marginal on the basis of the independent evaluation (the HEF).[7] Thus, although the marginal units examined at each site were not necessarily substandard by that agency's criteria, their condition was sufficiently questionable that inspection was necessary to avoid a serious risk of subsidizing substandard units.

For each marginal unit it was necessary to determine whether the agency inspection form contained information adequate to indicate that the unit's quality was questionable. The information on the form was considered adequate if the agency form cited two or more deficiencies (or one of the basic twelve) in the unit, or if the agency rejected the unit after reviewing the form, or if the agency required repairs to the unit. If a unit had been classified marginal because of a deficiency not clearly measured by the agency form, the unit was excluded from analysis.[8]

The analysis examined the proportion of marginal units in which professionals, generalists, and participants provided adequate information. For any approach a low proportion of cases with adequate information is taken to imply a substantial risk of approving substandard units.

Relative Effectiveness of Alternative Approaches

Trained professional inspectors assessed some dwellings in three of the eight AAE sites; only the Jacksonville agency used that approach exclusively. Inspections were performed by generalist staff members in seven sites.[9] Some units were approved on the basis of information provided by program participants in four sites; about two-thirds of the units in San Bernardino and between 83 and 98 percent of the units in Springfield, Salem, and Bismarck were inspected only by participants.

Trained professional inspectors were clearly more successful than either participants or generalists in providing the agency with adequate information on marginal dwelling units. As table 4–2 shows, the performance of generalist staff members was also better than that of program participants.[10] Trained professional inspectors met the analytic standard for effective performance in 87 percent of the cases. Generalists met that standard in 62 percent of the cases. Program participants met the standard in 36 percent of the cases examined.

Table 4–2. Relative Effectiveness of Inspector Types

Inspector Type	Number of Marginal Units Inspected	Proportion with Adequate Information
Trained professional	23	87%
Generalist staff member	116	62%
Program participant	64	36%

Source: Housing evaluation forms and agency inspection forms

Professional Inspectors.   Several factors help explain the apparent advantage of trained professional inspectors.[11] Professional inspectors recorded more detailed information, even when using open-ended forms that simply required a notation of the deficiencies observed.[12] The professional inspectors appeared to carry an effective mental checklist, presumably derived from a detailed understanding of the code or the agency standard. They tended to go systematically from room to room, from attribute to attribute, assessing each in terms of a clear set of preestablished criteria.

In contrast, program participants were clearly dependent on the agency checklist to define the information required and guide their assessment of particular conditions. Although generally conscientious in completing the inspection checklist, they apparently overlooked many deficiencies in units. Generalist staff members frequently ignored the detailed checklist and indicated only a summary judgment (standard or substandard) but missed major deficiencies less frequently than participants.

Professional inspectors also tended to be relatively stringent in their assessment of dwelling units. In both marginal and nonmarginal units professional inspectors tended to record more deficiencies per unit than either generalists or program participants. The professionals' advantage was greatest in identifying defects of a technical nature, as suggested in table 4–3. The table shows the number of deficiencies found by HEF inspectors and those recorded in agency data for specific classes of items.[13] The first column includes all items on which the HEF and agency forms provided reasonably comparable measures. The category structural and technical includes only measures of a unit's structural soundness and items of a moderately technical nature; these items would be expected to require a higher level of expertise in evaluation. Included in this category are items such as foundation, roof structure, and electrical hazards. Familiar items are those for which residence in the unit might provide an advantage in evaluation (such as infestation, adequacy of heating system, and leaky plumbing). Surface and amenity items include, for example, interior wall surface, floor surface, adequate shelves, and counter space; one might hypothesize that a future occupant of a house would be more sensitive to such items than would a current resident who wished to stay in the unit.

Table 4-3. Fail Ratios[a] for Specific Categories of Matched HEF/Agency Items, by Inspector Type

	All Items	Structural and Technical Items Only	Familiar Items Only	Surface and Amenity Items Only
Professional	283/310 0.91	59/34 1.74	61/47 1.30	113/101 01.12
Counselor	551/2,141 0.26	98/211 0.46	154/273 0.56	248/582 0.43
Participants[b] evaluating current residence	108/307 0.35	8/35 0.23	36/49 0.73	43/67 0.64
Participants[b] evaluating new unit	121/296 0.41	11/28 0.39	41/71 0.58	50/103 0.49

Source: Housing evaluation forms and agency inspection forms
[a]Fail ratio defined as total number of deficiencies cited by agency inspector divided by total number cited by HEF inspector.
[b]Springfield participant inspections excluded.

Professional inspectors were especially likely to identify structural, electrical, and plumbing deficiencies. Indeed the professional inspectors identified nearly twice as many deficiencies in this category as the independent HEF inspectors. The ratio of deficiencies identified by professional inspectors to deficiencies identified on the HEFs is from four to eight times as high as the ratio for staff generalists or program participants. Interviews and comments written on inspection forms indicate that both participants and generalists sometimes lacked the knowledge necessary to determine, for example, whether a hot water heater included a pressure relief valve or whether there were electrical hazards in a dwelling.

Finally it appears that professional inspectors had a limited, objective approach: they tended to view their task as applying a standard and recording information about deficiencies. Some generalist staff members tried to make "wise and appropriate" decisions about participants' selections, rather than objectively categorize units and their deficiencies. In their summary decisions many generalists reported that they attempted to take into account participants' preferences or needs, market conditions, and other factors. And program participants appear to have approached the task as consumers rather than inspectors; apparently a checklist can only partially overcome a tendency to focus on the attributes of a unit that make it "exactly what one wanted"—or at least better than what one had before.

None of these advantages is necessarily possessed by all professional inspectors or absent in all generalist staff members and program participants. In fact, some generalists and program participants were as detailed, as objective, and perhaps even as technically competent as professionals. Thus, although generalists or participants could not universally replace professional inspectors without a loss in the effectiveness of the minimum standards constraint, these alternative approaches might be satisfactory under special conditions.

Staff Generalists.   There is some evidence that generalists can be as effective as trained professionals. In Springfield, for example, a staff member without prior inspection experience was trained to take over the duties of a departing professional inspector. The analysis of marginal units showed this generalist to be as stringent and as detailed in his listing of deficiencies as his predecessor. In effect, the generalist became a professional; he became a licensed inspector after he left the program.

Although the Springfield case was not unique, most generalists in the AAE were not so effective. The AAE experience suggests three areas—staff training, management supervision, and staff assignments—where particular procedures might improve the generalists' effectiveness.

AAE agencies provided limited training for generalist staff members who would be required to inspect dwelling units.[14] The first was a series of orientation sessions to inform staff members about the checklist and the items it contained. Sometimes an expert provided practical advice on finding deficiencies in a unit. This training appears less suitable for generalists than for trained professionals, who might need only orientation to the particular standard adopted by the agency. Generalists were frequently dissatisfied with this type of training. Many later said that they were not sure how to assess a unit or did not have the expertise implicitly required by the checklist.

The second type of training was similar to the procedure commonly used in code enforcement programs. A staff member accompanied an inspector as an apprentice to learn the process of locating and recording deficiencies. Staff members in the AAE found this training helpful; a number indicated a desire for more of it.

Management support and supervision could play an important role in teaching technical expertise. A formal quality control procedure, for example, could allow review of staff members' work and provide incentive for good performance. This would involve reinspecting some dwelling units to identify and correct any tendency either to miss deficiencies or to be inappropriately stringent.

Combining responsibility for inspection with other duties, particularly supportive services, seems to have contributed to the weakness of the generalist approach in some agencies. There are three apparent reasons for this. Staff with significant other duties tended to do relatively few inspections and thus developed expertise slowly. Agencies that assigned staff members to multiple duties tended to provide somewhat less task-specific training. Most important, generalists with responsibility for providing supportive services apparently experienced role conflict—a difficulty in simultaneously attempting to help participants get into the program and to enforce program requirements that could prevent them from doing so. In at least some cases substandard units were approved not because the inspector did not locate deficiencies but because staff feared that particular families would not find acceptable units in the time allowed and chose to ignore the deficiencies.[15] Standards thus seem better implemented when staff members can specialize and especially when inspection and service responsibilities are not combined.

More intensive training and specialization appear likely to make generalists more effective but also to blur the distinction between them and professionals. Cost savings with generalists might be transitory: as generalists gained experience, they could be expected to command salaries equivalent to those of trained professionals. The generalist would then be mainly a pragmatic option, to be considered when professional inspections were not available.

Participant Inspection.   There appears to be less reason for optimism concerning the participant inspection approach. Some participants provided agencies with detailed information concerning deficiencies in dwellings, sometimes finding defects that required technical knowledge. However, participant inspection involves a large number of individuals with greatly varied expertise. In a housing allowance program an average participant would probably report on a very small number of dwellings, perhaps one or two a year, and could not be expected to have special knowledge beyond what the agency provides.

As a result, participants in the AAE were substantially less likely to provide adequate data on marginal units than either professional inspectors or generalist staff. Their weakness was particularly apparent on structural and technical items, as indicated in table 4–3. Participants tended to cite as many or more deficiencies in familiar items and amenity items (relative to the number identified by HEF inspectors) as the staff generalists, although still substantially less than the professionals.

The procedures that appear to make generalists more effective have less relevance for participants. A large investment in developing participants' skills for a one-time inspection seems impractical and unlikely to be cost–effective. A quality control spot check may provide some incentive to participants to give accurate information, but it does not offer much opportunity for learning and improved performance.[16]

Some improvement over the average performance for AAE participants might be possible, however. At most AAE sites participants received only limited training, generally a group session lasting less than an hour. During that session the agency's housing quality requirements were reviewed and the use of a checklist explained. A brief slide show might explain how to identify deficiencies to be reported on the form.

The Springfield agency offered more intensive training. Two one-hour voluntary workshops discussed the agency standards and the process of inspection in detail. About 20 percent of the participants in Springfield attended one or more voluntary sessions. A quality control spot check of units approved on the basis of information provided by participants indicated that session attendees were less likely to be living in substandard units and seemed to have provided the agency with more accurate information.[17]

Even with training and well-constructed checklists the participant inspection procedure appears to entail serious risk of approving substandard units, at least in some circumstances. A simple indicator of this risk is the proportion of approved dwelling units (based on information supplied by participants) that would have been rejected had an agency staff person inspected the unit. Staff at the Springfield and Bismarck agencies conducted systematic, random spot checks of units that had been approved after participant inspections; their results provide useful, if somewhat divergent, estimates of risk.

Springfield conducted two random spot checks, each involving more than one hundred previously approved dwellings. Each found that approximately 20 percent of the units were substandard, as shown in table 4–4. The Springfield spot check provides a reasonable test of the risk associated with participant inspection at that site. The criteria applied in the spot check were not artificial; in all cases where the spot check found a unit to be substandard, the participants were required to move or to have the deficiencies corrected within sixty days. Furthermore the units classified as substandard contained at least one and usually several deficiencies that the agency had characterized as serious. Units with technical violations of the code or minor problems were classified as standard with minor deficiencies. Thus one of every five units approved in Springfield on the basis of participant information did not meet the standard and would not have been approved by an agency staff member. In Springfield the participant inspection procedure clearly weakened the minimum standards constraint.[18]

Table 4–4. Results of the Springfield Spot Check
on Units Initially Inspected by Participants

Classification of Unit[a]	First-Year %	Spot Check N	Second-Year %	Spot Check N
Standard	31	35	32	35
Standard with minor violations	47	53	48	53
Substandard	21	24	20	22
Number of units in spot check		112		110

Source: Springfield "Narrative Progress Report," June 1974 and July 1975.
[a]Classification into three categories follows agency practice. Only units listed here as substandard were in violation of the Springfield agency's program requirements. The two spot checks were independent.

In Bismarck a similar spot check of units approved on the basis of participant information was done in the second year, with strikingly different results. In a random sample of one hundred units (approximately

20 percent of those in the program), the agency found only two that violated program requirements. One unit was probably standard when approved but developed problems after the initial inspection. The second unit was in satisfactory physical condition, but the participant shared basic facilities with the landlord, a violation of one program requirement.[19]

Because of the striking differences between the results in Springfield and Bismarck, a spot check was simulated using data from the Housing Evaluation Form. Information on the HEF does not correspond precisely to the agency standard, so simulation results must be regarded with caution. However, results were roughly comparable with those reported by the agencies. In Springfield 19 percent of the units in the sample were classified as substandard, and in Bismarck, 6 percent.

The differences between the Springfield and Bismarck spot checks thus appear to reflect real differences in the effectiveness of participant inspection (although the limited training and experience of the persons who did the spot check in Bismarck may also have influenced the outcome). The differential effectiveness seems to result from two factors. First, most housing stock in Bismarck met all the agency requirements. In addition, the Bismarck agency's simplified checklist covered relatively few attributes of a unit and generally asked questions that could be answered easily by persons without special training or expertise.[20] In contrast, much of the housing stock in Springfield did not comply with the standard adopted by that agency. And the Springfield checklist, while simplified in form, required a detailed assessment of many attributes of a dwelling unit.

The choice of an inspection procedure, then, may depend on both the quality of the local housing stock and the nature of the housing standard adopted. In a program whose standard is intended to exclude or force the upgrading of a substantial portion of the existing housing stock, AAE evidence suggests that participant inspection would entail a significant risk of diminishing the effectiveness of the minimum standards constraint. But where most of the stock is in generally good condition and the standard is defined to classify most housing as acceptable, a participant inspection approach might be satisfactory.

INSPECTION COSTS

The finding that participant or generalist inspections posed a substantial risk of approving substandard units is quite consistent with the concerns of some of the early planners of the housing allowance program. Had the costs of professional inspection been as high as some feared—perhaps hundreds of dollars per participant—program designers would have been confronted with a difficult choice indeed. They could rely on costly professional inspection, which might drive total administrative costs as high as 40 or 50 percent of the annual value of the subsidy, accept less costly participant inspection, with a risk that one of every five units subsidized might be substandard, or they could look for some alternative to the physical quality standard.

As it turned out, the costs of professional inspection fell near the lowest of the early estimates. Thus even though participant inspections were cheaper, professional inspections could be considered an "affordable" procedure in an ongoing program. This section presents estimates of inspection costs and possible strategies for minimizing cost.[21]

Inspecting a Dwelling Unit

Three factors determine the costs of inspection: the average cost of inspecting a dwelling unit, the costs of other activities needed to determine standardness, and the number of required inspections.[22] The cost for an agency inspection[23] in the AAE is estimated to be approximately $34 ($16 in direct costs and an estimated adjustment of $18 to cover management support, record keeping, and all other indirect costs).[24] The greatest part of this cost results from getting to and from the dwelling unit and physically examining it.

The average inspection required slightly more than one and one-half hours of staff time. Somewhat less than half that time (about forty-five minutes) was spent at the dwelling unit; the rest was spent on scheduling and travel. Little time was spent on follow-up activities, compared with the time commonly spent on follow-up in code enforcement programs. Handwritten comments on inspection forms were generally inserted directly into agency files, and in most cases, even when repairs were required on a unit, follow-up paperwork was a clerical task.

The limited follow-up activity contributed to the relatively low average cost of AAE inspections. The inspection itself was also relatively simple and short. Assessing housing attributes did not require boring into walls, detailed examination of electrical wiring, or access to remote plumbing connections. It was generally possible to determine whether a dwelling unit met the agency standard by examining easily accessible attributes.[25]

Other Inspection Activities

Four other activities add to the total cost of implementing a minimum standards requirement: training for participants, staff training, time required to communicate and explain decisions to participants, and management support. Only the last of these appears to add substantially to the total costs of inspection.

Training for participants in the AAE was generally minimal. In Springfield, which offered the most extensive inspection-related training, the direct cost was estimated at about $2 (or $4 including indirect costs) for each enrollee attending the sessions. The sessions were voluntary, and only about 20 percent of the enrollees attended them, so the average cost of all enrollees was considerably less. Staff training generally included a few orientation sessions and sometimes an apprenticeship to an experienced inspector. No cost estimates are available from the AAE for either method, but when amortized over large numbers of inspections, neither should add much to the average cost.

With a minimum standards requirement, some time must be spent informing a participant of the inspector's or agency's decision. An approval required very little additional time and could be combined with efforts to schedule whatever steps remained to be completed by the participant. More time was taken to explain why a unit failed and what repairs it required to be approved. On the average, the decision and discussion were estimated to take about sixteen minutes. This time represented the major agency expenditure in the case of a participant inspection. The estimated cost of a single participant inspection is about $5, including $2.11 of direct and $2.45 of indirect costs.

Management, record keeping, and other indirect costs required to support the inspection function are a substantial part of total inspection costs. In the AAE, costs for management supervision and maintenance of records were not allocated to specific administrative functions. The adjustment for management support and other indirect costs included in the estimate of total costs per inspection may underestimate the relative cost of the inspection function; inspection was reported to require considerable supervision and record keeping, but the adjustment assumes a constant relationship between direct and indirect costs for all functions.

There is no reason to believe, however, that this adjustment would seriously understate administrative costs.

The Number of Inspections

The number of units to be assessed is the final element determining the cost of inspections. In the AAE an average enrolled household required slightly more than one inspection, 1.07 in the median agency. Thus the average cost per enrolled household would be $36 for agency inspections and $5 for participant inspections. Some enrollees did request inspections on several dwelling units before one was approved by an agency. Units that required repair were also supposed to have at least one additional inspection (though this was not always done). The primary reason for the low average number of inspections in the AAE was that many enrolled households never requested an inspection of any dwelling unit. The most outstanding case was Jacksonville, where over 50 percent of the enrolled households failed to request an inspection. But at other sites as well, most enrollees who did not become recipients appear to have terminated without ever requesting an inspection.

The low average number of inspections may be partly a condition of the experiment, however. As a new program, the AAE's requirements were not well known. Most households had limited information about the agency's housing quality requirements when they enrolled; some who did not request inspections might never have enrolled if they had been better informed.

The highest conceivable number of inspections per household consistent with the AAE experience is 1.5, assuming that every prepayment terminee would request the same number of inspections as the average family that met program requirements. Preliminary data from the Supply Experiment tend to support an estimate of less than 1.5; for example, in Brown County during the first year 1.3 inspections were done for each participating family. Not all these were required for program operations, however; some were done solely for research purposes.[26]

These numbers refer only to inspections performed to allow enrollees to qualify for payments. There was no consistent policy in the AAE with respect to inspections for families already receiving payments. An ongoing program would probably require a regular assessment of dwelling units after some period of time, as well as inspections for families who moved after becoming recipients.[27] A policy frequently followed in housing programs (and one that seems logical in a program requiring one-year leases) is annual reinspection. The analyses that follow assume a policy of annual reinspections.

Strategies for Controlling Inspection Costs

At $36 per enrolled household, the average cost of inspections in the AAE was far lower than early planners had feared and was apparently within an acceptable range. Even so, participant inspections at $5 per household would represent a significant cost savings if this procedure could be used without substantial risk of approving substandard dwelling units for subsidization.

The most promising approach would be to combine the procedures—to conduct agency inspections on some units and to accept participants' information about other units. In fact, this combination occurred at all agencies using participant inspections; sometimes agencies had to inspect units because participants were unable or unwilling to do so themselves, and sometimes agencies inspected approved units as a quality control measure. (This fact reduces the apparent cost difference between the agency and participant inspection procedures; if participant inspections were used in 90 percent of the cases and agency inspections in a partially overlapping 20 percent, the average cost per enrolled household is $12 rather than the $5 associated with a "pure" participant inspection.)

Table 4-5 shows that reducing the number of inspections conducted by the agency can reduce average costs substantially. The analysis assumes that nearly all participants bring in data on the units selected and that the agency also inspects a (variable) proportion of the selected units. The figures in table 4-5 can be compared with a cost of $35 per enrolled household for agency inspection of all dwelling units selected by program participants.

Note that this assumed procedure differs from those used by the AAE agencies. The assumed procedure involves inspecting some units after participants have provided information on them, while the AAE agencies treated agency inspection as an exceptional procedure. The agencies inspected units only when participants were unable to do so or when their information was not sufficient to classify a unit.[28] One agency imposed a different decision rule: San Bernardino required all participants who wanted to stay in their preprogram units to have an agency inspection, although participants' information was accepted for units to which enrollees wanted to move.

Table 4-5.   Cost per Enrollee of Mixed-Method Inspection Strategies

Cost per Enrollee	Proportion of Assessments with Agency Inspection[a]			
	90%	75%	50%	20%
Direct[b]	17.22	14.69	10.50	5.42
Total	37.20	31.73	26.68	11.71

Source: Cost simulation model. See Budding et al., *Inspection*, appendix C, for description of model and parameter values chosen.
[a]All methods assume participant inspection in 90 percent of the cases.
[b]Enrollees are assumed to require an average of 1.075 inspections.

The version of this hypothetical procedure involving the least risk of subsidizing a substandard unit would require agency inspection of all units that appeared to be standard based on information provided by program participants. Such a policy would allow units to be rejected, but not approved, on the basis of participant inspection. The policy would involve no increased risk, regardless of participants' effectiveness. This method would yield a saving only if the cost of the avoided inspections were greater than the cost of the staff time involved in reviewing participants' information. The analysis assumes that this method would require agency inspection of 90 percent of the units selected by program participants. The estimated cost is about $37 per enrollee, actually higher than the average for agency inspections in all cases.[29]

To produce cost savings, then, an agency would probably have to approve some units based solely on information provided by participants. In the AAE most dwelling units that were inspected met agency standards. Using available information on rent and the quality of stock in various neighborhoods, an agency might be able to "predict" the standardness of a unit. A unit with a high probability of being standard and for which participant information concurred could be approved. If all dwelling units in the AAE that rented at or above the payment standard[30] were approved based on participant information, agency inspections would then have been required on between 37 and 87 percent of the units, depending on the site. Such a policy would have resulted in an agency inspection of at least 88 percent of the marginal units in each site (using the definition of marginal discussed earlier).

Potential cost savings from such a method can be illustrated by two examples, a mixed method that requires agency inspection of 75 percent of the units passed by participants and one that requires agency inspection of 50 percent of those units. The estimated costs per enrollee are $32 and $23, respectively, the latter representing a substantial saving. Thus, although the professional inspector appears most effective and not unduly expensive, it may be possible to carry out a reasonably low-risk inspection procedure with costs about one-third lower than those of the agency inspection.

APPLYING THE HOUSING QUALITY STANDARD

Deciding who was to collect information on the condition of dwelling units—professional inspectors, staff generalists, or participants—was the agencies' most clear-cut option in enforcing the housing quality requirement. In addition to obtaining information, the agencies had to apply the information to determine whether the unit was standard. These determinations offered the opportunity for further, even subtle, administrative variations. The effect of these variations is not readily measurable in quantitative terms, such as the proportion of correct determinations. Indeed on-site observers' qualitative reports indicate that variations in the determination procedures affected primarily the agencies' definition of the housing standard.

The simplest determination of standardness is a mechanical application of the standard, given information about the characteristics of a dwelling unit. If the unit has the required characteristics, it is standard; if it does not have those characteristics, it is substandard. In an operating program, however, staff decisions to classify units as standard or substandard may not correspond exactly to the stated requirements. If staff practice differs significantly from the stated requirements, the practice becomes the de facto standard of the agency, whether or not there is an explicit change in agency policy.

Each of the eight AAE agencies selected a standard, usually a modification of an existing housing code, during the planning period of the program. These initial standards were described in varying degrees of detail in plans submitted to HUD. But the initial standards guided decisions throughout the experiment in only two agencies. In the remaining six the decision rule used to classify units was at least sometimes different from the initial standard. Some agencies made conscious policy decisions to adjust the original standard, adding or deleting particular housing quality requirements. In other cases the discrepancy between the initial standard and the operating decision rule was not the result of a conscious change in policy but the cumulative effect of actions taken by individual staff members.

The process of implementing standards in the AAE was rarely smooth or simple; the nature and stringency of the standard was frequently a matter of discussion and sometimes dissension among agency staff. This section presents analyses of qualitative data on the process and problems of implementing housing quality requirements, seeking administrative procedures that might enhance effective implementation.[31]

Adjustment or Erosion of Standards

The AAE agencies chose their initial standards hastily, in a brief planning period, often with little detailed knowledge of the condition of the local housing stock. When they began to apply their initial standards to actual dwelling units selected by program participants, a number of problems arose. Some agencies had to add a serious hazard or deficiency to their list of prohibited features. Others found that requirements that seemed reasonable caused an unexpectedly large number of units to be judged unacceptable. Each of these situations led to changes in the initial requirements. Some of the changes amounted to adjustments and refinements; others represented an erosion of the standard.

A process of formal policy adjustment to a standard was illustrated in the Springfield agency. In the planning period Springfield decided to use Article II of the State Sanitary Code of Massachusetts as the minimum standard for dwelling units selected by program participants. The requirements of Article II were embodied in the agency checklist. But attempts to use the checklist soon revealed that few dwellings in the area complied with all the provisions of Article II. The results of initial inspections triggered a heated debate among the program staff. The agency inspector, a professional with code enforcement experience, argued for full enforcement of Article II. "There is no such thing as a 'minor' violation," he argued. "It's clear in the code—and if I'm called to the stand to testify in court, I just have to call it the way I see it."[32] Despite the inspector's objections, the program standard was changed. Some requirements from Article II were classified as "major," such as serious structural, plumbing, or electrical hazards. Other items still included in the agency checklist were to be used primarily as guidance for participating families.

The Springfield agency's new requirements were applied consistently to determine the standardness of any dwelling unit. A unit with major deficiencies could not be approved unless they were corrected. Program participants were informed of minor deficiencies and told that they had the right under state law to request repairs from landlords. Minor deficiencies, however, rarely affected agency decisions on the acceptability of a unit for the housing allowance program.[33]

Tulsa, which also adopted a housing code, adjusted its initial standard differently. Its checklist covered each item in the code, which had more requirements than Article II in Massachusetts. As in Springfield, the initial inspections failed more units than expected. Unlike Springfield, however, Tulsa made no formal policy adjustment to the agency standard. Inspectors gradually decided to abandon the original agency checklist in favor of a memorandum of required repairs. Essentially each inspector in Tulsa then had to decide which elements of the code to enforce. There appears to have been an informal consensus among the inspectors concerning some items, such as the need for a pressure relief valve on a hot water heater, but in effect there was no agency-wide standard. Issuing a memorandum of required repairs required a reinspection of the dwelling unit, usually within thirty to sixty days of the initial inspection. Because these reinspections were often done by a different inspector, the agency staff became aware of serious inconsistencies among inspectors in the criteria used to approve units. At the end of the enrollment period the Tulsa agency decided to reinspect many dwelling units because it believed that at least one inspector had approved substandard units.[34]

In Tulsa the application of a minimum standard appears to have become both subjective and discretionary; units rejected by one inspector might well have been approved by another. The initial standard adopted by the agency was quite stringent and, like the Springfield standard, might have required adjustment. But the process of adjustment was outside the control of agency management, occurred inconsistently, and is better described as the erosion of a standard through the actions of individuals than as an adjustment or policy change.

The Tulsa case was neither unique nor the most extreme case of erosion. Only three sites, Bismarck, Jacksonville, and Springfield, were able to maintain a clear set of decision rules over the course of the experiment. In extreme cases the de facto standard for dwelling unit quality was the set of deficiencies that consistently caused units to fail, a least common denominator among the staff.[35]

Exceptions, Exemptions, and Ambiguity

In these examples the initial standard appears to have been misspecified. In each case it was considered so stringent that consistent enforcement would jeopardize the achievement of some program goals.[36] Standards were also adjusted when it became apparent that the original standard was not an adequate guideline for decision makers, when the available information did not allow staff to determine whether the unit met the agency housing quality requirements. In other cases the application of the implicit or explicit decision rule to individual cases produced an illogical result. Both situations could reveal the need for adjusting initial standards; the latter could reveal the need for exceptions or exemptions.

Staff members in a number of agencies discovered that the initial agency standard was not a clear guideline for classifying a dwelling. Sometimes it was merely the wording of one or more items on the agency checklist that caused ambiguity. Individual items could be so broadly construed that they provided no guidance to the unit's acceptability. Other items included in the checklist were apparently never intended to be a basis for the decision on a unit's acceptability.[37] For individual items it was possible to interpret policy, eliminate the ambiguity, or discard the item. None of these changes was particularly difficult.

In at least two agencies the inadequacies of the checklist resulted in more severe problems. Ambiguity was not simply the result of technical mistakes in the construction of the standard or checklist but the result of a failure to develop a sufficiently explicit standard. The difficulty faced by staff responsible for implementing policy in these two agencies can be illustrated by the following quotations:

> How do you evaluate whether a unit is acceptable or unacceptable? You can't say if you've got five bad or inadequate checklist items the house is out, because peeling paint and a series of things which need repairs don't make the house unsafe or unsanitary.[38]

> In most cases, a marginal unit was initially approved primarily on the basis of moral judgment. In other words, if a particular staff person doing the housing inspection felt that the new unit was better than the unit the family had previously lived in and the family desperately needed another unit, the unit was approved.[39]

In neither case had agency management provided the staff with a set of clear standards. Even with written statements and an agency checklist, staff members made their own subjective decisions on housing quality. Consistency could not be expected and was not achieved.

Although the standards of other agencies provided more guidance to staff, it would be naive to assume that reasonable decision rules can produce reasonable decisions in all cases. Some items on checklists applied logically to certain types of participants. In Springfield, for example, porch stair rails were ultimately required only for elderly households and the ban on lead paint was applied only to households with young children. Well-established exceptions to the standard can be made explicitly conditional on the characteristics of the household. But such conditions might take a long time to develop and might produce an inordinately complex set of requirements.

The Durham agency's procedure for handling exceptions or exemptions appears to have general merit. Where direct application of the standard seemed to result in an inappropriate decision, a formal waiver of one or more requirements could be requested. If approved by a staff supervisor, the nature of the exemption and the reasons for granting a waiver were specified on a form that became a permanent part of the agency records.

A formal exception procedure can provide agency management with an opportunity to review the exception process, possibly enabling them to distinguish among three very different situations: the case where an exception is legitimate only for a particular unit or household, the case where the nature of the exception indicates a need for change in agency policy, and the case where the standard is eroding. With a formal exception procedure for individual cases, management should find it easier to retain policy control over the implementation of standards.

Failed Units: The Repair Option

A family whose selected dwelling unit was not approved by the agency had two choices if it wished to receive a housing allowance: it could locate a new standard unit or have the rejected unit repaired. To administer the repair option, agencies required an explicit list of required repairs, a procedure to inform the landlord and secure an agreement that repairs would be made, and a reinspection of the unit after repairs were completed. These procedures were considered necessary for several reasons. The AAE regulations recognized that it might not be desirable to require repairs to be completed before the participant signed a lease and began receiving a housing allowance. But agencies also felt that landlords might be reluctant to repair units without a formal commitment. Further it might not be possible to complete repairs during the limited time allowed for an enrolled household to complete program requirements.

One experimental policy option allowed a family to receive housing allowance payments while repairs were in progress, provided that rent payments were placed in an escrow account and released to the landlord only after the repairs had been completed and the unit reinspected. Several agencies considered using the escrow account strategy, but it was actually adopted in only a few instances. In several jurisdictions the use of rent-withholding and escrow accounts was not legal. In one jurisdiction that permitted the practice, judicial approval was needed, and that was usually granted only after long delays. Thus the escrow strategy did not prove useful in the experiment. Legal authority for rent withholding is being adopted more widely, however, and the rent-escrow procedure might be useful to agencies in a future program. No reasonable alternative to the escrow strategy (other than requiring that all repairs be completed before payments were made) was observed in the experiment.

Most agencies in the AAE developed a repair strategy that appeared to conflict with program guidelines. Units were inspected, lists of required repairs were made, and participants were permitted to live in those units (and receive allowance payments) if the landlord agreed to do the necessary repairs. Some agencies permitted this strategy only when the deficiencies were considered minor. Two problems were observed in agencies that did not require repairs to be completed before families received payments.

First, pressures of the work load sometimes delayed or prevented reinspections of units. The available data make it difficult to determine whether repairs were actually completed, but some participants subsequently indicated that they were not. With no adequate follow-up procedure, program participants would not only live in initially substandard conditions, but the de facto approval of a substandard unit could persist until a participant complained or until a regular reinspection of the unit (often a year later) again raised the question of standardness. Thus any procedure that did not require units to be repaired before the start of allowance payments—or at least specify an early date for reinspection of the unit—could weaken the minimum standards constraint.

Second, use of the repair option without follow-up may have contributed to the erosion of an agency standard. In some agencies the possibility of repairs appeared to allow staff to avoid difficult decisions on units. In addition to "pass" and "fail" a third category emerged—"passed pending repairs"—that was attractive to staff members who did not like to fail units. When units were not reinspected or were reinspected only after long delays, the passed-pending-repairs decision became a pass, and the deficiencies in that unit became deficiencies that would be tolerated by an agency.

Implementation Problems and Management Quality Control

While nearly all public assistance programs find it difficult to enforce regulations consistently, a number of factors make implementing a minimum standard in a housing allowance program particularly problematic. The very nature of a housing allowance, which emphasizes relative freedom for participants to select dwelling units, created some tension. To enforce a standard meant, at least in some cases, to deny a participant's opportunity to select a particular unit and receive housing allowance payments. Some staff members indicated that they found the conflict between freedom of choice and a minimum standard difficult to resolve.

Because each AAE agency could define its standard, the housing quality requirement was essentially arbitrary; no law or regulation required an agency to enforce any of its requirements. Any staff feeling of arbitrariness could only be reinforced by the lack of national consensus on what constitutes standard housing. Inconsistent standards exist within the federal government and even within HUD,[40] and some argue against the whole concept of standards.

The staffs of the operating agencies tended to see the standard in relation to the attempts of individual families to qualify for program benefits. In other words, some agency staff perceived housing quality requirements as a barrier to helping families more than a means of increasing the program's effectiveness. Most staff members responsible for determining the acceptability of dwellings were also responsible for helping individual families complete program requirements. Because the agencies had to meet specific goals for the number of participants within specified time limits, many staff members felt caught between competing objectives: maintaining a quality constraint on the housing approved and meeting participation goals.[41]

When agency policy was clear and unambiguous, staff members could resign themselves to implementing the policy or attempting to change it. When agency policy became ambiguous and decisions subjective or discretionary, staff members could become confused and inconsistent in their decisions.

Some staff members felt responsible for making "wise decisions" in determining which elements of a standard were major and should be enforced and which could be ignored. Under these conditions many experienced confusion. Some tended to defer to the judgment of program participants; if a participant indicated a strong desire to live in a unit, staff would approve it despite violations of the agency standard. Sometimes a unit would be approved simply because a family was approaching the end of its time limit for finding satisfactory housing.[42] Or staff members might avoid the issue by describing a decision as passed pending repairs. Some staff members retreated to the relative posture noted previously: if the unit was better than the one the family previously had, it would be approved.

Not all such decisions ignored specific agency requirements; some staff members developed a personal standard that they implemented in lieu of an official agency policy. In one interview a counselor said that she tried to decide what each family needed and what was right for them; if the dwelling unit met *her* criteria for what was good for the family, then she would approve it. Given the burden implicit in making "wise" decisions in the face of such uncertainty, it is little wonder that some counselors described their inspection responsibilities as onerous.

Discretionary or subjective decisions did not necessarily lead to approval of inappropriate dwellings or to inconsistent judgments. Where a limited number of individuals were responsible for the decisions made by an agency, the results could be relatively consistent despite an ambiguous agency policy. However, ambiguous agency policy in an ongoing program is unlikely to result in a consistent standard. In many cases a discretionary decision process implies erosion of an agency's standard over time, diminishing and perhaps even eliminating the quality constraint on participants' choice of dwelling units.

It thus appears that effective implementation of a minimum standards requirement is likely to require leadership and supervision from the management of an agency. The first responsibility of agency managers would be to ensure that the agency standard is clear and unambiguous and that changes, when necessary, are made formally. Clear policy alone, however, could not guarantee effective implementation of a standard, given the pressures that agency staff members apparently felt within the AAE. A consistently implemented policy is likely to require continuous monitoring of staff decisions.

The AAE experience suggests some elements of an effective quality control procedure. The essential element is accurate information, accessible to agency management, on the characteristics of the dwelling units approved or rejected by staff members. Checklists would have to be designed so that detailed information concerning services and deficiencies could be recorded and easily reviewed. Efforts would also be required to ensure that such detailed information was actually recorded; in the AAE it was not uncommon for an agency inspector to ignore a checklist and record only the summary pass-fail decision. Quality control inspection of a sample of units assessed by staff members could ensure the accuracy of information on the inspection form. A formal procedure for waiving standards could be used where exceptions were required.

Finally an effective quality control procedure must include a process for impartial review of decisions. Much of the inconsistency in decisions observed in the AAE could be attributed to conflicting pressures felt by individual staff members. At least one agency (Springfield) developed a process whereby the recommended decision was reviewed by a supervisor before the agency communicated its official decision to a program participant. This procedure seems to have had the salutary effect of channeling doubts about the appropriateness of quality requirements into a debate over agency policy rather than allowing such questions to be resolved personally by individual staff members.

HOUSING STANDARDS AND PARTICIPANTS' HOUSING IMPROVEMENT—A TENTATIVE EXAMINATION

The analyses reported thus far have focused on the effectiveness and costs of the administrative procedures by which agencies enforce housing standards. But effective enforcement does not necessarily imply that participants' housing conditions will be improved. Housing standards vary. Two different standards, enforced with equal effectiveness, may therefore contribute differentially to housing improvement.

The Administrative Agency Experiment was not designed to study the effect of the housing standard, or variations in the standard, in an allowance program. Each agency set its standard in accord with the perceived condition and availability of local housing, making it impossible to separate with certainty the effects of the standard from those of the housing market. And the absence of a control or comparison group makes it impossible to judge how participant households would have behaved without the housing requirement or the subsidy.

The question how the standard affects participants is nonetheless interesting enough to merit a tentative examination of the AAE data, even though the study design precludes firm conclusions. This section presents such an analysis.

Expected Effects

A housing allowance program might improve the housing conditions of low-income families in several ways. First, participants might move to better units or obtain improvements to the ones they already occupy. In either case, they would experience an improvement in their housing's physical quality. Second, by acquiring larger units or by moving from shared quarters, families could reduce crowding. Finally, the allowance might alleviate the rent burden of families whose rent is too high a fraction of their income.

The nature of any immediate housing improvements for AAE participants depended in part on how they qualified for payments.[43] As table 4-6 suggests, families that qualified in their preprogram units would be expected to benefit in different ways from those that moved to new units. Those who move would be most likely to gain better-quality housing and reduced crowding. If one assumes that movers would have greater rent increases,[44] then reductions in rent burden would be larger for households staying in their preprogram units. Households obtaining repairs of their preprogram units would also benefit from some improvement in the physical quality of their housing, but major changes would not be likely.[45]

Housing standards might be expected to influence the way that participants qualify for payments. In a program with more stringent standards, other things being equal, one would expect fewer participants to be able to remain in their preprogram units without repairs and more to obtain repairs or move to new units. For those who obtain repairs or move, higher standards might be expected to result in greater improvements. Most specifically standards with stringent occupancy requirements might be expected to cause greater reductions in crowding than those with less stringent criteria. In any of these cases one might expect the nature of the housing standards to interact with the agency's policy of supportive services in determining the kind of benefits participants receive.

This section reviews the AAE data relevant to these hypotheses. The discussion of the stringency of housing standards uses a rough three-way

Table 4-6. Expected Benefits to Participants,
by Means of Qualifying for Payments

Benefit	Extent of Benefit by		
	Moving to new unit	*Staying in pre-program unit with repairs*	*Staying in pre-program unit without repairs*
Improvement in physical quality of housing	Major	Minor	None
Reduction in crowding	Major	None	None
Reduction in rent burden	Minor	Major	Major

categorization of the eight agencies. The categorization is based not only on the number and nature of items each agency initially included in its standard but also on the formal and informal modifications leading to a de facto standard and on the effectiveness of the agency's inspection procedure. Thus Jacksonville and Durham, whose initial standards were less stringent than others, were rated high because the standards were applied rigorously through effective inspection procedures. Springfield and Tulsa began with more stringent standards but modified them sufficiently and had sufficiently loose inspection procedures that they are classed as medium, along with Peoria and San Bernardino. Salem and Bismarck began with relatively nonstringent standards and implemented them through participant inspection procedures and are classified as low-stringency agencies.

Participants Moving to New Units

Participants whose units did not meet the agency standard usually had to move to qualify for payments. The higher the housing standard, then, the higher the proportion of recipients who would be expected to move. As chapter 3 shows, the tightness of the housing market and the extent of agency supportive services influenced the success of households attempting to move. Tighter markets generally reduced enrollees' chances of finding acceptable housing, but higher levels of responsive services mitigated the difficulties.

The influence of the quality standards is shown in table 4-7. Agencies with high quality standards had higher proportions of recipients who moved to qualify for payments than agencies with relatively low standards. High standards were most important for families occupying units in bad condition. At the agencies with high standards, four-fifths of the recipients whose preprogram units were of relatively poor quality moved. Since the agencies with the highest standards also faced relatively tight housing markets, the high percentage of recipients who qualified by moving seems to reflect, not easy access to new units, but a difficulty in qualifying for payments without moving. Where standards were lower, only about half the recipients with equivalent preprogram housing moved.

Table 4-7. Percentage of Recipients Who Moved to Qualify for Payments

	Better Preprogram Housing[c]		Worse Preprogram Housing	
	%	N	%	N
Tight housing markets[a]				
High standard[b]	48	120	80	50
Medium standard	39	170	58	52
Loose housing markets				
Medium standard	36	124	46	111
Low standard	36	205	53	53

Source: AAE payment initiation forms, first participant survey (FPS), first-wave housing evaluation forms (HEF)
Data base: Recipients in joint FPS/HEF sample (N=885)
[a]This categorization is based on vacancy-rate data in the 1970 census and local housing studies, as well as on narrative data. Vacancy rates in the submarkets where enrollees searched were estimated at 7–13 percent in the sites categorized as loose (Bismarck, Salem, San Bernardino, Tulsa) and 4–6 percent in those considered tight (Durham, Jacksonville, Peoria, Springfield).
[b]Categorizations are high, Jacksonville and Durham; low, Salem and Bismarck; medium, all others.
[c]Based on the number of selected deficiencies reported for each unit. The selected deficiencies were the presence of leaks or rodents (as reported by participants) and the presence of structural hazards, safety hazards, heating deficiencies, plumbing deficiencies, or other deficiencies causing independent inspectors to consider the unit unfit. Units with none or one of the seven deficiencies are categorized as better; those with two or more deficiencies are categorized as worse.

Even at the agencies with lower housing quality standards, the moving rate rose as housing quality declined. This implies that all the standards had the intended effect: participants in poor housing were more likely to move than those in better housing. An alternative explanation might be that dissatisfaction would have prompted the enrollees in poor housing to move even if there had been no standard. However, another AAE analysis has shown that the quality of enrollees' housing was related to their plans to move, even after their expressed satisfaction with the units was taken into account.[46]

The effect of the quality standard on success in qualifying for payments appears relatively small. In loose markets, where moving did not present unusual difficulty, the proportion of enrollees who moved to acceptable housing was not related to the standard. In tight markets, however, a higher standard may have added to the difficulty of moving. A slightly smaller proportion of enrollees moved and qualified for payments under a high standard than under a medium standard (20 percent compared with 26 percent, in agencies offering limited responsive services).

The interrelation of the quality standard with market tightness and agency services is shown in table 4-8, which presents the proportion of enrollees who became recipients by moving.[47] The effects of the market and of services are best demonstrated by comparing the success rates for agencies with medium-level housing standards. Among those agencies the success rate for enrollees in loose markets was higher than for enrollees in tight markets. But the variations between loose and tight markets was smaller among those agencies that offered higher levels of responsive services. In other words, moving was more difficult for enrollees in tight markets, but services removed some of the difficulty.

Table 4-8. Percentage of Enrollees Who Became Recipients by Moving

	Low Responsive Services[a]		High Responsive Services	
	%	N	%	N
Tight housing markets				
High standard	20	1,035	33	731
Medium standard	26	1,445	32	1,208
Loose housing markets				
Medium standard	38	1,004	38	1,066
Low standard	37	1,606	—	—

Source: AAE enrollment and payment initiation forms
Data base: All enrollees (N=8,095)
[a]This categorization is based on the allocation of staff hours to services and on narrative accounts. High-service agencies include Springfield, Durham, and Tulsa; low-service agencies include Jacksonville, Peoria, San Bernardino, Salem, and Bismarck.

Administrative decisions therefore appear to have a complicated but potentially important effect on enrollee attempts to move. Higher housing standards generally increased the probability that a household would have to move to qualify for payments, especially if the preprogram dwelling unit was in poor condition. In tight markets, however, the higher standard made moving more difficult, as well as more necessary. Thus in agencies with high standards the proportion of recipients who moved was greater, but the proportion of enrollees who planned to move and failed was also greater.[48] Finally high levels of responsive services tempered some of the difficulties of tight markets. By helping enrollees to find acceptable housing in these markets, services combined with the higher quality standard to increase the number of people who improved their housing conditions.

Improvement in the Physical Quality of Housing for Movers

A quality standard defines the portion of the local housing stock from which participants may choose units. Other things being equal, a higher standard might be expected to lead households to choose better housing. Supportive services might have the same effect, by educating participants or by helping them locate good units.

On the average, AAE households that become recipients by moving experienced marked improvements in the physical condition of their housing. But no strong patterns link the amount of improvement to variations in administrative procedures. Table 4–9 uses two rough indicators of housing quality: the number of deficiencies reported from a selected set[49] and the standardized rent, the ratio of actual rent to a payment standard.[50] Neither measure shows any clear correspondence to the housing standard. The increase in standardized rent was larger where the housing standard was high,[51] but no similarly large reduction in deficiencies was reported.

These measures of housing quality change are crude, and their imprecision may mask some differential effect of alternative procedures, particularly alternative housing standards. But different households doubtless had differing housing preferences and financial resources that affected their selection of housing. It seems likely that these factors produced greater differences than those introduced by variations in administrative procedures.

The indirect effects of choosing administrative procedures, then, seem greater than the direct effects. Higher housing quality standards induced more prospective participants to move, and higher levels of services helped them accomplish the move. Because housing quality gains were greatest for movers, these procedures increased the *average*

Table 4-9. Indicators of Housing
Improvements among Households That Moved

	Mean Number of Common Deficiencies[a]			Mean Standardized Rent[b]		
	At enrollment	At first payment	N	At enrollment	At first payment	N
High standard	1.3	0.5	87	0.74	1.25	374
Medium standard	1.6	0.7	169	0.76	1.11	1360
Low standard	1.0	0.3	92	0.76	1.11	522

Source: AAE enrollment and payment initiation forms; first and second participant surveys; first- and second-wave housing evaluation forms
Data base: For mean number of deficiencies, recipients who moved and were members of the joint survey/HEF sample (N=348); for standardized rent, all recipients who moved excluding those reporting no cash rent at enrollment or first payment (N=2,256)
[a]Based on the set of seven selected deficiencies identified in table 4-7, note c.
[b]The ratio of gross rent (R) to the locally estimated cost of housing meeting the agency's quality standard for a household of the given size (C^*); thus standardized rent = R/C^*. A value of 1.00 or more suggests that a participant's housing meets or exceeds agency standards.

improvement for all prospective participants. Whatever influence the procedures had on the housing that participants selected was apparently less than this indirect effect.

Households Obtaining Repairs to Preprogram Units

As the preceding discussion suggests, a change of residence was the principal means by which AAE households improved the physical quality of their housing. Obtaining repairs on the preprogram unit was another, less common, option. Overall, 12 percent of the AAE recipients stayed in their preprogram units with repairs, and 45 percent moved.

Agency staff members generally believed that the AAE's short duration made landlord interest in expensive repairs unlikely, so they did not pursue this option aggressively. Some staff members routinely encouraged participants to move rather than seek repairs. Nonetheless, four agencies made it their policy to obtain improvements, usually fairly minor repairs, for participants who did not move. The standards of Durham, Jacksonville, Springfield, and Tulsa included items that elsewhere were considered minor, were not enforced, or were excluded (for example, condition of window screens). Those four agencies generally asked that deficiencies in these minor items be repaired.

The four agencies that regularly sought repairs obtained them quite frequently. Over half the participants who stayed in relatively poor units at those sites had repairs, as did more than a quarter of those in better units (see table 4–10. Rates for repairs were substantially lower where the agencies did not seek them actively.

Table 4–11 shows that participants who stayed in their preprogram housing with repairs did improve their housing quality. Given agency expectations that only minor repairs were possible, it is not surprising that the changes in housing quality indicators are generally smaller than those for movers (see table 4–9). There is no clear indication, however, that the agency policy affected the extent of improvements.

Table 4–10. Percentage of Recipient Households
Staying in Preprogram Units Who Obtained Repairs

	Better Preprogram Housing		Worse Preprogram Housing	
	%	N	%	N
Agency sought repairs[a]	28	171	53	47
Agency did not seek repairs	5	206	23	70

Source: AAE payment initiation forms; first participant survey; first-wave housing evaluation forms
Data base: Recipients in joint survey/HEF sample who stayed in their preprogram units (N = 494)
[a]Based on narrative accounts. Agencies categorized as seeking repairs include Durham, Jacksonville, Tulsa, and Springfield; those not seeking repairs were Bismarck, Peoria, Salem, and San Bernardino.

Data limitations require that conclusions be drawn cautiously from these patterns. Other factors, such as the level of the agency's quality standard, the tightness of the housing market, and the services offered, might also influence the frequency with which participants obtained repairs.[52] These patterns imply, however, that an aggressive repair policy can lead at least to small improvements in the physical quality of housing for a substantial number of households that do not move, even when the incentive for landlord investment is small.

Reduction in Crowding

Housing standards can include occupancy requirements, which relate the size of the unit to the number of people in the household.[53] Six AAE agencies defined, as part of their standard requirements, a mini-

Table 4-11.   Housing Quality Improvement
for Recipients Who Obtained Repairs to Their Preprogram Units

	Mean Number of Selected Deficiencies			Mean Standardized Rent		
	At en-rollment	At first payment	N	At en-rollment	At first payment	N
Agency sought repairs	1.24	0.81	63	0.93	0.99	432
Agency did not seek repairs	2.04	0.88	24	0.91	0.93	221

Source: AAE payment initiation forms; first participant survey; first- and second-wave housing evaluation forms
Data base: For mean number of deficiencies, recipients who stayed in their preprogram units with repairs and were members of the joint survey/HEF sample (N=87); for mean standardized rent, recipients who stayed in their preprogram units with repairs, excluding those reporting no cash rent at enrollment or first payment (N=653)

mum number of square feet per person or a maximum number of persons per room.[54] Like other elements of the housing standard, occupancy requirements could determine which units participants who were moving could choose.

Households that moved in order to become recipients experienced a reduction in crowding, on the average, as shown in table 4-12. Of course, this condition did not change for households staying in their preprogram units.[55] Nor was there any evidence that crowding was reduced more in the agencies that had a formal occupancy requirement than in those that did not. In fact, improvements were slightly larger for agencies with no such requirement. This pattern suggests that, as with improvements in housing and neighborhood quality, the principal effect of procedural variations is on the proportion of recipients who move, while the families' preferences and resources determine how much reduction in crowding they achieve.

Reduction in Rent Burden

The size of reductions in rent burden depended on two factors: the size of the allowance payment and the extent to which recipients increased their expenditures for rent. No administrative procedures would be expected to have a direct effect on the reduction of rent burden. However, procedures that brought about other forms of housing

Table 4–12.   Reductions in Crowding for Allowance Recipients

Occupancy Requirement	Households Staying in Preprogram Units			Households Moving to New Units		
	Mean persons per room at enrollment	Mean persons per room at first payment	N	Mean persons per room at enrollment	Mean persons per room at first payment	N
Yes	0.63	0.63	2,393	0.82	0.71	1,982
No	0.62	0.62	778	0.79	0.64	600

Source: AAE enrollment and payment initiation forms
Data base: All recipients (N=5,753, missing cases, 3)

improvement would generally entail increased rent expenditures and therefore more modest reductions in rent burden.

Whether recipients moved had a great effect on changes in their rent burden, as table 4–13 demonstrates. Within subsidy categories recipients who moved had the lowest average rent burdens at enrollment. They experienced the largest average rent increases,[56] and they had the highest average rent burdens after becoming recipients. As with improvements, the administrative procedures that influenced the probability of a household's moving—that is, the quality standard and the level of agency services—therefore had an indirect but no discernible direct effect on improving participants' circumstances.

CONSIDERATIONS FOR POLICY AND FUTURE RESEARCH

The experience of the AAE offers insights into the implementation of housing standards in an assistance program as well as some possible directions for future research. In contrast with some of the other findings, the AAE findings on housing standards are not broadly applicable to the full range of income assistance programs. The application to the housing field is quite direct, however: the current Section 8 program for existing housing requires, as did the AAE, local housing authorities to determine that units meet quality standards before subsidies can be awarded. It is therefore appropriate for comments about the AAE research to assume a continuing policy and research interest in these issues.

Table 4-13. Reduction in Rent Burden

	Recipients Who Moved			Mean Rent Burden for Recipients Who Stayed with Repairs			Recipients Who Stayed without Repairs		
	At enroll-ment	At first pay-ment	N	At enroll-ment	At first pay-ment	N	At enroll-ment	At first pay-ment	N
Monthly allowance payment greater than $80[a]	0.44	0.25	1,348	0.51	0.14	283	0.57	0.15	777
Monthly allowance payment less than or equal to $80[a]	0.38	0.29	898	0.42	0.22	391	0.46	0.23	1,699

Source: AAE enrollment and payment initiation forms
Data base: All recipients, excluding those reporting no cash rent or zero gross income (N = 5,396)
Note: Rent burden at enrollment is computed as gross rent (R) divided by gross income (Y), or R/Y. Rent burden at first payment is computed as gross rent minus the allowance payment (S), divided by gross income or $(R - S)/Y$. (Note that an unconstrained transfer program, in which the subsidy would not be earmarked for rent, would compute rent burden as $R/(Y + S)$.)
[a]The average monthly payment was $81.

The Effect of Housing Standards

Although necessarily a secondary question in the AAE, the question of how participants are affected by housing standards in an assistance program is certain to become a more central issue in future research. The AAE experience suggests that the first place to look for effects is in participants' behavior as they enter the program. It appears that housing standards may help determine whether people move from their current dwelling unit (or get repairs to it) in order to receive program benefits. Further, it seems that housing standards, unless accompanied by adequate supportive services, can reduce participation levels among some groups of people, at least in tight housing markets. These effects can determine the pattern of benefits a program provides. An important task for future research will be to determine whether these behaviors are indeed affected by the housing standard or would occur in its absence, whether the effects persist over time, and whether similar effects occur at subsequent stages of program participation.

The AAE data imply that research cannot focus simply on the presence or absence of housing standards but must consider standards as a family of procedures varying in stringency. AAE agencies varied substantially in the stringency of the standards they implemented, and those variations appeared to have influenced at least participants' behavior as they entered the program. But stringency is likely to prove difficult to measure. A stringency measure must take into account not only the nature of the written standard but also de facto modifications that can occur in applying the standard to individual dwelling units and the level of error likely in data collected about the units.

Whether housing standards influence the amount of housing improvement a household experiences, apart from the indirect effects noted, is an important question for future research. AAE data do not reveal such effects in these tentative analyses. But a full test of the hypothesis will require more precise measures of housing quality, controlled variation of the stringency of the standard with respect to local housing market conditions, and control or comparison groups of nonparticipants. Such research could contribute a great deal not only to understanding the effects of housing assistance programs but also to more general knowledge of housing code enforcement.

Collecting Data on Dwelling Units

The AAE finding concerning the relative effectiveness of using professional inspectors, staff generalists, or program participants to obtain information on the quality of dwelling units would come as no surprise to practitioners. Although there was some risk of approving substandard units with any of the three procedures, the risk was substantially higher with generalists or participants than with professional inspectors.

Some aspects of the findings were less obvious, however, and may have implications in contexts such as the Section 8 program. For example, staff generalists with sufficient training and experience can become as effective as professional inspectors. But effectiveness depended on motivation as well as expertise. Staff members with additional responsibilities, particularly those responsible for helping participants in their efforts to qualify for program benefits, were likely to respond to a perception of the participants' needs rather than to the specifications of the housing standard. For an agency that must help participants qualify for benefits and at the same time apply a housing standard, this finding implies that a functional staff organization (for example, with some staff specializing in inspections and others in services) incurs less risk of subsidizing substandard units than would be likely with staff organized on a casework basis.

The cost analysis provided the greatest divergence from prior expectations. Administrative costs for professional (or staff specialist) inspectors were much lower than originally feared. The AAE inspections were less detailed and required much less follow-up effort than is typical of code enforcement inspections and enrolled households did not request as many inspections as anticipated. Although these costs make it feasible to use professionals or specialists (as is most commonly the case in the Section 8 program), the findings also suggest that it may be possible in some cases to reduce administrative costs by relying on information from participants. For example, if the AAE agencies had accepted participant information for adequate housing, administrative costs for inspection would have been at least 30 percent lower than those for professional inspections in all cases.

AAE analysis substantiated previous research, however, in indicating the fallibility of all procedures for measuring housing quality. The evaluation contractor performed two waves of inspections on the same sample of units about six months apart, and produced quality judgments with a correlation coefficient of 0.45—about the same level as that found in Census Bureau reliability studies.[57] The implication is that a program incorporating a housing standard cannot avoid a substantial risk of subsidizing substandard units and that carefully designed forms, quality control procedures, and periodic reinspection may be needed to minimize the risk. For research purposes the implication is that there is no absolutely accurate measure of a particular unit's condition; analyses must be carefully designed to avoid assuming that information is accurate because it is independent, and extensive data manipulation is likely to be needed to minimize the incidence of artificial discrepancies in paired measures.

Setting and Applying Standards

Just as it substantiated the difficulty of measuring housing quality, the AAE experience illustrated the problems that public agencies have faced for decades in formulating housing standards. Part of the difficulty amounted to a debate about the role of housing standards in an assistance.program. Given the existing condition of the local housing stock, should the standards be sufficiently stringent to force participants to improve their housing quality, or should the standards be loose enough to allow most interested families to meet them easily and at least alleviate their rent burdens? The prevalence of the debate and the variety of local resolutions that resulted suggest that program regulations must specify housing standards more tightly than was the case in the AAE if the standards are to serve the same goals in all locations. The Section 8 program is in fact considerably more specific than past programs about the nature of the housing standard to be applied.

The most striking pattern in the observational data was the need for—and frequent absence of—local procedures to ensure that the housing standard was consistently applied in determinations of the acceptability of individual units. (This is a particular strength of the long-term, open-ended observational procedures used in the AAE; briefer observations would probably not have captured the process through which de facto standards developed.) Further research would be required to allow quantitative determination of the most effective actions, but the AAE experience suggests a need for three classes of procedures. The first is a procedure for formal modification of items within the standard; even if a standard is specified relatively fully at the national level, it is likely that local circumstances will make minor modification desirable. Second, exception procedures are required to recognize and allow individual deviations from the standards but to avoid making such deviations a matter of staff members' discretion. Finally, monitoring or review procedures seem desirable as a means of ensuring that determinations of standardness are made consistently and in accordance with program policy.

NOTES

1. In common parlance, standard housing means housing that complies with the requirements of whatever housing code is locally applicable. In this discussion a standard can be any set of housing quality requirements, including those adopted by an AAE agency or those existing in some other regulations, such as a code. The specific standard referred to is established in the context of each discussion.

2. Oscar Suttermeister, "Inadequacies and Inconsistencies in the Definition of Substandard Housing," *Housing Code Standards: Three Critical Studies,* National Commission of Urban Problems Research Report No. 19 (Washington, D.C.: U.S. Government Printing Office, 1969).

3. Chester W. Hartman, Robert P. Kessler, and Richard T. LeGates, "Municipal Housing Code Enforcement and Low-Income Tenants," *Journal of American Institute of Planners* 40, no. 2 (March 1974): 91. See also Bruce Ackerman, "Regulating Slum Markets on Behalf of the Poor: Of Housing Codes, Housing Subsidies, and Income Redistribution Policy," *Yale Law Journal* 80, no. 6 (May 1971); and National Commission on Urban Problems, "Housing Codes," in *Housing Urban America,* ed. Jon Pynoos et al. (Chicago: Aldine Publishing Co., 1973), p. 502.

4. Analysis attempting to disentangle these issues is being conducted in the Housing Allowance Demand Experiment, which includes both a control group and experimental groups that do not have to meet housing standards to receive payments.

5. Joel A. Rosenblatt, "Housing Code Enforcement and Administration: An Organizational and Political Analysis" (Ph.D. thesis, Massachusetts Institute of Technology, 1971).

6. The author is indebted to Walter Stellwagen for this account of early discussions of the design of EHAP. Some of these early "expert" judgments were solicited by Abt Associates and are recorded in notes taken by staff members at various meetings. Costs are identified as central to the earmarking question in *Evaluation Manual: Administrative Agency Experiment* (Cambridge, Mass.: Abt Associates, 1973, revised) and *Experimental Design and Analysis Plan of the Demand Experiment* (Cambridge, Mass.: Abt Associates, 1974, revised), sections 2, 6. Cost issues in inspection were raised extensively in correspondence between the evaluation contractor and HUD during the preparation of the *Agency Program Manual* (1972). See also Henry J. Aaron, *Shelter and Subsidies: Who Benefits from Federal Housing Policies* (Washington, D.C.: Brookings Institution, 1973) and Anthony Downs, *Federal Housing Subsidies: How Are They Working?* (Lexington, Mass.: D.C. Heath, Lexington Books, 1973).

7. Since each agency chose the items to be included in its standard, no common definition of substandard was possible. The sample described was selected on the basis of items that would have caused a unit to be considered substandard in most but not necessarily all agencies. The term *marginal* is used to indicate that the final classification of the unit would depend on the agency's standard. For example, the unit was considered marginal if the independent inspector gave a rating of "seriously deficient, beyond repair, requiring replacement" to features such as the roof, wall, or floor structure or if the unit lacked items such as hot water, heat, bathroom, or kitchen. If the HEF inspector's overall rating of the unit was good or excellent, four deficiencies were required to consider it marginal. Of 1,237 units for which sufficient HEF and agency data existed to apply the criteria, 365 (30 percent) were classified as marginal.

8. The measure of adequate information is not equivalent to an item agreement comparison. If a unit was classified as marginal and not excluded from the analysis, any two deficiencies recorded on the agency form (not just those deficiencies cited by the HEF inspector) sufficed to categorize the information as adequate. (An analysis of item agreement among inspectors is contained in Budding et al., *Inspection*, appendix B.) Because housing inspectors tend to judge units rather than to record data about all features of the units, it was felt that focusing the analysis on judgments about units rather than item agreement would reduce problems of reliability between raters.

9. Inspections in Tulsa and Jacksonville were performed under subcontracts; for purposes of this discussion, subcontractor staff are not distinguished from agency staff.

10. Results reported in table 4–2 represent the most reliable comparison of inspector types. Other tables representing a somewhat different sample and larger numbers of cases are reported in Budding et al., *Inspection*, appendix B, and show results consistent with those reported in this single summary table (see table B3-2, p. B-28).

11. The analysis reported in the following paragraphs is based on reports provided by on-site observers, interviews with agency staff members, and comments recorded on agency inspection forms.

12. A closed-ended checklist, requiring an explicit judgment on each of a set of items, was more commonly used.

13. The table includes all units, not just those classified as marginal.

14. More information on training for staff and participants is included in Budding et al., *Inspection*, appendix D.

15. For a fuller discussion of this issue see Budding et al., *Inspection*, appendix A and chapter 4.

16. Spot checks were performed in Bismarck and Springfield but explicitly conceived as a research tool. In Springfield, however, the spot check was also used to correct participant errors by forcing them to move or to have deficiencies corrected. In neither case was the spot check envisioned as a training device.

17. See Budding et al., *Inspection*, appendix D.

18. Results of the Springfield spot check were reported to HUD in the agency "Narrative Progress Report" of June 1974 and July 1975. It was feared that the first spot check was not random; however, the second spot check confirmed the results of the first. Some staff members at the Springfield agency would disagree with this interpretation of the results of the spot check. Several people interviewed there continued to express satisfaction with the participant inspection approach, despite the results of the spot check.

19. Information on the results of the Bismarck spot check is contained in the "Final Report of the North Dakota Experimental Housing Allowance Project" (April 1976), p. 20.

20. In fact, nearly all the "error" cases in the simulation involved a single general question on the form regarding structural soundness. This question gave little guidance to the participant and encouraged a general summary judgment on structural soundness rather than careful attention to specific defects. The question was later revised by the agency for its own spot check.

21. This section focuses on the alternatives of professional inspection and data collection by participants. The staff generalist approach yielded results—in costs as well as effectiveness—midway between those of participants and professionals. Because considerable variation is possible in the degree of training and specialization for staff members, and therefore in the costs and effectiveness of that procedure, it is reasonable to focus on the professional and participant procedures as upper and lower bounds.

22. For a full presentation of the analysis summarized here see Budding et al., *Inspection*, appendix C.

23. Costs for generalists and professionals were not estimated separately. To the extent that differences could be observed in the AAE, they were small. The estimate may thus slightly understate the cost for professionals and slightly overstate the cost for relatively untrained generalists.

24. Costs were estimated by two procedures, one using agency reports of their expenditures and numbers of inspections performed and one using a simulation model to estimate time spent on component tasks (see chapter 6 for further discussion of both data sources). The estimated total from both procedures was quite similar: $15.36 using agency data, and $15.75 using the simulation model. Cost figures presented in this discussion are primarily from the simulation model. An indirect cost rate of 116 percent of direct costs is used here and in most other analyses using the simulation model.

25. The definition of the standard determined both the nature and amount of information an inspector collected. If a simplified checklist were adopted, an average inspection would obviously require less time and be less costly. Estimates of the unit cost of an agency inspection throughout this analysis have been kept conservatively high, and it is quite possible that the observed cost per inspection in an operating program would be lower. See Budding et al., *Inspection,* appendix C, for a further discussion of this issue.

26. See *Second Annual Report of the Housing Allowance Supply Experiment* (Santa Monica, Ca.: Rand Corporation, 1976), pp. 107–113.

27. No information was collected in the AAE to allow assessment of relative benefits of requiring reinspections at different intervals.

28. Random spot checks were also performed but not as a regular part of the procedure for deciding whether a participant would be eligible for payments in a particular unit.

29. Obviously the percentage of substandard units as reported by participants would depend on a variety of factors: the stringency of the standard, the quality of the local stock, the availability and price of housing, the extent of training, quality of the inspection checklist, and so on. The assumption of 10 percent here is based on the fact that about 30 percent of the units in the sample were classified as marginal and that participants provided adequate information on about one-third of the marginal units they examined.

30. The payment standard was an estimate of the average cost of housing in each program area that would meet the agency standard. Separate estimates were prepared for households of various sizes.

31. More detailed information on the problems and procedures of implementation is presented in Budding et al., *Inspection,* appendix A.

32. Adell Johannes, "Draft Case Study of the Springfield, Massachusetts, Experimental Housing Allowance Program" (Cambridge, Mass.: Abt Associates, June 1976), p. 73. The inspector was accurate in his interpretation of Article II. What he and others in Springfield sometimes failed to recognize was that the choice by the agency of Article II was voluntary. The debate thus concerned not the proper interpretation and enforcement of Article II but whether the agency would continue to use Article II as its standard or adopt a new standard based on Article II but not requiring conformance to all its provisions. Agency inspectors continued to use Article II as a reference for their decisions even though they shifted their criteria for approval in compliance with the agency decision; hence the category standard with minor violations used in the agency spot check.

33. The revised standard allowed a unit to be classified as substandard if it contained multiple minor deficiencies. It was later reported that ten minor deficiencies were required to fail a unit.

34. Most of the information on Tulsa comes from field notes and logs of the on-site observer. No formal report on the results of the reinspections could be located, and few reinspection forms were included in the forms provided to the research contractor. It is known, however, that some participants were forced to move or to have units repaired as a result of these reinspections.

35. Some indication of which deficiencies were permitted in approved units and which deficiencies were likely to cause units to fail is included in Budding et al., *Inspection,* appendix A.

36. In Springfield the results of the agency spot check confirm the judgment of the agency. Seventy-nine percent of the units actually approved by the agency would have failed the requirements of Article II (Substandard and Standard with Minor Violations, see table 4-4). In Tulsa there is no objective confirmation of the agency belief in a need to change the standard, but the stringency of the original standard makes the agency position credible.

37. In Durham, for example, the first page of the original agency checklist was intended for the use of staff in advising participants about the choice of housing. The "minor" violations in Springfield as defined later also fit this description.

38. Staff interview with senior agency official, 1975.

39. *Final Report,* Durham County Department of Social Services, 1976.

40. See Suttermeister, "Inadequacies and Inconsistencies."

41. Agency staff members encountered situations where the minimum standard failed a unit and a family dropped out of the program. There is some evidence from staff interviews in 1974 and 1975, however, that staff members tended to underestimate the possibility that participants who had one or more units failed could find standard housing, thus increasing the perceived pressure to relax the minimum standards constraint.

42. AAE participants were given sixty days after enrollment to locate standard housing. An additional thirty-day extension could be granted by an agency. Some of these exceptions are discussed in Budding et al., *Inspection,* appendix A.

43. The analysis here focuses solely on improvements in housing conditions that occur at the beginning of a household's participation—that is, when an enrolled household begins to receive payments. It does not deal with the duration of those improvements. Nor does it consider subsequent improvements, which might well be substantial. Evidence from the Demand Experiment, for example, suggests that households might delay five years or more before fully adjusting their level of housing expenditures in response to a housing allowance. See Stephen K. Mayo, *Housing Expenditures and Quality, Part I: Report on Housing Expenditures under a Percent of Rent Housing Allowance* (Cambridge, Mass.: Abt Associates, January 1977).

44. Other research has shown that a move is often the occasion for an increase in rent, even with quality factors held constant. See Sally Merrill, *Draft Report on Hedonic Indices as a Measure of Housing Quality* (Cambridge, Mass.: Abt Associates, 1977).

45. The AAE's short duration and limited scale were not expected to make landlords willing to undertake major rehabilitation, although observers reported a few major improvements. Table 4–6 therefore assumes that repairs amount to correcting generally minor defects rather than major problems.

46. William L. Holshouser, *Supportive Services in the Administrative Agency Experiment* (Cambridge, Mass.: Abt Associates, 1977), appendix B.

47. Because the market, standard, and services variables are all measured at the agency level, most cells in table 4–8 represent only one agency. (The loose market, low standard, low services cell includes two agencies.) The patterns reflected in the table must therefore be interpreted cautiously.

48. Of enrollees who planned to move, 60 percent failed to become recipients in the high-standard agencies, 34 percent in the medium-standard agencies, and 19 percent in the low-standard agencies.

49. The selected set of seven deficiencies is discussed in note c, table 4–7.

50. At each site a panel of local experts estimated an average cost for housing that met the agency's quality standard for different household sizes. This figure was used in computing the payment for which a household was eligible.

51. The figure in question depends on the pattern in the Jacksonville site. High standards in combination with a very tight market may have led participants to spend more in Jacksonville than in other locations. Agency staff also believed that the payment standard was too low and that very little standard housing could be obtained at the estimated levels (the payment standard was subsequently revised upward). For more discussion of this issue, see Marian F. Wolfe and William L. Hamilton, *Jacksonville: Administering a Housing Allowance Program in a Difficult Environment* (Cambridge, Mass.: Abt Associates, 1977).

52. These factors are too much confounded with the repair policy categorization for examination here. For example, three of the agencies with active repair policies were in tight markets, and three of the other four were in loose markets. Similarly the two agencies with high housing quality standards had aggressive repair policies, and the two with low standards did not.

53. Program guidelines required that the agencies, in formulating their standards, give consideration to the "size, number of rooms, and furnishability to adequately accommodate the size and types of families to be housed." *Agency Program Manual* (Cambridge, Mass.: Abt Associates, 1972), appendix IV.

54. Bismarck and Salem were the two agencies without such requirements.

55. In a few cases, but not enough to affect the mean substantially, the number of persons per room was reduced in households staying in their preprogram units.

56. The average rent for recipient households that moved increased by $56, compared with $7 for recipients who stayed in their preprogram units with repairs and $3 for those staying without repairs.

57. However, the six-month interval between measurements introduces a source of discrepancies unrelated to reliability between raters.

5

Certification of Eligibility and Income

Payment errors, especially erroneously large payments and payments to ineligible persons, are the bane of income assistance programs. Sensational cases periodically become a public embarrassment to program operators. Less sensational are the statistics constantly indicating that some percentage of program resources is not allocated in accordance with program goals.

Concern with payment errors has generated considerable discussion and development of procedures for avoiding or correcting them. The Department of Health, Education, and Welfare has established elaborate quality control procedures for measuring and responding to error in AFDC and related programs.[1] Critics and administrators of the welfare system have debated for decades the appropriate procedures for obtaining and validating information pertinent to recipients' eligibility or payment status, seeking simultaneously to minimize payment error, to contain administrative costs, and to treat individuals with dignity.

Like other organizations administering assistance programs, agencies in the Administrative Agency Experiment had to implement procedures intended to minimize payment error. These procedures, illustrated in figure 5-1, were associated with three administrative functions. When people applied to the program, the agency conducted a prelimi-

---

Most of the material in this chapter is taken from Donald E. Dickson, *Certification: Determining Eligibility and Setting Payment Levels in the Administrative Agency Experiment* (Cambridge, Mass.: Abt Associates, 1977).

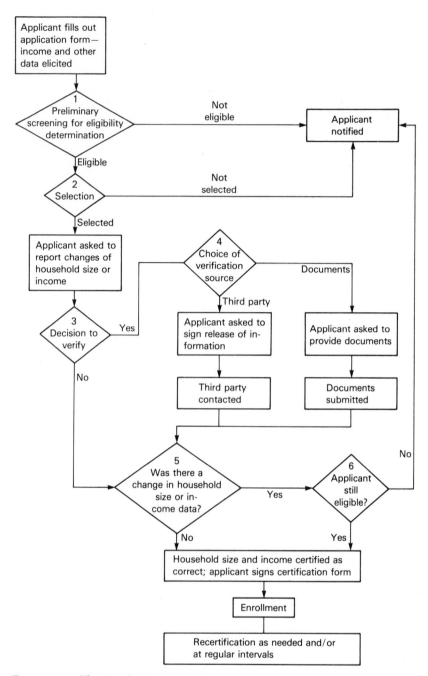

Figure 5-1. The Certification Process

nary screening to remove obviously ineligible persons from the applicant pool. After the agency selected a family for possible participation in the program,[2] certification procedures were performed to validate the information determining eligibility status and payment amounts. After participants began receiving allowance payments, periodic recertifications were performed to confirm or adjust eligibility status and payment amounts. Although the functions are similar to those of most income assistance programs, the AAE agencies were given the unusual option of designing their own procedures for implementation. This chapter discusses the results of the varying procedures that the agencies chose.

Discussions of payment error generally use the definition implicit in the HEW quality control process. In that process a sample of cases active at a particular time is selected, and independent audits of the participants' circumstances are performed. An error is a difference between the amount that should be paid according to the figures obtained in the audit and the actual payment issued by the agency. Payment error may thus arise from four sources.

Audit error, that is, a discrepancy between the figures reported by the audit and the true situation. There is little empirical literature to suggest the likely size and nature of this kind of error.

Participant reporting error, a discrepancy between information provided by the participant and the true situation at the time of the report. A number of studies have examined in a nonprogram context the reporting error associated with information of the kind used to determine eligibility and set payment levels.[3] U.S. Census studies have shown low error rates for household size and composition, for example. Higher error rates have generally been found in income reporting, with the prevailing error being an understatement of true income.

Administrative error, a discrepancy between the payment that should have been made on the basis of the information provided by the participant and the actual payment. Administrative error might result from incorrect recording of the information, erroneous information obtained in validating that reported by the participant, or error in the computation or issuance of payments. Quality control reports have attributed a portion of error to administration,[4] but there has been little effort to model the factors associated with this error.[5]

Changed circumstances, a discrepancy between the true situation at the time of the last report and the true situation at the time of the audit. Incomes of the low-income population are subject to considerable short-term instability, and a number of demographic factors are associated with that instability.[6] Quality control analyses therefore show an increase in "error proneness" with increasing lengths of time since the last report.[7]

Because the AAE did not include a routine quality control audit, the analysis does not deal with payment errors. Rather the analysis focuses on the results of the agency procedures for obtaining and validating information from participants. These results—determinations of ineligibility, for example, or adjustments to the amount of income reported by participants—might be regarded as avoided payment errors. The analysis generally assumes that potential payment errors are distributed randomly with respect to the administrative procedures under analysis and that the frequency with which each alternative procedure identifies potential error reflects the procedure's relative effectiveness.

Much of the analysis concerns the procedures for validating participant-supplied information on income and household size. Would-be participants filled out an application that included information on their income and household size. If this information did not indicate that the household was ineligible, and if the household was selected for possible participation, the agency would carry out some further procedure to certify the accuracy of the information. If the information entered on the certification form was changed from that on the application form, the agency was assumed to have identified and avoided a potential payment error.[8] For analytic purposes the amount of payment error avoided is seen as a function of the effectiveness of agency procedures and changes in participants' circumstances (proxied by the amount of time between application and certification and by demographic characteristics generally associated with income instability).[9]

A more limited analysis examined the results of eligibility determination procedures. In this case, administrative procedures might have some effect on the number of ineligible people who apply to the program as well as the number who are identified and excluded. The frequency with which an agency determines applicants to be ineligible is therefore a function of agency variations in the eligibility criteria and outreach efforts as well as the procedures for obtaining eligibility-related information and applicants' demographic characteristics. The results of this analysis are discussed in the next section; subsequent sections review the analyses of procedures for certifying information and household size data.

ELIGIBILITY DETERMINATION

Three features of a housing allowance program (or other income transfer program) might have important influences on the number of applicants who will be declared ineligible: (1) the nature of the eligibility standards; (2) the amount of information about eligibility in program outreach messages; (3) the procedures used to determine applicants' eligibility. In the AAE the most important influence on the number of ineligible applicants came from the set of eligibility rules used by the agencies. The specific procedures used to determine whether each applicant was eligible were the least important of the three factors.

Eligibility Rules

HUD guidelines established seven eligibility criteria, which were applied almost uniformly by all eight AAE agencies. The most important criterion was the income limit, which was defined to reflect the local price of housing that met the minimum quality standards established for the program. Income limits varied according to the number of people in the household,[10] with higher limits for larger families.

A second criterion established by HUD required the agencies to consider limitations on financial assets, but the agencies differed considerably in applying this criterion. Six set a limit on assets, some with a different limit for elderly applicants. Two agencies set no asset limit.

Five other HUD criteria were applied consistently by all agencies: applicants living outside the program area, households consisting of a single-person under sixty-two years of age, households headed by a full-time student, home owners, members of the armed forces, and applicants living in HUD-subsidized housing[11] were not eligible for the program.

In addition to these standard criteria, additional eligibility rules were imposed by five agencies. Four agencies rejected application forms that were not completely filled out. Salem and Tulsa rejected applicants whose income statements could not be verified through contacts with income sources, including those who declared zero income. Finally,

Tulsa rejected applicants who had lived in subsidized housing and had a "bad record"—problems in rent or with neighbors, for example.

Overall, the AAE agencies determined that about 8 percent (the median for the eight agencies) of the applicants to the program were ineligible. The income limits accounted for more than 40 percent of the cases in which applicants were found ineligible. The exclusion of non-elderly, single-person households accounted for a substantial proportion of the ineligible applicants in most locations, as did the restrictions on full-time students and nonresidents. But no general criterion other than the income limit accounted for more than 10 percent of all ineligibility cases.

Some of the major reasons for ineligibility at particular sites are related to unique applications of the eligibility rules. The most striking example is Tulsa, which had by far the highest rate of ineligible applications of the eight sites (see table 5-1). Approximately 19 percent of the Tulsa applicants were found ineligible at each of two steps in eligibility determination, preliminary screening and certification. An unusually large number of applicants were eliminated because they had lived in subsidized housing and had some negative experience with the local housing authority (which operated the experimental agency as well). Tulsa also excluded applicants whose incomes could not be verified by a third-party source. During the certification step, these two local eligibility rules were responsible for nearly 60 percent of all applicants ruled ineligible in Tulsa.

The effect of eligibility determination can be seen not only in terms of the number of applicants excluded but also in terms of the allowance payments those households might have received had they not been excluded. In total, those excluded for reasons other than income[12] at screening might have received annual payments of $354,000,[13] and those excluded at certification might have received $329,000,[14] if all of them had become recipients. The combined value of these exclusions[15] was about 3 percent of the total payment bill in the median case, or about $29 annually per recipient household. In Tulsa, due largely to the local eligibility criteria, exclusions amounted to about $230 per recipient household per year.

Eligibility Information in Outreach

The main purpose of outreach in the AAE was to make potentially eligible families aware of the program's existence and interested in par-

Table 5-1. Eligibility Results from Screening and Certification

Site	Screening			Certification			
	Number screened	Total ineligible (%)	Over income limit (%)	Number certified	Total ineligible (%)	Over income limit (%)	Adjusted ineligible[a] (%)
Salem	2,527	3.7	1.3	1,107	1.4	1.0	5.0
Springfield	2,478	5.8	3.5	1,210	0.0	0.0	5.8
Peoria	2,242	7.9	3.9	1,459	1.0	0.8	8.8
San Bernardino	2,050	6.0	2.8	1,008	0.1	0.1	6.1
Bismarck[b]	—	6.1	—	665	14.3	4.5	14.3
Jacksonville	1,806	6.1	3.0	1,160	1.6	0.8	7.6
Durham	1,337	7.9	3.4	803	2.7	1.9	10.4
Tulsa	2,283	19.0	9.7	1,375	18.8	2.7	34.2
Total	14,723	8.1	4.0	8,787	4.8	1.3	12.5
Median		6.1	3.5		1.5	0.9	8.2

Source: AAE application and certification forms

Data base: Applicants (N=15,388; missing cases, 11), certified applicants (N=8,787)

[a]Estimated as 100 percent minus the product of the eligibility fraction at screening and certification.

[b]Bismarck's actions might be considered either screening or certification, since the steps were combined. Since this review resulted in the "official" finding on eligibility, it is considered as certification.

ticipating. But outreach may also have an exclusionary purpose: to convey eligibility criteria to families who would not be eligible, or simply not to reach ineligible families with word of the program's existence.

Because it was a new program, the major thrust of the AAE outreach was to kindle awareness of the program. There was little room in the outreach message for detailed information on eligibility, especially when the message was delivered in paid advertisements or public service announcements on television, radio, or in newspapers. Yet with the exception of the income limits, the message seems to have been remarkably clear. For example, the agencies found only thirty-eight home owners among more than fifteen thousand applicants, even though the low-income populations to whom the outreach message was broadly directed included a substantial proportion of home owners.

Explaining income limits was a difficult task for outreach, and it is not surprising that this is the largest category of ineligibles. The limits were complex and difficult to communicate in brief messages. The limits depended on family size[16] and on net income, the computation of which was described in several pages of rules about deductions. The outreach message could seldom be precise on such points.

The difficulty of communicating eligibility criteria was compounded by the AAE agencies' objective of enrolling a representative cross section of the eligible population. Because households in the upper eligible income categories proved difficult to attract in representative numbers, most agencies emphasized the program's applicability to those groups. Attempting to attract those near the income limits while unable to communicate the precise limits, outreach was bound to attract numerous applicants whose income was too high.

Tulsa is a case in point. Tulsa's outreach campaign was aimed deliberately at households with relatively high incomes, because the agency felt that referrals from its public housing waiting lists and from other social service agencies would probably generate a disproportionately large number of low-income applicants. A mobile unit circulating among middle-income neighborhoods and a collegiate cartoon character in printed promotional materials were intended to counteract the expected imbalance. Tulsa's outreach campaign was effective in its aim, but it also attracted the largest number of applicants over income limits.[17]

Tulsa also illustrates a case of outreach directed to a group likely to include many households that would be ineligible for reasons other than income. The agency sent publicity materials to people on the public housing waiting lists. Because many of them had already lived in subsidized housing at some time, and because the agency was itself the local housing authority and was careful to check its records on previous tenants, many applicants were found ineligible because they were already in subsidized housing or had "bad tenant" records with the agency.

Different outreach techniques might be expected to have different capacities to carry detailed eligibility information and hence to result in different numbers of ineligible applicants. For example, a detailed set of eligibility criteria could be sent to other social service agencies, so applicants referred by those agencies might less frequently be ineligible than those responding to a brief message in the mass media. Referrals to the AAE in fact included a smaller proportion of ineligibles than other applicants, but the difference seemed to result from the fact that the referring agencies' clientele were generally in the lower-income categories, not from more precise screening. When demographic characteristics are taken into account, there is no important difference in the proportion of ineligibles among applicants from different outreach sources.[18]

As a new program, the AAE was especially likely to attract ineligible applicants. Not only did outreach have to focus on creating awareness rather than on communicating eligibility criteria, but there was little "common knowledge" in the community about who might be eligible. In an ongoing program outreach could probably shift its focus toward providing more precise information about eligibility and the community would probably have a greater general understanding about the program criteria. There is some evidence that such a pattern developed even within the limited duration of the AAE. Although applications were accepted for a maximum of eight months, a smaller proportion of ineligible households applied in later months than in the initial months.[19] As such a program became more established, then, formal and informal outreach would probably become more effective in minimizing the number of ineligible applicants.

Eligibility Determination Procedures

Compared with program eligibility criteria and outreach, the specific procedures used to determine eligibility had little measurable influence on the proportion of applicants found ineligible in the AAE. What difference there is can be identified only in the contrast between Bismarck and the other seven agencies. As table 5-1 showed, the median proportion of ineligible applicants was about 8 percent. The most extreme departure from this norm was Tulsa. The second largest departure from the norm was Bismarck, probably because of a procedural difference between this agency and the others.

Seven agencies asked applicants to fill out an application at the agency, which was screened immediately and certified later. Preliminary screening allowed the agency to inform obviously ineligible applicants immediately, which kept applicants from having to wait for a response and saved the agency the cost of further processing. Bismarck, in contrast, accepted applications by mail. Most applications were certified by the agency as soon as they were received. This procedure seldom included direct contact with prospective applicants, so there was little opportunity to explain the eligibility criteria in any detail,[20] and consequently there was a relatively high proportion of ineligible applications.

Beyond this basic procedural choice involving both application procedures and preliminary eligibility screening, there was little measured variation in procedures used by the other seven agencies. With the exception of income and household size information, agencies did not attempt to verify eligibility data; they simply asked participants for the information and assumed it was correct.[21] Likewise, there was little variation in the results of eligibility determination. Aside from Bismarck and Tulsa, the rate of ineligible applications ranged narrowly between 5 and 10 percent. Agencies generally verified income information, and sometimes information about household size, during the second step of eligibility determination (certification). The procedures used for checking those items have little bearing on the proportion of applicants found ineligible, as shown in table 5-2.[22]

The variation across procedures, whether for certifying household size or income, was very small. However, the very small number of people found ineligible severely limits the power of analysis to reveal differences among the procedures. While the AAE offers no evidence that some certification procedures are more effective than others in identifying ineligible applicants, it does not prove that such a difference does not exist.

Most eligibility criteria were applied simply on the basis of participant statement. Because certification involved a review of the accuracy of income and household size data, it is worth examining separately the effect of this review in terms of households found to exceed the income limits. In fact, only about 1 percent of all certifications exceeded income limits. This had a fiscal impact[23] of about $5 per recipient per year in the

Table 5-2. Rates of Ineligibility by Method of Certification

Method	Household Size Ineligible[a] No.	%	Certified	Income Ineligible[a] No.	%	Certified
Complete[b] third party[c]	1	0.8	119	17	0.8	2,059
Complete documentation[d]	10	1.4	717	14	1.3	1,081
Complete mixture[e]	0	0.0	22	6	2.7	226
Partial third party	2	1.6	128	1	0.6	169
Partial documentation	9	1.3	691	11	1.4	769
Partial mixture	0	0.0	8	0	0.0	11
Self-declaration[f]	135	2.5	5,414	102	3.3	3,053
Total	157	2.2	7,099	151	2.0	7,368

Source: AAE application and certification forms
Data base: Certified applicants (N=7,412, excluding 1,375 certified applicants for Tulsa; missing cases, 313 household size; missing cases, 44 income)
[a]Includes applicants found ineligible for all reasons, including income and household size, full-time students.
[b]Complete verification meant checking all reported items (household members or sources of income). With partial verification some items were verified and a signed statement (or declaration) was accepted for others.
[c]In third-party verification the agency checked on participant-reported data by directly contacting other persons or organizations (such as an employer or welfare agency).
[d]For documentary verification the agency requested the participant to provide substantiating evidence for reported information (such as birth certificates, tax returns, or paycheck stubs).
[e]Mixture refers to the practice of verifying some items by documents and some by third parties. AAE agencies did not use redundant verification, that is, documentary and third-party verification of the same item.
[f]In a declaration or signed statement participants attested to the accuracy of the information they had provided.

median case.[24] Again the numbers are too small to show differential effects for different certification procedures.

Analytic limitations notwithstanding, there is little evidence that agency variations in the procedures for determining eligibility affected the accuracy of such determinations. The major effects seem to spring from procedures that influenced the number of ineligible people who were likely to apply (the outreach message and local eligibility criteria) rather than from procedures for identifying those who did apply.

ADMINISTRATIVE ALTERNATIVES FOR INITIAL CERTIFICATION

In the AAE all agencies began certification procedures with a general policy. Five agencies departed from the general policy in a relatively small percentage of cases, and three departed from the general policy so frequently that decisions appear to have been made on a case-by-case basis. This section discusses a number of considerations to be taken into account in establishing a general policy toward certification. Some of the grounds on which case-by-case variations might be made will also be discussed.

The primary consideration in selecting procedures for certification of household size and income is accuracy. A second is total program cost, especially whether the administrative costs of particularly accurate methods overshadow their greater effectiveness.

Certification and the Accuracy of Payments

AAE agencies could use three possible methods of certification:

(1) Self-declaration. Agencies could accept a signed statement from the applicant attesting to the accuracy of information.

(2) Verification through documents. Agencies could ask participants to supply documents such as check stubs or tax returns to substantiate the reported data.

(3) Verification by third parties. Agencies could ask participants to supply the names of knowledgeable third parties, for example, an employer that the agency could contact to verify earned income.

An agency could choose any of these certification sources for an individual applicant.[25] If there were multiple items of information (multiple sources of income, for example), the agency might choose to verify some items and accept a signed statement for others. Thus the completeness of verification was a second dimension along which the agency had three choices:

(1) Self-declaration. Acceptance of a signed statement for all information items.

(2) Partial verification. Substantiating some items through documents or third parties, but accepting the participant's statements for others.

(3) Complete verification. Checking all items either through documents or third parties (or checking some items by third parties and others by documents).

The stringency of a certification procedure might be assumed to be determined by the extent to which it relies on the participant rather than an independent source. Accepting a signed statement for all information items would be considered the least stringent procedure, and verifying all items through third parties the most stringent. Thus both the method and the completeness of certification can be summarized into the single broad question of how stringent certification procedures should be.

Assumptions about Sources of Error.   For several agencies the appropriate degree of stringency depended on their assumptions about the likely sources of error in participant-reported data. None of the AAE agencies was very stringent in certifying household size information. Complete verification was used in about 10 percent of the cases and partial verification in another 26 percent. Even planners who chose relatively stringent means of certifying income tended to feel that participants would report their household size accurately.

Two agencies, Bismarck and Springfield, elected to certify all applicants' income by the self-declaration method. Planners there felt that most applicants would be honest and accurate in reporting both their household size and income. Errors, they felt, could be identified by a careful review of the reasonableness of the information provided or by discussion with the participant. Both agencies also planned a quality control audit of a sample of households, mainly to test assumptions about accuracy than to identify errors.

Three agencies, Tulsa, Durham, and Salem, selected very stringent income certification policies. Based on their previous experience with income certification, staff at these agencies felt that applicants were not likely to report their incomes accurately. They felt that stringent certification would result in more accurate income determination, and by extension, more accurate payments. Some also felt that more stringent measures would deter deliberate misrepresentation.

However, the three agencies differed in their assessment of the honesty of applicants. Staff at one stringent agency felt that fraud on the part of applicants was a serious possibility and that only strict certification procedures could prevent significant abuse of the program. On the other hand, staff at another stringent agency felt that misreporting was usually the result of oversight, not deception; they felt that applicants usually tended to forget occasional sources of income, such as part-time or temporary work or Medicare payments. Staff at this agency felt that participants were as likely to overreport as underreport their income and that it was important to avoid both types of error. This agency considered certification necessary to ensure accuracy but not to prevent fraud.

The experience of the AAE provides some evidence on the hypotheses implied by these assumptions. For example, participants seemed to report household size information accurately. Certification resulted in changes to the household size data supplied on the application form in only 5 percent of all cases.[26] Applicants were more often inaccurate in reporting incomes; certification resulted in an adjustment to reported income in about 51 percent of all cases.

Applicants tended to underestimate their incomes: certification resulted in an upward change in about two-thirds of the cases of income change. Whether underreporting occurred as an effort to maximize benefits or an honest error cannot be determined from the AAE data. Other studies have shown, however, that errors in income reporting tend to be understatements, independent of any financial consequences of the reporting behavior.[27] Although the AAE data do not allow assessment of the incidence of deliberate misreporting, the agencies reported only a handful of suspected cases.

Changes in reported income and household size can reflect actual changes in participants' circumstances[28] as well as corrections of misreporting. Whatever the reasons for the changes, the principal effect of certification was to adjust reported income, not household size, and the most common adjustment was an increase in the income figure reported at application.

Stringency of Certification and Changes in Projected Income.   The AAE also provides some support for the presumption that more stringent certification procedures yield more accurate income data. As a test of the hypothesis, income data on application forms were compared with the figures that the agencies subsequently certified as correct. The analysis rests on the assumption that any change[29] is an increase in accuracy (but not necessarily that the certified figure is perfectly accurate—an independent audit of participant circumstances would have been required to assess accuracy in an absolute sense).

The analysis shows that all procedures involving verification of reported income resulted in more changes—that is, more improvements in accuracy—than did the acceptance of participants' signed statements. Table 5-3 demonstrates this overall pattern: most verification procedures resulted in changes nearly twice as often as self-declaration.[30] Multivariate analysis, taking into account factors such as household characteristics and the length of time between application and certification, confirms the relationship.[31]

The stringency hypothesis also suggests that verifying all reported data would be more effective than verifying only some and that third-

Table 5–3.   Certification Method and Changes in Income Data

Certification Method	Number of Certifications Performed	Certifications that Resulted in a Change of Income Data (No.)	(%)
Complete third-party verification	3,038	1,979	65
Complete documentation	1,101	669	61
Complete mixture	231	191	83
Partial third-party	288	189	66
Partial documentation	767	420	55
Partial mixture	11	8	73
Self-declaration	2,411	844	35

Source: AAE application and certification forms
Data base: Certified applicants (N=7,847; excluding 665 applicants in Bismarck, which did not perform a separate certification procedure; excluding 246 applicants declared ineligible for reasons other than income, for whom certification was usually not completed; missing cases, 29)

party sources would be more effective than documents. The AAE data support these hypotheses, but the relationships are not as strong as the general difference between verification and self-declaration. Table 5–3, for example, shows that third-party verification resulted in more changes than documentary verification but fails to reveal a consistent pattern in comparing complete with partial verification. Multivariate analysis shows both patterns somewhat more clearly,[32] but several exceptions to the overall patterns can be found in particular sites.

In addition to yielding more improvements in accuracy, complete third-party and documentary verification also seem to be more precise in that they were able to detect smaller changes of income. The complete verification techniques resulted in a greater number of both large and small changes than self-declaration, but the greatest difference was in the number of small changes. Because of the greater number of small changes, the average size of changes detected by complete third-party verification and complete documentation was about $200 less than the average for self-declaration.[33]

These certification techniques represent only one step—the most readily measured—in a larger system of procedures. The importance of the unmeasured dimensions is illustrated by the fact that even the strongest pattern observed, the association of self-declaration with few changes, was not consistent at all sites. The pattern was quite strong in cross-site analysis and in some single-site analyses; but in one site self-declaration yielded about as many changes as the verification techniques. It is reasonable to conclude that the general hypothesis of a relationship between stringency and accuracy is supported, but as one site demonstrates, less stringent techniques may have equal or greater effectiveness in some situations.

Stringency of Certification and Changes of Household Size Data. Although AAE planners devoted considerable attention to selecting procedures for certifying income and much effort to verifying income data, they gave far less attention and effort to certifying household size. This may have been based on the expectation that household size was not as subject to change, confusion over definitions, or error. Alternatively planners may have expected that more stringent procedures would not be more effective in detecting errors or changes than the simpler procedure of self-declaration.

The AAE data do not allow a conclusive judgment about either of these expectations but provide some support for both. That changes in household size data were made in only 5 percent of the cases, compared with 51 percent for income data, suggests that errors occurred relatively infrequently. It could be argued that the absence of stringent verification of household size leads to an underestimate of these changes. But some verification of household size was performed in 36 percent of the cases, compared with 65 percent for income data, which makes it unlikely that the frequency of verification alone could account for more than a small portion of the disparity. Thus the evidence strongly indicates that inaccuracies in household size data occurred less frequently than in income data, even though the absolute frequency of inaccuracies is unclear.[34]

Analysis was unable to reveal any important differences among procedures for certifying household size in the frequency with which they resulted in changes.[35] In both cross-site and single-site analysis all procedures yielded roughly equivalent numbers of changes. However, the small number of cases in which change was observed limits the power of the statistical analysis; further research would be required to demonstrate conclusively that stringency does or does not matter in certifying household size.

Total Allocation Effects of Certification. AAE allowance payments were based on the difference between the locally estimated cost of "modest, standard housing" and the rent that a given household could afford to pay. Specifically the payment formula was

$$P = C^* - 0.25Y_{net}$$

where

P = monthly payment amount

C^* = the estimated cost of housing for a household of a given household size

Y_{net} = the monthly net income of the household after subtracting certain allowable deductions

Certification could change the amount of payment in several ways: changing the household size would change the estimated cost of standard housing, changing the total income would change the net income figures, and either household size or income changes could change the amount of allowable deductions from gross income (as could a review of the deductions themselves). Thus an upward change in income would increase both the total income and the deductions, so the total payment reduction would be slightly less than one-fourth of the change in income.

The effect on allowance payments of all these factors can be seen by comparing the payment that would have been made on the basis of original data with the payment that would be made on the basis of the certified data. Some of these payment changes were upward, and some were downward. In measuring the total effect of certification on payments, upward and downward changes can be added to estimate the total reallocation of payment funds.

On the average, certification resulted in a reallocation of $116 in annual payments per certified applicant, as shown in table 5–4. In other words, had certification been omitted for an average household, the expected result would have been erroneous monthly payments (either overpayments or underpayments); the error would have totaled $116 by the end of a year.[36] All methods of actively verifying income produced a greater reallocation of payment funds than did self-declaration. The verification methods reallocated an average of $13 to $86 more than the average for self-declaration ($97). Multivariate analysis shows that, holding other factors constant, complete third-party verification reallocated $34 more than self-declaration; complete documentary verification reallocated $28 more than self-declaration; and partial third-party verification reallocated $24 more.[37]

Table 5–4.   Allocation Changes by Income Certification Method

Method of Certification	Mean Allocation Effect	Number of Certifications
Complete third party	$110	3,038
Complete documentation	139	1,101
Complete mixture	183	231
Partial third party	134	288
Partial documentation	137	767
Partial mixture	123	11
Self-declaration	97	2,412
Total	$116	7,848

Source: AAE application and certification forms
Data base: Certified applicants (N = 7,848, excluding 246 applicants ineligible for reasons other than income; excluding 665 Bismarck applicants, missing cases, 28)

In summary, all procedures involving verification of participant-reported income seem to yield more accurate information than that obtained by self-declaration, although there is no equivalent effect for household size data. These differences in the accuracy of information are translated into differential improvements in the accuracy of payments, seen as a reallocation in the distribution of funds. However, the relationship of the different income certification procedures to payment reallocations is weaker than their relationship to the frequency of income changes; payment changes resulting from changes in household size and deductions attenuate the impact of income certification procedures.

The Impact of Initial Certification on Program Costs

Two factors determine the net cost of certification: first, the administrative cost of performing the certification and, second, the tendency of certain certification procedures to result in more decreases in payments than increases (if certification results in more upward changes in reported income than downward changes, there could be a net decrease in the total amount of payments). These factors must be combined to estimate the total cost of certification.

Estimated Administrative Costs of Certification.   Administrative costs of certification in the AAE were estimated by a simulation model, which took into account the amount of time required to perform certain tasks, standardized wage rates paid in the AAE, and other factors related to administrative costs. Based on the average number of income sources checked in the AAE, the direct cost[38] estimate for certification using third-party verification is $5.53. The estimate for documentary verification is $4.46 and for self-declaration, $2.60.[39]

Although these estimates are useful for analysis, actual costs in the AAE varied substantially and in patterns were not always consistent with the estimates produced by this method. For example, the average direct cost per certification[40] in Tulsa, which used third-party verification almost exclusively, was $4.21. Springfield, which relied almost entirely on self-declaration, had an average cost of only about a dollar less, $3.50, and Jacksonville, which used different techniques in different cases, recorded an average cost of $9.83.

Further, other analyses of the agency costs (in contrast with the simulation estimates) suggest that verification by documents was more expensive than third-party verification. Thus, while the simulation estimates are probably reasonable reflections of the costs of the alternative income certification procedures defined here, it is clear that other aspects of agency procedures can have an important impact on costs.

Costs Compared to the Allocation Effect.   Verification of income yielded annual allocation changes per certified applicant averaging $24–$34 more than those yielded by self-declaration, as reported above. The additional cost of third-party verification compared with self-declaration, however, was only about $6; the increment for documentary verification was about $4 (including direct costs). Apparently the greater accuracy of the verification procedures does not cost substantially more.

However, certification costs and improvements in accuracy, even though both have been measured in dollars, are qualitatively different. Improvements in accuracy do not represent a cash flow to or from the government. To say that an increase in accuracy is greater than the associated costs is not proof that the increase is "worth" the costs; conversely an improvement in accuracy that was smaller than the associated costs might still be considered worthwhile. Nevertheless, the comparison suggests that the active verification method can yield a fairly substantial improvement in accuracy for a small increment in absolute cost over self-declaration.

Net Cost Effects of Various Certification Methods.   Some methods of certifying income had a tendency to result in more upward changes in income (potential payment decreases) than others. Multivariate analysis showed that most active verification methods identified more upward changes than self-declaration.[41] Because the active verification techniques also resulted in more total changes in income, both upward and downward, these methods yielded a larger average net increase in reported income than self-declaration.

Other things being equal, then, the active verification techniques would have yielded a greater net reduction in allowance payments than self-declaration. Table 5-5 shows that certification resulted in an overall net reduction in potential annual payments of approximately $17 per certified applicant[42] and that most verification techniques resulted in larger average potential payment reductions than self-declaration. However, when changes due to factors besides income were taken into account in multivariate analysis, the active income verification methods proved not to be substantially different from self-declaration.[43] Changes in household size and deductions attenuated the income changes to the point that the impact of income certification methods was indistinguishable.

Table 5-5. Net Payment Effects of Income Certification by Method

Method	Net Payment Effect ($)	Number of Certifications
Complete third party	−23.02	3,038
Complete documentation	11.30	1,100
Complete mixture	−52.74	231
Partial third party	−47.56	288
Partial documentation	−35.82	767
Partial mixture	−43.59	11
Statement alone	− 8.98	2,412
Total	−16.94	7,847

Source: AAE application and certification forms
Data base: Certified applicants (N=7,847, excluding 246 applicants ineligible for reasons other than income; excluding 665 Bismarck applicants, missing cases, 29)

This analysis does not disprove the hypothesis that more stringent income certification procedures will result in greater net payment reductions. Greater reductions in fact appear to be the "pure" effect of at least some verification procedures. However, the impact of other factors on the total payment bill is sufficiently large that varying administrative costs cannot usefully be matched with payment reductions to demonstrate a differential net financial impact on the program.

MATCHING CERTIFICATION METHOD
TO APPLICANT CHARACTERISTICS

Whatever general policy an agency adopts toward certification, exceptions must sometimes be made. An agency using self-declaration might routinely select certain kinds of applicants for more thorough verification. An agency that generally verifies applicants might choose not to verify certain types of applicants. An agency might establish no universal policy toward verification but set up guidelines indicating which types of households are to be verified and which are not. Even if exceptions are normally not made for groups of households, an individual staff member may believe that an extraordinary situation requires a nonroutine response.

The AAE provides some evidence on the types of households that were most likely to experience changes in the recorded income and household size data between application and certification. It also shows which factors tend to influence agencies' choices of certification procedures in particular situations. Both points may be useful in deciding whether and how to apply certification procedures selectively.

Household Types with High Rates of Change

Certification workers might feel that certain applicants should be verified more thoroughly for three kinds of reasons. First, the staff member may believe that there is an error on the application form. This perception might be linked to the age or an infirmity of the applicant or to a language barrier between the applicant and the staff member who assisted in filling out the application form. The household situation must be complex, and it might be hard to determine whether certain sources of income or members of the household should be included by the program definitions of income and household. A perceived need for verification might even result from a belief that the staff member who took the application did it incorrectly. Second, the staff member may suspect misrepresentation on the application form. A staff member might suspect that a particular applicant has been evasive or dishonest in an effort to qualify for a larger payment than he or she would be entitled to. Third, there might be some indication that the household situation had changed since the application form was filled out. In the AAE a period of four to six weeks commonly elapsed between application and certification; during this time households could gain or lose members or increase or decrease the total household income. Some households might be more subject than others to this kind of instability.

AAE data do not separate the reasons for a recorded change in income or household size data. Therefore no estimate can be made of the frequency of each of these situations. However, the data describe the likelihood of a recorded change in income or household size for certain types of applicant households, for whatever reason the change occurred. Among the household characteristics recorded for each AAE applicant, the percentage of income derived from grants was the strongest predictor of the likelihood of an income change. Applicants who received about 40 percent of their income from grants (e.g., welfare) were the most likely to have an income change. These individuals were probably marginal wage earners, often unemployed or working at part-time or seasonal jobs. In general, applicants who were receiving income from two or more sources were more likely to have a change than those who received all their income from a single source, either earned or grant.

Changes in household size were also strongly associated with changes in income. Presumably the income change represented either the earnings of the additional (or departing) person or a change in grant entitlement directly responding to the altered household size.

AAE data confirm the findings of previous studies that older applicants are less likely to have income changes than younger applicants. Elderly applicants who did have an income change tended to have smaller changes than nonelderly applicants. These findings are consistent with the expectation that many elderly persons are living on fixed incomes.

AAE applicants at the lowest income levels had more income changes than those at middle and higher levels. These changes tended to be upward rather than downward, and they also tended to be smaller than the changes observed for higher income levels.

Finally, male-headed households tended to have more income changes than female-headed households. The race of the household head, however, was not a predictor of income changes: white, black, and Spanish-American households all had about the same proportion of changes.

Other Situations with High Rates of Change

Many of the recorded changes in income data in the AAE reflected actual changes in the household's situation between application and certification. Thus the more time that passed between application and certification, the more likely that a change would be recorded. Although the data do not identify the number of actual changes in household situations, some sense of their frequency can be obtained by comparing cases that were certified almost immediately after application with those that took longer. Certifications completed within one week of application resulted in changes in income data in 36 percent of the cases; the rate climbed to 66 percent in the cases with a three-month delay, and 74 percent with a delay of four months or more. The elapsed time between application and certification was the most consistent predictor of a change in income data in cross-site and single-site multivariate analysis. The analysis of changes in household size revealed a similar pattern.

The local unemployment rate was another factor linked to the incidence of changes in income data. Applicants in areas with high rates of unemployment were more likely to experience an income change at certification, and their changes were larger, on the average, than those at sites with lower unemployment rates.[44]

Patterns of Verification in the AAE

The AAE agencies did not generally verify income data selectively for particular types of applicants. Five of the eight agencies followed a consistent verification policy for almost all applicants. Three agencies did not have a consistent policy—some applicants were verified and some were not. But applicant characteristics recorded in the AAE data were not consistently important in determining the procedures used in individual cases. Although some patterns were found at individual agencies—one agency, for example, tended to verify Spanish-American applicants more than others—the patterns were not highly consistent even within the agencies. No important cross-site patterns were found.

Administrative Convenience in the Choice of Verification Source

Two administrative factors seem to have affected the choice of certification procedures at agencies without consistent policies: pressures arising from the need to process many applicants in a short time and the ease of obtaining information from alternative sources.

The AAE agencies were allowed to enroll participants for only a limited period (eight or nine months), and within that period they attempted to enroll enough households to meet prespecified target numbers of recipients. Most agencies received fewer applications than they anticipated in the early months and consequently were under considerable pressure in the later months to select, certify, and enroll a large number of households.

The three agencies that did not have a consistent policy[45] tended to do less verification. The agencies performed some verification for 72 percent of the applicants certified in the first two months of operations, compared with 59 percent of the cases in the last two months. Program month was the only predictor of verification that was consistent in multivariate analysis for all three sites.[46]

For applicants with some portion of their income from grants, third-party sources (the granting agency) were relatively easy to contact. The grant agency was often part of the same bureaucracy as the AAE agency. Even when it was not, only a few working relationships had to be established to process a large volume of verifications. For applicants with earned rather than grant income, third-party contacts with employers were more difficult to establish, if only because of the number of contacts that would be required. Documentary sources, such as pay slips and check stubs, were easier to obtain. At the five agencies that did not follow a consistent policy toward verification sources, the presence of grant income was a strong factor in the choice of third-party verification. The absence of grant income was likewise associated with the choice of documentary verification. This was the strongest predictor of the verification source in multivariate analysis for each of the five sites.[47]

The AAE experience thus suggests that the local administration, given substantial discretion in the choice of procedures, will not usually choose to match certification methods to applicant characteristics. Where procedural variations occurred, the major reasons were administrative pressures or convenience. In view of the absence of strong relationships between participant characteristics and changes in reported data, more consciously selective procedures do not seem warranted.

OTHER ISSUES IN THE CHOICE OF CERTIFICATION PROCEDURES

Although quantitative analysis in the AAE focused mainly on the issues of effectiveness and costs of the alternative certification procedures, two other considerations are important in designing and implementing the certification function. One is the possible intrusiveness and reporting burden that some certification methods are presumed to pose for the applicant. The other involves the interactions between certification procedures and two other features of the enrollment process: the degree of detail with which income and household size data are elicited at application and the timing of certification in relation to application and formal enrollment.

Intrusiveness and Reporting Burden

When designing certification procedures some of the AAE planners were conscious of the impacts that certification might have on the lives of applicants. Agencies that selected self-declaration considered it less intrusive than third-party verification because no outside sources would be made aware that the applicant was seeking government assistance. Self-declaration was also considered less burdensome than verification by documents.

Such concerns have been common in income-dependent assistance programs for over a decade. During the late 1960s many welfare organizations adopted self-declaration of income and household size on the basis of a directive from the U.S. Department of Health, Education, and Welfare. This method was argued for in terms of dignity and justice toward low-income households, in addition to more traditional grounds of cost and efficiency.

The only evidence from the AAE that bears on this issue is a question from a sample survey of enrollees conducted shortly after enrollment: "Do you feel the agency does too much checking, not enough, or about the right amount of checking?" The timing and context of the question implied a reference to certification, because at that point no other kinds of checking had been conducted.

Of the nearly twelve hundred participants sampled, only 1 percent said the agency did too much checking, while 97 percent said that the amount of checking was about right. The remainder either felt that the amount of checking was not enough or believed the agency did not check. The results of this question did not vary substantially within or between agencies, and the attitudes of participants toward the AAE agencies seem to have been overwhelmingly positive.

These findings confirm the impression from other programs[48] that verification of payment-related data for an individual household is seldom resented by the household. In any case all methods of certification used in the AAE seem to have been well within the tolerance levels of participants.

Interactions between Application, Certification, and Enrollment

Certification takes place between filling out the application and formal enrollment in the program. In fact, the application-certification-enrollment sequence was an integrated system in which the choice of certification method had important implications for the overall design.[49] The certification system consisted of three interrelated elements: first, the method of certification, which may be self-declaration, documentation, or third-party verification; second, the level of detail demanded in the elicitation of income data at application, which may range from brief, unspecific, and aggregated to lengthy, specific, and detailed by source and amount; third, the timing of certification, which may be early, perhaps simultaneous with application, between application and enrollment, after selection but before the enrollment conference; or late, often during the formal enrollment conference. The three configurations of these elements that occurred in the AAE are illustrated in figure 5-2.

The sequential certification system was chosen by three AAE agencies: Tulsa, Durham, and Salem. These agencies elicited only brief and

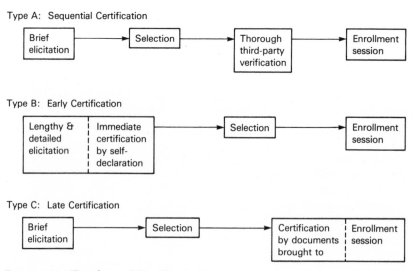

Figure 5-2. Typology of Certification Systems

unspecific income data at application, concentrating mainly on income sources rather than precise income amounts. After applicants were selected for participation, a thorough certification procedure was performed. In two of the agencies using this configuration (Salem and Tulsa), certification by documents was initially specified for all or most cases, but if the documents were not furnished or were insufficient, third-party contacts were made to verify income data. At Durham the plan specified third-party verification unless an applicant expressed a preference for bringing in supporting documents. In practice all three agencies relied principally on third-party verification. After satisfactory completion of the verification of income, applicants were invited to the formal enrollment session.

Two agencies, Bismarck and Springfield, chose an early certification system. These agencies used a supplemental application form that requested detailed information on income, disaggregating it by source, amount, and family member. The agency usually certified this information immediately by having the participant sign the required statement attesting to the truth of the information. Normally no further verification was conducted. When the selected applicants were invited to the formal enrollment session, they might be asked whether there had been any change in their income or household size, but again this information was normally not verified and it became the basis for computing allowance payments.

The late certification system was chosen by three agencies, Jacksonville, Peoria, and San Bernardino. These agencies generally collected only brief and nonspecific income data at application. Selected applicants were then invited to the formal enrollment session and told to bring documentation to support the income data given at application. At the enrollment session certification was performed using these documents. If insufficient documentation was provided, staff members had to decide whether to delay enrollment long enough for the applicant to bring the required documents, to contact a third party for income verification, or to accept the signed statement alone. No specific back-up plan had been devised for such a situation. Thus although late certification agencies planned to have thorough verification (as in sequential certification), they were often forced to accept self-declarations (as in early certification).

Implications of Certification Systems.   The sequential certification system, with third-party verification performed consistently, seems to result in the most accurate distribution of payments. It is probably more costly and time-consuming. The delay involved in third-party contacts[50] might impede the flow of assistance payments, creating an administrative problem for an agency faced with an enrollment deadline and perhaps a hardship for an applicant suffering an emergency or unusual situation.

The early certification system has the advantage of timeliness. It results in little if any delay between application and payment initiation, especially if the quality control procedure is allowed to follow enrollment. This system could result in more errors in payments, because self-declaration is a less accurate method of certification than active verification. However, the detailed elicitation procedures used in this system seems to reduce the level of error.

The late certification system may have some of the advantages of both other types. That is, it can be timely and responsive because there is usually no need to contact third parties and await their response, and it can be reasonably accurate because documentary verification is generally more accurate than the signed statement alone. However, if the applicant is not able to furnish the required documents, as frequently happened, this system does not have a reliable backup procedure. Agencies using late certification had neither the detailed and specific income data elicited at application by early certification agencies nor the verified and accurate income data produced by sequential certification agencies. If the applicant was asked again to furnish the required documents, an unplanned delay occurred. If the agency decided to proceed on the basis of the signed statement, payments were calculated with less specific information. These conditions can be expected to cause the greatest amount of payment error. The greater the pressure of time or hardship, the more likely the agency would be to accept a signed statement, with no verification of income data.

Detailed Elicitation and the Avoidance of Error.   One would expect agencies using detailed elicitation systems to experience fewer errors in recording income data than agencies using only brief and unspecific elicitation systems. Table 5-6 shows that more changes occurred at the agencies that used less detailed elicitation methods.[51] The only major exception was the Jacksonville agency, which had an unusually detailed elicitation procedure even though it was a late certification agency.

Although AAE data are too limited to examine the possible effect of elicitation procedures in detail,[52] this effect could be an important topic for future research. Three questions would be important: To what extent can detailed elicitation prevent payment errors when participant declarations are accepted? To what extent can detailed elicitation prevent payment errors when participant information is verified? What is the incremental cost of a detailed elicitation procedure? Answers to these questions could indicate whether detailed elicitation would be a cost-effective substitute for or supplement to verification procedures.

Table 5-6. Elicitation Detail and Income Changes

Agency	Number of Income Items Elicited by Source[a]	Changes in Income Data at Certification (%)
Sequential certification agencies		
Salem	0	82.7
Tulsa	0	72.3
Durham	3	60.9
Late certification agencies		
Peoria	3	56.7
San Bernardino	7	26.2
Jacksonville	10	50.5
Early certification agencies		
Springfield	5	34.1
Bismarck	13	0.5

Source: AAE supplemental application forms
Data base: Certified applicants (excluding ineligibles)
[a]This index was derived from a count of specific supplemental income questions asked at application; see table A3-2 in Dickson, *Certification*, appendix A, p. A-19.

RECERTIFICATION

Although this analysis has concerned the initial certification required for an applicant to enroll in the program, the AAE also provides some insight into the procedures and results of both routine and ad hoc recertification of household size and income. This section briefly reviews the results of annual and interim recertifications and the procedures used. It also discusses the recertification period, the length of time between mandatory recertifications, on the basis of the limited AAE data bearing on that point.

Participant-initiated Recertification

All eight AAE agencies chose to have no more than the required annual mandatory recertifications. In addition, all eight established policies for dealing with interim changes in participant circumstances, but these varied substantially.

The variation in interim recertification policies reflected differing emphases on three concerns. The first was that payments be as accurate as possible. This would require that participants report all changes in their status as they occur and that payments be adjusted accordingly. The second and third concerns were related to the recipients' one-year lease and their fixed monthly expenditures for housing. Agencies feared that a fixed subsidy might force the household to break its commitment if its income decreased. To avoid this possibility participants would have to report all decreases in income so that payments could be adjusted. On the other hand, agencies feared that even if the household's financial circumstances improved, its disposable income might not show a real immediate and continuing increase. A reduction in the subsidy, though technically appropriate, might thus also force the family to break the commitment. To avoid this possibility, increases in income should be reflected only in the annual recertification, not in interim adjustments.

Two AAE agencies (Springfield and Jacksonville) explicitly told recipients that they should not report increases in income but should report income decreases. Salem and Tulsa, both local housing authorities, followed their existing procedures, permitting recipients to report income changes if they wished; one would expect that mainly decreases would be reported under this policy. San Bernardino requested recipients to report increases and permitted them to report decreases, but the form supplied for the purpose provided only for an increase in the allowance payment, which implied reporting decreases of income only. Bismarck, on the other hand, clearly instructed recipients to report all income changes, up or down. Durham told most participants to report all changes, but one staff member told recipients to report only decreases. There is limited documentation of Peoria's instructions to recipients, but it appears that they were told to report all income changes.

The pattern of interim recertifications is generally what would be expected to result from agency policies. Agencies that instructed participants to report all changes, on the average, recorded more changes and more upward changes in income (payment decreases) than the agencies that encouraged primarily reports of downward changes. Table 5–7 presents these patterns. The direction of differences in recertifications performed is not surprising, but it is somewhat surprising that the differences are not larger. Overall income decreases accounted for 48 percent of the changes in the sites requesting that all changes be reported, compared with 67 percent in agencies that encouraged the reporting of decreases only. A decreases-only policy doubtless allows more error than one requiring all changes to be reported, but the AAE patterns suggest that neither policy is likely to be perfectly followed and that the difference in errors allowed is therefore smaller than would logically be expected. Agencies generally maintained verification policies for interim recertification similar to those used for initial certifications. The three agencies that had been most thorough at initial certification were also the most thorough during participant-initiated interim certifications; the relative thoroughness of the other five agencies was also unchanged. However, even though the relative stringency of the agencies remained about the same, some were substantially less likely to verify participant-initiated reports than they had been at initial certification. San Bernardino and Jacksonville verified about 25 percent fewer interim than initial certifications, while Salem and Peoria were about 15 percent less likely to verify interim reports. The other agencies continued to verify at about the same rate as at initial certification.

Table 5-7. Interim Recertifications during First Year of Payments

Site	Total Number of Recipients	Number of Interim Recertifications of Income	Average Interim Recertifications per Recipient	Percentage of Downward Changes in Income
Group A: Recipients told they should report income decreases only				
Springfield	851	172	0.20	65
San Bernardino	822	152	0.18	61
Jacksonville	339	30	0.09	77
Salem	948	65	0.07	82
Tulsa	915	24	0.03	75
Subtotal	3,875	443	0.11	67
Group B: Recipients told to report all income changes				
Bismarck	430	259	0.60	38
Peoria	935	202	0.22	51
Durham	516	60	0.12	77
Subtotal	1,881	521	0.28	48
All sites	5,756	964	0.17	57

Source: AAE (re)certification forms
Data base: All participant-initiated recertifications of income in first twelve months (N = 964)

Annual Recertification

All AAE agencies were required to recertify participants' income and household size at least once a year. Between 91 and 99 percent of all recipient households showed a change of income, as shown in table 5–8. From 70 to 82 percent of these changes were upward, and the average amount of the income changes ranged from about $900 to $1,370.

At most agencies the degree of stringency used to verify income changes at annual recertification remained about the same as in the initial certifications. As with initial and interim certifications, three agencies, Salem, Durham, and Tulsa, were the most thorough, verifying virtually all income data. Again Bismarck and Springfield were the least thorough, accepting self-declarations from most recipients, although Bismarck performed somewhat more verifications at annual recertification. The remaining three agencies were in between, verifying from 12 to 68 percent of their households. The overall rate of active verification was 64 percent, virtually identical to the 65 percent rate at initial certification. The rate of income changes was high and nearly uniform across all sites. All certification procedures generally revealed changes of income after a year. This does not contradict the previous findings that active verification is more effective than self-declaration, but it cannot further confirm that finding.

Income Reporting Periods

One of the issues to be determined in the design of a certification system is the frequency with which participants are required to report income. More frequent reporting would be expected to detect changes of income earlier and thus keep payments more accurate, but more frequent reporting also increases the administrative costs to the program and the reporting burden on the recipient.

Monthly, quarterly, semiannual, annual, and biennial reporting periods have all been used by various operating or experimental income transfer systems. In this case all eight AAE agencies used the annual reporting period that HUD specified as the minimum required. The AAE, therefore, can provide no direct comparison of costs and benefits of alternative reporting periods. Nonetheless, some parts of the AAE experience may help provide a framework for decision making.

The policymaker may want to choose a reporting period in which the expected benefits of each certification would outweigh the administrative cost plus the cost to participants of complying with the certifica-

Table 5–8. Results of Annual Recertification

Site	Number of Recertifications Performed	Percentage Showing Change in Household Size	Percentage Showing Change in Income	Percentage of Upward Changes in Income	Mean Size of Income Change
Salem	712	18.1	98.5	81.7	$1,030
Springfield	738	18.2	97.6	72.5	1,032
Peoria	625	16.6	95.7	79.9	1,062
San Bernardino	688	17.9	98.3	73.4	896
Bismarck	305	21.0	98.4	79.0	1,230
Jacksonville	230	18.7	90.9	69.9	1,369
Durham	430	14.9	97.2	73.7	962
Tulsa	640	16.3	98.9	77.9	1,202
All sites	4,368	17.5	97.4	76.5	$1,063

Source: AAE certification forms
Data base: Recertified recipients (N=4,368, excluding 34 recipients declared ineligible for reasons other than exceeding income limits)

tion procedure (assembling and mailing in information or making a trip to the agency office, for example). While the cost to participants is not measurable with AAE data, the administrative cost can be estimated at about $32.

Two benefits may result from income certification: an increase in the accuracy of payments (allocation effect), which may be measured by adding payment increases and decreases, and a reduction in the total amount of payments (net payment effect), which may be measured by subtracting payment increases from payment decreases. One approach to determining the reporting period, then, would be to choose a system in which the incremental benefit (allocation effect and/or net payment effect) outweighs the incremental cost of performing certifications.

The AAE data do not support a precise estimate of the effects of different reporting periods, but they can be used to illustrate this decision logic. Table 5-9 uses the AAE data on the changes resulting from annual recertification, together with some restrictive simplifying assumptions, to compare monthly, quarterly, semiannual, and annual reporting periods.

Comparing payments after annual recertification with those at initial certification[53] shows an average allocation effect of about $220 per recipient household per year (combining increases and decreases in annual payments) and an average net payment reduction of about $92 per household per year (subtracting payment increases from decreases).

These figures can be taken as the annualized value of payment errors existing on the date of annual recertification. If the events leading to these errors—that is, the changes in participant circumstances—were evenly distributed through the twelve months between initial and annual recertification, then the average error allowed during that year would be exactly half the preceding figures—errors of $110 in total mispayments, or $46 in net overpayments. Cutting the reporting period in half would reduce the allowed errors by half, if one assumes that certification always identifies the errors existing at any point in time.

Thus the illustrative data in table 5-9 indicate that semiannual recertification might be a cost-effective alternative to an annual reporting period: the incremental cost is $32 compared with an increment of $55 in total avoided errors and $23 in net payment reductions. The quarterly system, compared with the semiannual, would add costs of $63 and yield an additional reduction in overall error of $28 and net payment reduction of $12 compared with the semiannual recertification. The monthly system would clearly add more costs than benefits.

Table 5-9. Hypothetical Illustration of the Effects of Varying Frequency of Recertification

Recertification Period	Cost[a]	Average Error Allowed[b]	Average Net Payment Reduction Foregone[c]	Increase in Cost Compared to Annual Recertification[d]	Decrease in Error Compared to Annual Recertification[d]	Net Payment Reduction Compared to Annual Recertification[d]
Annual	$ 32	$110	$46	—	—	—
Semiannual	64	55	23	$ 32	$ 55	$23
Quarterly	128	28	12	96	82	34
Monthly	384	9	4	352	101	42

[a]During the period when most (interim and annual) recertifications were performed, the direct costs of recertification amounted to $75,425. During this period the agencies performed a total of 7,243 (interim and annual) recertifications, at an average cost of $10.41. Total indirect costs for the same period amounted to 204 percent of total direct costs. Thus the total cost per recertification can be estimated at $31.65. (Cost figures taken from Charles M. Maloy et al., *Administrative Costs in a Housing Allowance Program: Two-Year Costs in the Administrative Agency Experiment* (Cambridge, Mass.: Abt Associates, 1977), tables A-14, A-6. The total cost is substantially higher than the estimates discussed earlier (about $12 with third-party verification). This results from two factors: the average direct cost per recertification was about 80 percent higher than the average for initial certifications, and the indirect cost rate after the enrollment period (204 percent) was much higher than the rate of 116 percent used in the earlier estimate. Substituting a $12 cost in the illustration would mean that the incremental costs would exceed the incremental benefits for monthly but not quarterly recertifications.

[b]The average absolute difference in payments (computed from the initial certification and annual recertification forms) was $220.56 per household per year, for those households that had annual recertifications. The figures assume that the changes in household situations causing the $220 difference occurred evenly throughout the year (and that none were reflected in interim recertifications). Thus one-twelfth of the changes are assumed to occur in the first month and to result in twelve months of payment errors; one-twelfth occur in the second month and result in eleven months of errors, and so on. With annual recertification the average error allowed is therefore assumed to be half the difference between certification and annual recertification, or $110. For semiannual recertification it is assumed that recertification corrects all the errors existing at the six-month point, so the maximum duration of an error is six months.

[c]The average difference in annual payments computed from initial certification and annual recertification was a reduction of $92.36 per household (for those with annual recertifications). The averaging logic is the same as that described in note b.

[d]Semiannual, monthly, and quarterly figures in columns 1–3 are subtracted from annual figures.

This illustration omits many factors, three of which are worth noting. First, the sum of errors existing during the year is probably greater than the total at the end of the year, because some individuals will encounter multiple or counterbalancing changes during the year; leaving this factor out tends to bias the example in favor of the longer periods. Second, any system has a lag time between the identification of a change and its implementation in payments; this tends to bias the example in favor of the shorter periods. Third, the example does not include the potential impact of eligibility determination at each recertification. The shorter the reporting period, the greater the possible flow of households into and out of the program, as their income fluctuates above and below the limits or as other conditions change. This fluctuation affects not only the payments but also administrative costs. A family found ineligible must be terminated, which incurs an administrative cost but no longer requires the performance of other administrative services and functions. A family that becomes eligible again incurs the substantial[54] administrative costs of application, enrollment, and so on. In the absence of data on the number of families likely to enter and leave the program under alternative reporting periods, these factors cannot be usefully estimated.

FURTHER RESEARCH

Like any other single research project, the AAE does not answer all the questions it might have addressed; and it raises questions that suggest directions for further research.

One such question concerns the relative effectiveness and costs of various methods of certifying household size. Most of the AAE agencies chose not to verify household size. This lack of significant variation prevents any conclusions about whether some methods might have been more effective than others. The low number of changes in household size observed at initial certification might have been an accurate reflection of the accuracy and stability of the household sizes reported at application or it might merely be a result of the lack of verification. This question requires further systematic investigation under more carefully controlled conditions before reliable answers will be available.

The findings on income certification are somewhat more conclusive but still limited. Most important, an independent audit of participant incomes, conducted at about the same time as agency certification, would be required to assess the absolute accuracy of any of the procedures used. It would also be required to shed further light on the various sources of error in income data, most importantly to separate actual changes in participant circumstances from error and deliberate misreporting.

Another subject for further investigation is the relative effectiveness of a certification system that uses both detailed and elaborate elicitation procedures at application *and* a thorough verification process. This option falls outside the range of procedures used by the AAE agencies. The evidence of the AAE, however, suggests that this system would be the most accurate of all. Whether this improved accuracy would be worth the increased time and cost would be a suitable question for future research.

The cost of alternative certification procedures has been estimated for analytic purposes, but the considerable variation in average costs across agencies (and the limited power of the analysis to explain that variance) indicate that much is still unknown about how certification costs are incurred. Further data and observation of agency procedures in a variety of operating situations would be required to obtain estimates that could be confidently used in program budgeting.

Finally, the AAE at best provides suggestive information on the issue of the optimum reporting period for income-conditioned transfer programs. More detailed analysis requires a data base with monthly income data with which the procedural and cost data available from the AAE might be combined.

Because the prevention of payment errors in a universal concern of income assistance programs, the experience of the Administrative Agency Experiment may be relevant to a much broader context than that of housing programs. The AAE shows that there is substantial cause for concern about payment error and that the choice of administrative procedures can be an important determinant of how much error is allowed. It would be inappropriate to assume that the AAE findings apply equally well to AFDC or other programs. Indeed, limitations of the research design argue that the findings should be interpreted with caution even in the context of housing assistance.

An Overview of Errors Avoided

The potential for payment error at the time a household applies for assistance is high. AAE agencies found a median of 8 percent of the applicants to be ineligible. Among eligible applicants errors were seldom found in the data on household size. But the agencies had to adjust the initially reported income data in more than half the cases. Had these adjustments not been made, the average participant's annual benefits would have included an error (either overpayment or underpayment) of $116.

Payment error tends to be equated in the public mind with dishonesty—with attempts by participants to obtain benefits to which they are not entitled. The consequent assumption is that eliminating error will substantially reduce public expenditures. In the AAE, however, agency efforts to adjust income data would have reduced the average payment by $17 per year if all those certified had received allowance payments; for those who actually did receive payments, the effect of certification was a reduction of less than $1. The reason for this small effect was that the agencies found many errors that increased payments as well as errors that reduced them. Although the source of error cannot be measured in the AAE data, the pattern appears to be dominated by honest error. Agencies reported a handful of cases of deliberate misreporting, and additional cases doubtless went undiscovered. But the major contribution of agency certification was not to save money by identifying instances of fraudulent behavior[55] but to allocate program resources more equitably among deserving households.

If the role of the agency is principally to correct honest error, it may well be fruitful to focus future research and development work on understanding the reasons for reporting error and mechanisms for preventing it. The wording of the questions about a particular kind of income, the sequence of questions, and the nature of the interaction between the applicant and the agency staff member might be more important determinants of error than any of the factors analyzed here. In fact, there is some evidence in the observational data that the level of detail with which information was elicited helped determine how much error subsequently had to be corrected, and future research might well begin with this hypothesis.

Income Verification

Verification—checking participant-reported income data by examining documents or contacting knowledgeable third parties— proved an important means for avoiding error in the AAE. Any procedure for reviewing income data resulted in a substantial number of adjustments to participants' reports, but verifying the information through documentary or third-party evidence produced markedly more adjustments than merely reviewing the information with participants. On average, spending an additional $4–$6 for verification avoided $28–$34 in annual payment errors.

The high rate of error avoidance and the low marginal cost seem to argue that income data at application should normally be verified. But three points suggest further analysis of this policy. First, although verification did predictably reduce errors, it did not yield a predictably greater reduction in total payment expenditures. In other words, universal verification would result in an increase in total government expenditures because the administrative cost would not be offset by payment reductions.

Second, the value of error avoidance depends on the length of time the error is assumed to exist before it is corrected. Because the AAE had an annual recertification policy, a twelve-month duration was assumed. But in a program with more frequent verification, the expected payment error would be smaller: with semiannual recertification the marginal value of third-party verification would be $17 in avoided payment error; the value would be $9 with quarterly recertification, and $3 in a monthly system. The incremental administrative cost would always be $6, regardless of the frequency of recertification.

Both points argue for additional analysis of the consequences of alternative income certification policies in the context of specific programs. Thus a third argument is posed by the limitations of the research design underlying this analysis. In the absence of an independent audit of participant incomes, conducted at the same time as the agency certification, it is impossible to judge the absolute effectiveness of the various procedures in eliminating potential payment errors. Research incorporating such a design could make an important contribution to the administration of income assistance programs.

Other Procedural Options

Apart from the certification of income data, few administrative variations observed in the AAE appeared to make a substantial difference in the avoidance of payment error. However, data limitations may have masked differences that further research could measure.

Alternative procedures for obtaining and reviewing data pertinent to eligibility, for example, resulted in little apparent difference in eligibility findings. But this finding is clouded by indications that other administrative variations, particularly the adoption of local eligibility requirements and the content and targeting of outreach, can influence the number of ineligible people who apply to the program. Research involving independent measurement of participants' eligibility-related characteristics would be required to separate the effects of procedures that produce potential error from procedures that remove it.

Certification of data on household size also appeared to yield roughly constant results regardless of the procedures used. Only a small fraction of the cases had adjustments to household size data, whether the participants' reports were verified or not. This may imply that it is more important to establish procedures for capturing changes in household size that occur during the period a family is participating than to check the information filed at application. Again, however, research with independent measurement of participants' status, and preferably with more cases than the present analysis had, would be necessary to confirm this finding.

The AAE analysis found few participant characteristics strongly associated with the presence or amount of potential payment error and little indication that a policy of selective verification would be useful. This finding conflicts with one of the current trends in AFDC administration, in which some states are reporting significant improvement in error rates as a result of selective checking. The conflict may result from features of the AAE design, such as the absence of a quality control audit to measure participant incomes independently, the consequent analysis of avoided error rather than existing error, or the analytic focus on initial certification. Any of the types of further research described earlier could contribute to a greater understanding of the utility of selective error-avoidance procedures by focusing separately on individual sources and kinds of error.

A final issue is the nature and frequency with which eligibility and payment-related information should be recertified. The Administrative Agency Experiment allowed only superficial examination of this issue, but some interesting indications are found in the data. Nearly all AAE participants had adjustments to their income data at the time of annual recertification; most adjustments, reflecting a general increase in incomes over time, led to payment reductions. This pattern suggests that recertification might well be more frequent in order to capture changes in income more quickly and that verifying income data at the time of recertification, unlike initial certification, might yield savings in overall program expenditures. In this vein, monthly reporting of income is currently required of AFDC recipients in some states and has been included as an element of the national program in the Carter administration's welfare reform proposals. Whether monthly reporting yields an appropriate match of error reduction and administrative costs can certainly not be determined from the AAE data; it is clear from those data, however, that reducing the interval between reports will reduce the amount of error avoided in any given action while increasing the level of administrative expenditures. Hence there appears to be a need for careful analysis of the alternatives.

NOTES

1. See, for example, *Quality Control in AFDC* (SRS) 76-0410 (Washington, D.C.: Social and Rehabilitation Service, U.S. Department of Health, Education, and Welfare, 1976).

2. Because the AAE agencies could serve only a limited number of households, most put apparently eligible applications into a pool from which potential participants would be selected as the opportunity arose. Thus there was generally a time lapse between screening and certification, which would not be typical of programs that could serve all eligible applicants.

3. For a review, see Seymour Sudman and Norman M. Bradburn, *Response Effects in Surveys* (Chicago: Aldine Press, 1974).

4. For example, approximately half of all payment error is attributed to agency error, which approximates the above definition of administrative error in *Aid to Families with Dependent Children Quality Control Findings*, January–June 1977 (Washington, D.C.: Social Security Administration, 1978).

5. A partial exception is found in Marc Bendick, Jr., Abe Lavine, and Toby H. Campbell, *The Anatomy of AFDC Errors* (Washington, D.C.: Urban Institute, 1978). In this analysis a number of administrative factors are included in an equation explaining overall error rate; the administrative error rate is not separately analyzed, however.

6. James N. Morgan et al., *Five Thousand American Families: Patterns of Economic Progress*, vol. 1 (Ann Arbor, Mich.: Institute for Social Research, 1974).

7. *Aid to Families with Dependent Children Quality Control Findings.*

8. It is not necessary to assume that the information developed by the agency was a completely accurate reflection of the true situation but simply that it more closely approximates the true situation than does the participant's initial report. Note that sources of administrative error that occur between recording of the data and issuance of the check (for example, erroneous computation of the payment amount) are excluded by this analytic treatment.

9. Of the four components of payment error as usually defined, only changed circumstances and (some kinds of) administrative error are explicitly represented. Audit error, as distinct from administrative error, is not measured. Participant reporting error is assumed to be randomly distributed with respect to the variables of analytic interest (although some variation in that pattern is probably captured by the demographic variables included in the analysis), and no attempt is made to estimate the absolute level of this error component.

10. In the median case a family of four was eligible with an annual "net" income up to $6,575 (certain deductions, such as medical expenses, were subtracted from total income to compute net income). The median limit was $4,600 for a one-person household and $8,825 for a household of nine or more.

11. Agencies differed slightly in applying this criterion. Some accepted applications from families in subsidized housing, with the proviso that they would have to move to become allowance recipients. Others did not accept applications from people in subsidized housing. Similarly home owners were allowed to apply but had to move to rental units to qualify for payments.

12. Applying the payment formula to households over the income limit would yield a zero or negative payment (or a very small payment where agencies established a minimum payment limit). These households are therefore excluded from the calculation.

13. Based on income and household size data on the application form.

14. Based on income and household size data on the certification form.

15. Adjusted for the proportion of applicants and certified applicants who did not become recipients. Note that in the AAE, the effect of excluding an ineligible applicant was not to reduce the total volume of allowance payments but to make it possible for an additional eligible household to participate. Thus another way to look at these figures is to say that excluding ineligible applicants made it possible for about 3 percent of those who ultimately became recipients to do so—about 162 of the 5,756 recipient households in the AAE (at the average payment level).

16. There were six household size categories, each with a different net income limit.

17. Tulsa had lower income limits than most other agencies (reflecting the lower cost of living there), which may have exaggerated this pattern.

18. Table E-1, appendix E, displays the results of a logit analysis of eligibility findings. For a complete discussion, see Dickson, *Certification*, appendix B.

19. This factor is significant in multivariate analysis; see table E-1, appendix E. There are, however, alternative explanations for the pattern: for example, agency staff may have been less careful in the later months, as the pressure

to meet enrollment deadlines intensified. However, analyses of other aspects of the certification process, even where procedures are shown to change over time, do not show any changes in results (such as the number of changes in income data) that correspond to the pattern in eligibility determination.

20. AAE agencies were requested not to prescreen; that is, they were to take applications from all interested households, even those that might appear ineligible. Nonetheless, individuals could walk into (or telephone) an agency office, ask a few questions about eligibility, decide they would probably be ineligible, and not apply. Bismarck's mail-in procedure tended to limit this self-screening.

21. Some information would be coincidentally corroborated, for example, a listing of income sources would confirm or contradict a statement about whether the applicant was a member of the armed forces.

22. Because the high ineligibility rate in Tulsa was mainly related to that agency's special eligibility criteria and outreach procedures, Tulsa is excluded from the table.

23. Adjusted to reflect the proportion of certified applicants that did not become recipients.

24. Alternatively, these exclusions allowed about twenty-nine eligible families to participate (at the average payment level).

25. In the case of multiple items of information, the agency could verify some items through third parties and others through documents. In some analyses, this is separately identified as a mixture procedure.

26. The use of nonstringent procedures could mean that this figure is an underestimate. However, the rate was not substantially different in the cases where stringent procedures were used.

27. See, for example, Sudman and Bradburn, *Response Effects in Surveys.* Analysis of income reporting in the Housing Allowance Demand Experiment revealed no significant difference between households that stood to gain from underreporting and those for whom income had no impact on benefits. See David C. Hoaglin and Catherine A. Joseph, *Draft Report on Income Reporting and Verification in the Housing Allowance Demand Experiment* (Cambridge, Mass.: Abt Associates, 1978).

28. An average of about six weeks elapsed between the time the participant filled out the application form and the time income and household data were certified.

29. Most analyses excluded changes of less than $48 in annual income. A change of $48 would yield a change of $1 in the monthly allowance payment, other things being equal. Changes of less than $48 amounted to 13 percent of all changes.

30. The complete-mixture technique appears to result in substantially more changes than other methods. However, this procedure was used in only about 3 percent of the cases, and these were, by definition, cases with more than one income source (and thus multiple opportunities for change).

31. Table E–2 in appendix E gives the results of a logit analysis of adjustments to reported income. For a complete discussion of the analysis see Dickson, *Certification.*

32. See table E–3, appendix E.

33. Table E–4, appendix E, gives the results of a regression analysis of the magnitude of income changes.

34. U.S. Census studies have shown low error rates for household size information and higher rates for income data. See Sudman and Bradburn, *Response Effects in Surveys.*

35. Dickson, *Certification,* appendix C, section VII.

36. A one-year period was chosen for examining payment effects to correspond to the annual cycle of mandatory recertification.

37. See appendix E, table E–5. Methods used in fewer than 5 percent of the cases were excluded from the multivariate analysis. For a full discussion of this analysis see Dickson, *Certification,* appendix E.

38. The estimates do not include indirect costs such as management, record keeping, office supplies. The indirect cost rate used for most simulation analyses presented here was 116 percent of direct costs. Applying this ratio to the estimates would yield total cost estimates of $11.94 for third-party verification, $9.63 for documentary verification, and $5.62 for self-declaration.

39. For a full discussion of this analysis, see Dickson, *Certification,* appendix F.

40. Average cost per certification (including some interim as well as initial certifications) is computed for the enrollment period (the first eight or nine months of agency operations).

41. Complete documentation identified somewhat more upward changes than self-declaration, but the relationship was not statistically important (appendix E, table E–6).

42. A more accurate picture of the impact of certification on the AAE payment bill is obtained by computing the net payment effect only for those 5,756 households that became recipients. By this computation the net payment effect is an average reduction of about $1 per participant per year.

43. See Dickson, *Certification,* appendix E.

44. This relationship was only observed after taking agency verification practices into account.

45. Peoria, San Bernardino, and Jacksonville. Durham and Salem were not consistent in the source of verification used but did consistently perform some kind of verification.

46. See table E–7, appendix E.

47. See Dickson, *Certification*, appendix D.

48. See, for example, Joel F. Handler and E. J. Hollingsworth, *The "Deserving Poor"* (Chicago: Markham, 1971).

49. For a full presentation of this analysis see Dickson, *Certification*, appendix A.

50. The reported delay varied substantially, both within and across agencies. Staff at one agency indicated that third-party verifications were usually complete within one week; at another agency delays of four weeks were considered common.

51. The general relationship between stringency of procedures and level of changes is maintained when detail of elicitation is taken into account.

52. The number of items on the form is a crude proxy for the level of detail required. Further, because this information is available only at the agency level, it is confounded with other procedural (such as stringency and timing of certification) and environmental factors. In a preliminary analysis a term reflecting the detail of elicitation was added to the basic model shown in appendix E to examine the effects of certification procedures. Both the elicitation variable and the verification variables were significantly associated with the incidence with which income data were adjusted.

53. For each household that became a recipient and stayed in the program long enough to have an annual recertification, two annual payment figures were computed. The first was based on income and household size data on the certification form, the second on the recertification data. A payment increase, in this discussion, means that the annual recertification payment was higher than the certification payment. Interim recertifications are ignored: change that was first recorded on an interim certification form and merely confirmed at annual recertification is treated as though it had first appeared at annual recertification.

54. In the AAE the median cost of bringing a family into the program was estimated at $253. See Charles M. Maloy et al., *Administrative Costs in a Housing Allowance Program: Two-Year Costs in the Administrative Agency Experiment* (Cambridge, Mass.: Abt Associates, 1977).

55. It is of course possible that agency actions had some deterrent effect on deliberate misreporting, and this is unmeasured in the data.

6

Administrative Costs

In the debate about housing allowances in the late 1960s and early 1970s, advocates argued that one of the program's major advantages would be lower administrative costs than for existing housing subsidy programs. Accordingly, designers of the experimental programs attempted to limit the requirement for administrative actions, and the Administrative Agency Experiment took as a major objective the measurement and understanding of administrative costs.

Because the administrative mission of the AAE agencies resembled that of welfare and other income transfer programs, and because those programs now have a substantial operating history, it might be expected that they would offer a methodological framework for analyzing the AAE costs. But the literature on welfare and related programs contains surprisingly little work on administrative costs. Indeed, it is only in the 1970s that the administrative cost of welfare has become a significant policy issue and hence has begun to receive serious research attention.[1] That research is still far from providing a complete understanding of administrative costs, however, as illustrated by the following comment in a report by the Congressional Reference Service:

From 1973 to 1974, New York's AFDC administrative costs as reported by HEW in its annual State expenditure reports, decreased

Most of the material in this chapter is taken from Charles M. Maloy et al., *Administrative Costs in a Housing Allowance Program: Two-Year Costs in the Administrative Agency Experiment* (Cambridge, Mass.: Abt Associates, 1977).

from $95 million to $85 million. This is a particularly striking occurrence in light of the fact that their AFDC employees nearly doubled in 1974 and the entire AFDC staff received a 7 percent across-the-board salary increase. The following year, AFDC administrative costs went from $85 million up to $251 million. . . . HEW officials are unable to explain this fluctuation.[2]

The AAE research effort on administrative costs thus represented a sizable step into poorly charted territory, especially at the time the effort was designed.[3] Two primary concepts underlay the research: a hierarchical structure of agency functions and a work measurement approach to measuring costs. Neither of these concepts was new, but the scope of the effort in which they were applied was unusual.

FUNCTIONS AS A FRAMEWORK

The set of administrative functions defined to categorize agency activities has been partly visible in previous chapters; in fact, this framework is the basis for the entire AAE research design, but it was most comprehensively and explicitly used in the cost analysis. The framework is illustrated in figure 6-1.

Administrative costs are categorized for analysis into *direct* and *indirect* costs. Direct costs were incurred to perform the activities necessary to bring participants into the program and to provide payments and ongoing services. These activities accounted for about 40 percent of administrative costs in the AAE. The remainder was indirect costs, incurred for support of the direct cost activities; they result from management, planning, providing facilities and equipment, and related activities.

Direct costs are further divided into *intake* and *maintenance* costs. Intake activities are the one-time actions required to bring eligible families into the program. These costs, which were incurred only in the first year of the AAE, amounted to nearly 60 percent of direct costs for the two years. Maintenance costs were incurred mostly in the second year, to distribute monthly payments and provide other required services to allowance recipients. Maintenance activities are repetitive and continue as long as the family remains in the program.

Intake activities are subdivided into two processes and six functions:

Process 1: Generating enrollees. Performing administrative tasks necessary to generate an enrollee group that is determined eligible to par-

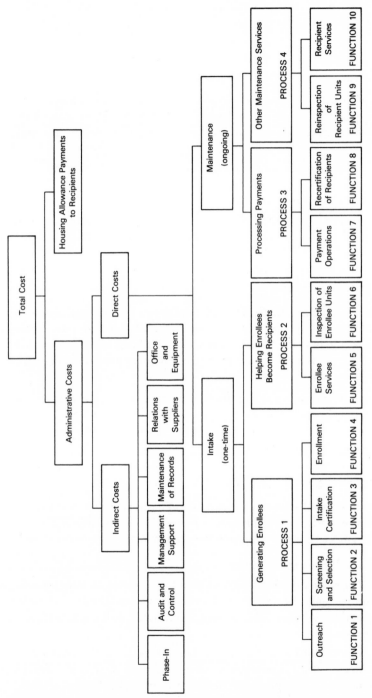

Figure 6-1. A Model for Disaggregating Housing Allowance Program Costs

ticipate in the program. This process is composed of four intake functions, which were performed only during the first year.

1. *Outreach.* Making the eligible population aware of the program and inducing them to apply. Outreach was the most costly function in Process 1, accounting for about 20 percent of all intake costs.

2. *Screening and selection.* Taking applications, screening to determine applicant eligibility, and selecting applicants to receive an offer of program participation.

3. *Intake certification.* Certifying income and household size for eligibility and determining the amount of the housing allowance payment each eligible household could receive.

4. *Enrollment.* Explaining program rules and participant rights and responsibilities and signing an enrollment form.

Process 2: Helping enrollees become recipients. Providing services to the enrollee group to assist them in the search for housing and determining that the housing selected meets agency requirements for quality. This second intake process includes two administrative functions, performed during the first year.

5. *Enrollee services.* Providing housing market information and assisting with problems the participants encounter. Services accounted for 30 percent of all intake costs, more than any other intake function.

6. *Inspection of enrollee units.* Inspecting housing units to ensure they meet agency standards for decent, safe, and sanitary housing.

Maintenance activities began as soon as families reached recipient status, in some cases early in the enrollment period. After the first year, however, AAE activity was exclusively devoted to maintenance activities.

Process 3: Processing payments.

7. *Payment operations.* Includes all procedures required for the disbursement of funds to recipients. About a third of maintenance expenditures went for payment operations, with little variation across sites.

8. *Recertification of recipients.* Includes an annual recertification of income and household size for all recipients as well as a routine agency- or participant-initiated interim recertification.

Process 4: Other maintenance services.

9. *Reinspection of recipient units.* Includes inspection of new units for recipients who move while in the program and reinspection of units already occupied.

10. *Recipient services.* Assisting recipients with problems or questions encountered during their tenure in the program.

Indirect costs involved administrative functions not related to providing services or assistance to families at any specific stage of their participation. The following six administrative functions include costs collectively termed indirect.

Management support. Includes all management activities necessary to support and direct each aspect of agency operations. Management support, together with maintenance of records and office and equipment, accounts for about 85 percent of indirect costs.

Maintenance of records. Includes all gathering, storing, and reporting of information required by the AAE.

Office and equipment. Includes all costs for physical space and equipment not directly or specifically allocable to other administrative functions.

Audit and control. Includes all activities such as meeting staff payroll and paying bills related to the management of program funds.

Relations with suppliers. Includes contacts that an agency makes with individuals and organizations other than program participants.

Phase-in. Includes monitoring of the demographic characteristics of the participant profile to ensure representativeness of participants from the eligible population. This function was performed only during the first year.

With the exception of phase-in, which was an indirect cost associated only with intake activities, all other indirect cost functions were performed throughout the entire period covered by the analysis.

DATA COLLECTION AND ANALYSIS STRATEGY

The research followed a dual strategy within the common framework provided by the functions just defined. The first part of the strategy was to collect and analyze data on what were generally called actual costs or reported costs. The second was to construct a simulation model to project agency costs under hypothetical situations.

Key to the analysis of actual costs was the monthly financial reporting form. With this form each of the eight agencies allocated each staff member's time (apart from paid leave) among the functions. Nonpersonnel costs were likewise allocated.[4] Analysis of the data generally focused on time rather than accounted costs in order to reduce the effect of regional wage variations and other distorting factors. The analysis proceeded through two stages. The first attempted to produce reliable measures of unit costs (or time) for each function, such as enrollment costs per enrollee. The second attempted to explain cross-agency variation in unit costs as a function of the specific administrative procedures chosen—and thus to estimate the cost of alternative administrative procedures—usually by means of multiple regression analysis.

The simulation model was for the most part independent of the reported cost data base. For each of the direct cost functions, staff at each agency were asked to estimate how long it took them to perform particular tasks in particular ways. For example, staff were asked to estimate the amount of time it would take them to complete a certification under a self-declaration procedure, under a procedure involving document checks, and with third-party verification. Each function was then represented by a set of equations multiplying staff time requirements by typical wage rates for staff at that skill level and multiplying the resulting unit cost by the number of times the function would have to be performed for a given number of participants. Time and cost estimates produced by the model were then validated against the reported cost data base (except for the indirect cost functions, in which the reported cost data base was used to develop regression equations that were directly incorporated in the model).[5]

The following sections present results from the actual cost analysis and the simulation model. Actual costs are used primarily to describe the overall levels of cost and variation in costs observed in the AAE, while the simulation results are used to explore some of the factors influencing costs.

AGGREGATE COSTS

During the two years covered by this analysis, the eight experimental programs spent a total of nearly $10 million.[6] This section presents an overview of the major components of that expenditure, separating payments from administrative costs and describing the distribution of administrative costs in terms of program phase, the functional components of intake and maintenance costs, and direct versus indirect costs. The aggregate cost figures are also used to derive summary statements of the cost of assisting an average family in the AAE.

Administrative and Payment Costs

The costs of the first two years of operation at the AAE sites are shown in table 6-1. The total program cost for the two years combined was $9.96 million, including $7.10 million of housing allowance payments to recipients and $2.86 million of agency administrative costs. In the first two years, then, administrative costs amounted to 29 percent of the total expenditures of the AAE agencies combined. Across agencies and over time, however, the ratio varied substantially. Administrative costs in the first year made up a substantially greater proportion of total costs than in the second year, 42 percent compared with 18 percent. Because the first year was devoted largely to bringing people into the program, administrative costs were higher and payment costs lower than in the second year.

First-year administrative costs varied across agencies, ranging (if Jacksonville is excluded) from 31 percent of all costs at Peoria to 51 percent at Springfield. Jacksonville's extraordinarily high proportion of administrative costs (60 percent) was caused by a very high attrition rate. The number of applications to the Jacksonville agency was much lower; there were only nineteen recipients per hundred applicants at Jacksonville, compared with thirty-seven per one hundred at all eight sites combined.[7] Thus Jacksonville's first-year administrative costs were not unusually high, but the payment costs were unusually low. In the second year the administrative costs ranged from 13 percent of total expenditures at Salem to 27 percent at Bismarck.

Administrative Costs over Time

The total administrative costs for all eight agencies during their first two years of operation are summarized in table 6-2 by time period. Total first-year administrative costs were nearly 80 percent higher than second-year levels, reflecting the shift from predominantly intake to pure maintenance activities.[8] For the two years Bismarck and Durham had the

Table 6-1. Administrative Costs and Total Program Costs

Site	Administrative Costs		Housing Allowance Payments		Total Program Cost		Ratio of Administrative Costs to Total Program Costs	
	Year 1	Year 2	Year 1	Year 2	Year 1	Year 2	Year 1	Year 2
Salem	$224,475	$105,523	$429,140	$729,651	$653,615	$ 835,174	0.34	0.13
Springfield	269,354	219,892	257,953	884,052	527,307	1,103,944	0.51	0.20
Peoria	219,017	144,146	479,607	691,079	698,624	835,225	0.31	0.17
San Bernardino	291,662	135,276	436,809	689,133	728,471	824,409	0.40	0.16
Bismarck	114,713	98,541	222,223	264,136	336,936	362,677	0.34	0.27
Jacksonville	216,306	87,455	143,161	321,992	359,467	409,447	0.60	0.21
Durham	175,095	119,219	216,074	372,630	391,169	491,849	0.45	0.24
Tulsa	320,196	118,761	350,244	616,418	670,440	733,179	0.48	0.16
Total for eight sites	$1,830,818	$1,028,813	$2,535,211	$4,569,091	$4,366,029	$5,597,904	0.42	0.18

lowest costs. These sites, with targets of 400 and 500 recipients respectively, were planned as the two smallest agencies. Jacksonville had a higher target (900) but actually achieved the fewest recipients (339) during the first year and consequently showed the lowest second-year cost.[9] Tulsa incurred first-year costs almost $30,000 higher than those of the next closest agency; the reasons for this difference include a higher level of activity on some intake functions (especially outreach) and the use of subcontractors.

Table 6-2. Total AAE Administrative Costs

Site	First Year Enrollment	First Year Transition	First Year Total	Second Year	Two-year Total
Salem	$181,410	$ 43,065	$224,475	$105,523	$329,998
Springfield	195,847	73,507	269,354	219,892	489,246
Peoria	170,801	48,216	219,017	144,146	363,163
San Bernardino	204,945	86,717	291,662	135,276	426,938
Bismarck	79,167	35,546	114,713	98,541	213,254
Jacksonville	171,625	44,681	216,306	87,455	303,761
Durham	120,349	54,746	175,095	119,219	294,314
Tulsa	248,039	72,157	320,196	118,761	438,957
Totals for eight sites	$1,372,183	$458,635	$1,830,818	$1,028,813	$2,859,631

Cross-site comparison within the enrollment and transition periods (during the first year) is somewhat misleading because of site variation in the number of program months in the two phases. To permit a more incisive comparison of the levels of activity at the various sites, the average monthly administrative costs by time period are given in table 6-3.

Table 6-3. Average Monthly Administrative Costs

Site	First Year Enrollment	First Year Transition	First Year Total	Second Year	Two-year Average
Salem	$20,157	$14,355	$18,706	$ 8,794	$13,750
Springfield	21,761	24,502	22,446	18,324	20,385
Peoria	18,978	16,072	18,251	12,012	15,132
San Bernardino	25,618	21,679	24,305	11,273	17,789
Bismarck	9,896	8,886	9,559	8,212	8,886
Jacksonville	19,069	14,894	18,026	7,288	12,657
Durham	15,044	13,686	14,591	9,935	12,263
Tulsa	31,005	18,039	26,683	9,897	18,290

Average monthly expenditures at all sites but Springfield decreased between the enrollment and transition periods. Springfield's monthly expenditure rate increased, for two reasons. First, a disproportionately high number of this agency's recipients (44 percent) got their first payment during the transition period, requiring greater agency activity in some functions. Second, Springfield provided recipients with more intensive maintenance services than other agencies, which meant that the staff was not reduced as much after enrollment.

The most dramatic change in expenditure rates was at Tulsa, where monthly costs dropped nearly 40 percent between the enrollment and transition periods. The magnitude of this reduction was amplified by the high costs for contracted services incurred by the Tulsa agency during the enrollment period.

Cross-site comparisons illustrate the variability of administrative costs during the enrollment period. For the six sites with targets of 900 recipients total monthly expenditures ranged from $18,978 at Peoria to $31,005 at Tulsa. Although the totals are smaller in the second year, the proportional variation was even larger.

Intake and Maintenance Costs

Of the total $2.9 million administrative costs of the AAE, $1.2 million (41 percent) is considered "direct costs." These costs are directly attributable to services required either to bring families into the program or to maintain services and make payments to recipients. Intake, bringing families into the program, accounted for 57 percent of all direct costs in the two-year period and nearly 80 percent of the first-year direct costs.

Figure 6–2 disaggregates intake costs into the two processes and six functions defined earlier. The process of generating enrollees incurred the largest share (58 percent) of total intake costs; helping enrollees become recipients accounted for the remainder (42 percent). Two administrative functions accounted for about half of the total intake costs: supportive services to enrollees (30 percent) and outreach (20 percent).

The remaining direct administrative costs in the first two years of the AAE were incurred in dealing with households that were receiving housing allowance payments. Maintenance activities accounted for all second-year direct costs and 21 percent of those in the first year. Disaggregate maintenance costs are shown in figure 6–3.

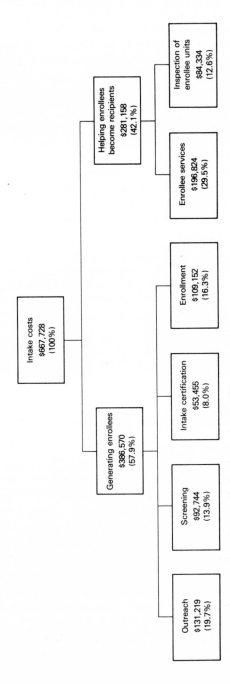

Figure 6-2. Allocation of Intake Costs in the AAE

Almost half of all maintenance costs went to making monthly payments to recipients, including both the mechanical process of delivering
checks and recertification (updating information on participant eligibility, income, and household size). The other half of maintenance
costs was divided between inspection or reinspection of units for recipients and supportive services provided to recipients (including assistance
in disputes with landlords, in relocation to new units, and in other nonroutine situations). Recipient services accounted for the largest segment
of maintenance costs (46 percent), followed by payment operations (32
percent). Recipient inspection accounted for less than 7 percent of maintenance costs in the AAE; however, an ongoing program might well
place more emphasis on ensuring the maintenance of housing quality
over time and thus on the reinspection function.

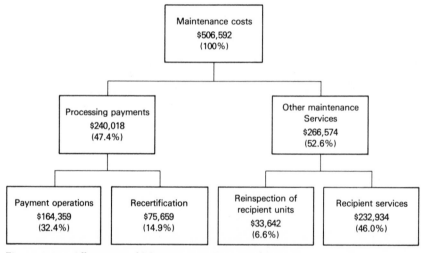

Figure 6-3. Allocation of Maintenance Costs in the AAE

Indirect Costs

Indirect costs were incurred for various managerial, accounting,
equipment, and office space items necessary to support the agencies.
Over the two years these costs amounted to nearly $1.7 million, or
approximately 59 percent of total administrative costs. Figure 6-4 disaggregates total indirect costs for the AAE according to administrative
function. Nearly 40 percent of all indirect costs are incurred in management support. Office and equipment expenditures (26 percent) and costs

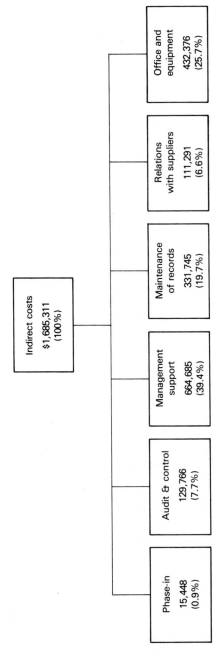

Figure 6–4.   Allocation of Indirect Costs in the AAE

for maintenance of records (20 percent) are the other two major functions. Total expenditures within these three functions amounted to approximately $1.4 million and represented 85 percent of total indirect costs.

Indirect costs increased during the two-year period from 50 percent of administrative costs during the enrollment period to 68 percent during the second year (table 6-4). Managerial and overhead costs did not decline as sharply as the number of staff and the direct costs. The increase in importance of indirect costs as total administrative costs declined suggests that scale of agency operations may be a significant factor in program costs.

Table 6-4. Direct versus Indirect Costs
in the AAE by Time Period, Eight-Site Total

| Period | Agency Administrative Costs | | | Indirect Cost as Percentage of Total |
	Direct	Indirect	Total	
First year total	$840,067	$990,751	$1,830,818	0.54
Enrollment	685,334	686,849	1,372,183	0.50
Transition	154,733	303,902	458,635	0.66
Second year	334,253	694,560	1,028,813	0.68
Total both years	$1,174,320	$1,685,311	$2,859,631	0.59

Cost per Family

To plan a housing allowance program, or to compare the costs of such a program to alternative means of providing housing assistance, aggregate AAE figures must be translated into unit costs—the cost of providing a family with decent, safe, and sanitary housing for one year. Such a summary figure must include three elements: the annual benefit payment, the annual administrative cost for maintaining a family in the program (including indirect costs), and some portion of the administrative cost of bringing a family into the program (including indirect costs). Annual benefit and maintenance costs for an agency can be derived simply by dividing total AAE expenditures by the number of recipient-years[10] of service.

Determining the appropriate proportion of intake costs to include is somewhat more difficult. Intake costs should be amortized over the number of years a family will stay in the program, but the limited duration of the AAE prohibits precise estimation of the expected length of participation. About 20 percent of the AAE recipients dropped out of the program within one year of their first payment. For this analysis, then, the average tenure of a family in a housing allowance program has been estimated at five years, and amortized cost estimates include one-fifth of the total intake cost per recipient.[11]

The average annual cost in the AAE of providing a family with decent, safe, and sanitary housing is presented in figure 6–5.[12] The figure

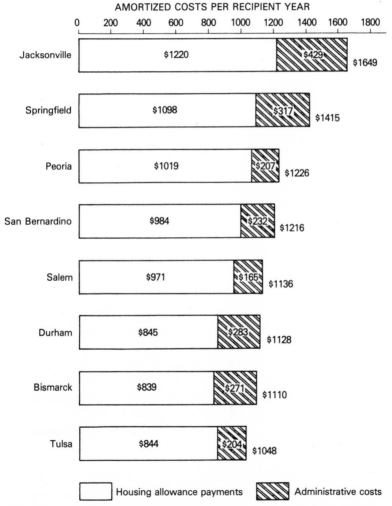

Figure 6–5. Amortized Costs per Recipient-Year by Site (dollars per year)

for each agency includes the average benefit payment and maintenance cost, plus one-fifth of the average intake cost per recipient. The highest-cost site (Jacksonville) had a cost per recipient year of $1,649. Jacksonville had both the highest average payments[13] and the highest administrative costs. The lowest-cost agency (Tulsa) spent an average of $1,045 to provide families with decent housing for a year, 37 percent below the Jacksonville cost.

The totals shown in figure 6-5 reflect the particular combinations of intake, maintenance, and payment expenditures at each individual site. Examining the three cost components separately yields a somewhat better description of typical costs.

Intake costs per recipient and maintenance costs per recipient year (including indirect costs) for the eight sites are shown in figure 6-6. The median intake cost was $253, and the median maintenance cost $205.

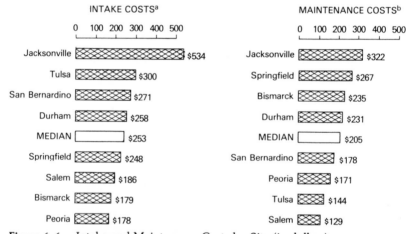

Figure 6-6.   Intake and Maintenance Costs by Site (in dollars)
[a]Intake Costs per new recipient, loaded to include indirect costs
[b]Maintenance Costs per recipient year, loaded to include indirect costs

The typical administrative cost per recipient year is thus $256 (the total maintenance cost plus one-fifth of the intake cost). The average annual allowance payment in the AAE was $969. Payment and administrative costs combined, the cost of providing a family with decent housing for a year is $1,225.

If the AAE experience were to be used to estimate administrative costs in a national housing allowance program, a more refined estimating procedure would be desirable. A first step might be to disaggregate further the intake and maintenance cost components. An estimate was therefore derived using the AAE median costs for each of the four direct cost processes,[14] the median indirect cost rate, and the median attrition rate.[15] This procedure estimates administrative costs at $276 per household per year, yielding a total program cost estimate of $1,245.

DIRECT COSTS

Most of the AAE analysis, as reported in previous chapters, focused on the administrative functions dealing directly with participants. Similarly the initial focus of the cost analysis was on direct costs, the personnel and other costs required to carry out those contact functions. This section examines the variation across the eight agencies in the unit costs they reported for each direct function and the extent to which the variation appears to have resulted from policy choices about procedures for carrying out the functions.[16]

Intake Costs

Most direct administrative costs for the agencies' first year were intake costs, that is, the costs of bringing families into the program. Intake costs ranged from 67 percent of the total at Bismarck to 86 percent at Tulsa; the median was 79 percent.

Costs per applicant for *outreach* varied dramatically (figure 6–7). Durham had exceptionally low costs (about $1 per applicant); the agency carried out a minimal outreach effort, relying heavily on informal presentations in the community and referrals from other social service organizations. By contrast, Tulsa incurred costs of about $27 per applicant, largely to pay for a professionally developed publicity campaign that used mass media extensively. Even if these two agencies are excluded, however, costs ranged widely around the median of $5.67 per applicant.

Local policy choices on several dimensions influenced the level of agency costs. Agencies determined the content of the outreach message, whether outreach materials would be designed by staff members or professionals in advertising agencies, whether to rely on institutional contacts or use the public media, and how much outreach to carry out. It was not possible with the AAE data to estimate the cost of alternative

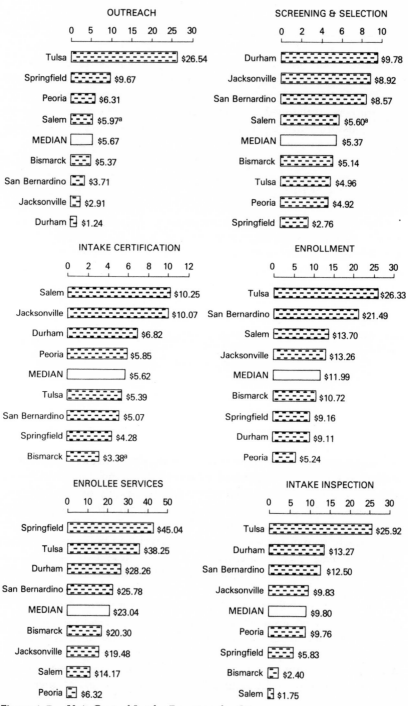

Figure 6-7. Unit Cost of Intake Functions by Site

[a]The number of applicants in the base of these ratios is 2,387, which excludes 142 applications received prior to the enrollment period at no cost.

[a]Bismarck's unit cost of certification is calculated as cost per applicant (rather than enrollee) because certification was done when applications were taken.

choices on each of these dimensions.[17] However, multivariate analysis demonstrated that outreach expenditures were directly related to the number of applications received—that greater expenditures led to predictably greater numbers of applications.[18] This analysis estimated the marginal cost per application at $5.74, very close to the median shown in figure 6–7.

Factors outside an agency's policy control were also shown to influence outreach costs. For example, costs per applicant were lower where the potentially eligible population was larger. Thus the analysis suggests that outreach costs are likely to vary from one location to the next as a function of the number of applicants sought, the agency's outreach procedures, and characteristics of the environment of each agency.

Screening and selection activities resulted in about the same median cost as outreach ($5.37), but the variation was much less. Two procedural choices contributed substantially to cost variation, however. Agencies could either take applications by mail or require people to apply at the agency office, and either manual or computer procedures could be used to maintain an applicant pool and select potential participants. The simulation model estimated a difference of approximately $4 between the least expensive combination (mail-in applications with computer selection) and the most expensive (in-person applications with manual selection).[19] Multivariate analysis also showed that costs were related to the difficulty of the agencies' task: the farther the agencies were from meeting their targeted numbers of recipients, the higher the average cost of screening and selection.

The *certification* function included agency activities to determine the eligibility of applicants and to ensure the accuracy of income and other information relevant to payment levels. The variation in unit costs for certification—from about $3 at Bismarck to about $10 in Salem, with a median of $5.62 per enrolled household—was slightly greater than the variation for screening.

According to simulation estimates, the choice of procedures for certifying income could account for variations of about $3.50 in direct costs per enrolled household, compared with the observed variation of about $7 in the agency averages.[20] It is evident that factors other than this procedural choice influence agency costs, however. In multivariate analysis of all agencies' reported costs, no stable estimate for the alternative certification procedures could be derived.[21] Moreover, analyses of single-site data sometimes indicated that verification by checking documents was more expensive than verification through third parties, although the simulation model and the all-site analysis show greater costs for the third-party technique. No environmental factors were hypothesized to have major impacts on certification costs,[22] so it seems likely that procedural variations not measured in the AAE analysis were influential.

Enrollment costs were incurred mainly in meetings between agency staff and prospective enrollees, where the latter were told of program rules and signed official enrollment papers. With a median of $11.99, these costs were generally larger than certification costs per enrollee. The variation in enrollment costs was substantial; Tulsa's high of $26 per enrollee was more than five times Peoria's low of $5.

Relatively little of the variation in enrollment costs can be explained by procedural alternatives that were measured in the AAE data, however. The major apparent distinction in procedures was the use of group or individual sessions for explaining the program to enrollees.[23] This distinction was estimated in the simulation model to cause a difference in direct costs of about $1.25 per enrollee.[24] A less precisely measured variation was an agency's special emphasis on enrollment, reflected in such site-specific procedures as developing a slide show or conducting enrollment in participants' homes. Multivariate analysis estimated that this special emphasis cost about $1.40 per household. A substantial amount of variation in enrollment costs thus comes from agency differences that are likely to be difficult to predict or detect.

Service costs ranged from 95 percent above the median of $23.04 to 73 percent below. As described in chapter 3, supportive services in the AAE took two forms: formal services, which were relatively routine presentations of information about the program's housing requirements and how to obtain housing in the local market, and responsive services, in which agencies responded ad hoc to individual families' problems. Procedures for formal services paralleled those for enrollment, with group sessions, individual sessions, and a combination of group and individual sessions. Responsive services varied along a continuum of emphasis, but agencies were simply categorized according to whether they placed a low or a moderate-to-high emphasis on making this service available.

These procedural options accounted for a substantial amount of the variation in average agency expenditures. Estimates from the simulation model ranged from $9 to $26 in direct costs per enrollee. Multivariate analysis of reported costs also took into account any special emphasis placed on formal services (such as preparation of unusually extensive materials) and showed an even wider range of estimated costs, from $7 to $35 per enrollee.[25] That analysis also indicated that tight or loose housing market conditions, which were an important determinant of effectiveness, also influenced costs; responsive services appeared to have higher costs per enrollee in tight markets.

Inspection costs also varied substantially, although the median of $9.80 indicates that the impact on total costs is smaller than that of services. The variation, from about $2 at Salem to about $26 at Tulsa, was strongly influenced by the individual agency's choice of administrative procedures. The simulation model estimated the direct cost of participant inspection (a determination of standardness based on information collected by the participant) at $2.11 per inspection. The cost for a full agency inspection was estimated at $15.75.[26]

The variation in inspection costs is also influenced by variation in the number of inspections that the average enrollee requested. Tulsa, for example, had the highest number of inspections per enrolled household of any agency, so the average cost is higher than the per-inspection estimate. Jacksonville used procedures similar to those of the Tulsa agency, but a much higher proportion of enrollees dropped out without requesting inspections.[27] Thus it is likely that inspection costs per enrolled household are influenced not only by the choice of inspection procedures but also by factors affecting enrollees' success in becoming recipients (particularly the tightness of the housing market and the nature of agency supportive services).

Agencies varied in all categories of intake costs, with extreme variation in some cases. Such variation can have important policy meaning. It can signal an opportunity (or need) for management control to hold costs in line with those incurred at the more cost-efficient agencies. Or it may mark the existence of an important administrative option—that is, a situation in which the choice of procedures can have a major influence on the budget, and perhaps a situation in which the policymaker faces a trade-off between higher administrative costs and the benefits associated with the more expensive procedure.

As a step toward assessing the potential for policy action, an "index of cost variation importance" was developed. The index ranks each intake function according to two factors: (1) the overall importance of each administrative function, indicated by its relative share of total intake costs for the AAE and (2) the dispersion or variation in observed agency unit costs.[28] To the extent that policy decisions such as the choice among alternative administrative procedures influence unit costs of functions, a higher score on the index tends to reflect a greater opportunity for policy control of total intake costs. Table 6–5 presents the index values for each intake function. These values are presented for two situations: the first includes all sites; the second excludes the extremes, the minimum and maximum unit costs, for each function. The second set is presented to eliminate the sensitivity of the dispersion measure to very high and low values at individual sites.

Table 6–5.   Index of Cost Variation Importance (Intake Functions)

Intake Function	Ratio of Function Cost to Total Intake Cost	Coefficient of Variation		Index	
		All sites	Excluding minimum, maximum	All sites	Excluding minimum, maximum
Outreach	0.196	1.04	0.420	20.0	8.0
Services	0.295	0.509	0.345	15.0	10.2
Inspection	0.126	0.757	0.463	9.5	5.8
Enrollment	0.163	0.513	0.360	8.4	5.9
Screening	0.139	0.388	0.295	5.4	4.1
Certification	0.080	0.398	0.329	3.2	2.6

Source: Abt Associates, *Administrative Costs of Alternative Procedures: A Compendium of Analyses of Direct Costs in the Administrative Agency Experiment* (Cambridge, Mass.: 1977), introduction.

Outreach and services to enrollees are the most important sources of variation in intake costs. Both functions account for major fractions of total intake costs, 30 percent in the case of services and 20 percent for outreach. Moreover, costs for both functions varied substantially across the eight AAE sites. The index scores for outreach and services, as shown in table 6–5, are therefore well above the scores for any of the remaining intake functions.

Although the index provides a useful indication of the relative influence of a function's cost variation on total intake costs, the index alone tells little about whether the variation can be controlled by policy. Table 6–6 gives a clearer impression of the policy leverage available. The first three columns present the eight-agency range of average costs and the range estimated between the least expensive and most expensive of the procedures analyzed directly. The last two columns standardize the procedural ranges to a cost per enrollee, allowing more direct comparison of the cost implications of the choice of procedures for each function.

Table 6–6. Variation in Direct Intake Costs Resulting from Procedural Choices

Function	Average Costs	Range Associated with Procedural Choices		Range of Costs per Enrollee[b] Associated with Procedural Choices	
		Observed	Simulated	Observed	Simulated
Outreach	$32 per eligible applicant	—	$ 2	—	$ 3
Services	$28 per enrollee	$19	17	$19	17
Inspection	$24 per enrollee	12[a]	14[a]	13	15
Enrollment	$21 per enrollee	4	1	4	1
Screening	$ 9 per applicant	1	2	2	4
Certification	$ 8 per certification	—	3	—	3

Source: Abt Associates, *Administrative Costs of Alternative Procedures: A Compendium of Analyses of Direct Costs in the Administrative Agency Experiment* (Cambridge, Mass.: 1977), introduction.
[a]Costs per inspection rather than per enrollee.
[b]Assumes overall AAE ratios of applicants to enrollee, eligible applicants to enrollee, certifications to enrollee, and inspections to enrollee.

Procedural choices for supportive services and inspecting partici-pants' units clearly have a greater impact on cost than the choices for enrollment, screening, and certification. Table 6–6 indicates that choos-ing a particular procedure for supportive services or inspecting units could increase or decrease direct intake costs by $13 to $19 per enrollee, compared with a maximum effect of $4 per enrollee for enrollment, screening, or certification procedures. The figures suggest that pro-cedural choices for outreach have an effect comparable to the enroll-ment-screening-certification group, but this is probably a misleadingly low number, resulting from the estimation procedures used.[29] Note that the actual range of average costs across agencies was considerably larger than the range associated with procedural choices. The additional varia-tion, which exists for all functions, is presumably associated with pro-cedural differences not captured in the analysis, with efficiency differ-ences, and with differential wage and skill levels.

Maintenance Costs

Making payments to recipients entails operating a system that pro-cesses information and sends out checks (payment operations) and

periodically updating that information (maintenance certification). Costs
are incurred in these activities for individual events such as printing and
mailing a check or recertifying a family's income. For convenience of
estimation, however, it is useful to combine all events occurring within a
one-year period. The unit costs for all maintenance functions therefore
use recipient years[30] in the denominator and total second-year[31] direct
costs for the function in the numerator.

The median cost of *payment operations* was $13.04, or slightly over
$1 per month (most checks were distributed monthly). Costs did not
vary greatly,[32] and the choice of administrative procedures appears to
contribute relatively little to the variation observed. The major procedural distinction concerned the means that agencies used to determine
whether participants had paid their rent.[33] Adopting procedures that
required formal action, such as participant submission of rent receipts,
was estimated to add $4–$5 in direct costs.[34] The variation in figure 6–8
also reflects the varying difficulty that agencies experienced in establishing their routine for processing payments; first-year costs were estimated
at $10–$14 higher per recipient-year than second-year costs. Variation in
the frequency with which payment amounts had to be changed, due to
annual or interim recertifications, also influenced costs.[35]

Maintenance certification, the performance of annual and periodic
recertifications as participants reported changes in their status, showed
costs varying through a somewhat greater range, around a median of
$15.92.

These costs were substantially higher than the average cost of intake
certification per enrollee, an outcome that should not be unexpected
because a recipient-year of service normally includes some interim recertifications as well as the mandatory annual recertification. The number
of interim recertifications actually performed in the AAE would account
for only a portion of the cost difference, however. Thus the lower cost
for intake certification may reflect some economies associated with the
large volume of certifications carried out in the first few months, but no
clear reason for the difference emerged from the analysis.

Other maintenance activities carried out during the second year
included the inspection of units for recipients (some agencies reinspected
units periodically, and when participants wanted to move to new units
those had to be inspected) and the provision of supportive services
(generally assistance in disputes with landlords or in moving to new
units).

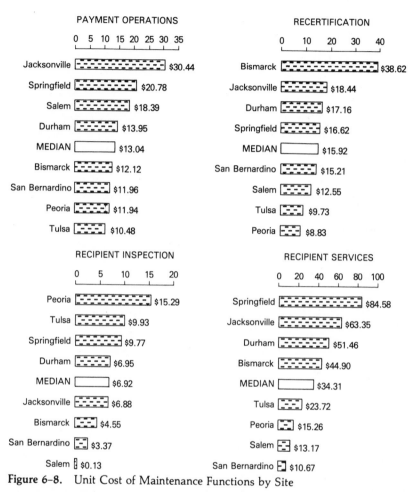

Figure 6–8.   Unit Cost of Maintenance Functions by Site

The *recipient services* function generally resulted in relatively high expenditures, with a median of $34.31 per recipient-year. Moreover, the costs varied dramatically across agencies, from $11 to $85 per recipient-year. Multivariate analysis indicates that the variation in agency costs reflected housing market conditions as well as agency policy. Among the agencies with a relatively high emphasis on responsive services to recipients, services which were largely directed to helping recipients who wanted to move, the cost per recipient-year was estimated to be $38 in tight housing markets and $32 in loose markets. Agencies with a low emphasis on responsive services had an estimated cost of $20, regardless of market condition.

The costs of *inspecting recipient units* also varied significantly but around a much smaller median ($6.92). These costs are probably artificially low, reflecting the experimental nature of the program. Because a dwelling unit's condition can deteriorate over time, an ongoing program would be likely to have a policy of routine periodic inspections to ensure continued compliance with the agency standard. Because the AAE was of short duration, however, most agencies did not schedule regular reinspections, and most inspections carried out after the enrollment period concerned units to which recipients desired to move.

Again, it is useful to summarize the extent to which the cost variation for particular functions can affect total administrative costs by considering both the variation and the proportion of maintenance costs that each function constitutes. This information is examined in table 6–7 with the index of cost variation importance described earlier for the intake functions.

Table 6–7.   Index of Cost Variation Importance (Maintenance Functions)

Maintenance Function	Ratio of Maintenance Function Cost to Total Maintenance Cost	Coefficient of Variation		Index	
		All sites	Excluding minimum, maximum	All sites	Excluding minimum, maximum
Recipient services	0.460	0.706	0.590	32.5	27.1
Payment operations	0.324	0.415	0.257	13.5	8.3
Maintenance certification	0.149	0.545	0.218	8.1	3.2
Recipient inspection	0.066	0.654	0.385	4.3	2.5

Supportive services to recipients clearly contribute the greatest variation to maintenance costs and thus may reflect a significant opportunity for cost control. The payment operation function has a much lower value in the index, even though it accounted for about one-third of all maintenance costs; the limited variation here means that the AAE experience reveals that policy can probably have little impact on the costs of this function.

The cost range associated with procedural choices was in most cases much smaller than the observed range of averages, as shown in table 6–8. (The exception is the inspection function, where the estimation procedure assumed an annual reinspection of each subsidized dwelling unit, a policy that most AAE agencies did not follow.) The difference between the range of averages and the procedural range is considerably larger than that seen for the intake functions, suggesting either that there were greater differences in the efficiency with which the maintenance functions were carried out or that there were more procedural variations not captured in the analysis.[36]

Table 6–8. Variation in Direct Maintenance Costs
per Recipient-Year Resulting from Procedural Choices

	Range of Average Costs	Range Associated with Procedural Choices	
		Observed	Simulated
Recipient services	$74	$15	$13
Payment operations	20	4	5
Maintenance certification	30	—	4[a]
Recipient inspection	15	14	16[b]

Source: Abt Associates, *Administrative Costs of Alternative Procedures: A Compendium of Analyses of Direct Costs in the Administrative Agency Experiment* (Cambridge, Mass.: 1977).
[a]Assumes one annual recertification and 0.27 interim recertifications per recipient-year.
[b]Assumes one annual reinspection and 0.16 move-related inspections per recipient-year.

Even though procedural choices had a small range relative to the total, the choices for supportive services and inspection had potential cost impacts of $13 to $16 per recipient year, similar to the variation in costs per enrollee for the most important choices on the intake functions. Moreover, because the cost of the intake functions must be amortized over the length of a participant's tenure in the program, the importance of influencing intake costs is diminished relative to controlling the maintenance functions (under the assumption that participation lasts more than one year). Table 6–9 shows the relative impact of intake and maintenance functions under the assumption that participation lasts an average of five years. After amortization, the smallest of the cost ranges for maintenance functions is nearly as great as the largest range for an intake function.

Finally, the figures in table 6–9 provide an overall perspective on the significance of procedural choices for administrative costs. The differ-

Table 6-9. Total Administrative Cost
Variation Associated with Procedural Choices

	Simulated Direct Costs	Simulated Total Costs[a]
Intake		
Outreach	$ 1	$ 2
Services	5	11
Inspection	4	9
Enrollment	—[b]	—
Screening	1	2
Certification	1	2
Total intake	$12	$ 26
Maintenance		
Services	$13	$ 28
Payment operations	5	11
Certification	4	9
Inspection	16	34
Total maintenance	$38	$ 82
Total	$50	$108

[a]Assuming indirect costs at 116 percent of direct costs.
[b]Less than $0.50.

ence between choosing the least expensive and most expensive procedures analyzed in the AAE amounts to direct costs of $50 per household per year, or about $108 in total administrative costs. Given the estimated average AAE cost of $1,225 per household per year (including allowance payments and administrative costs), it is clear that the choice of procedures could have a significant impact on the total cost of a housing allowance program.

INDIRECT COSTS

To the extent that administrative procedures become policy issues, procedures associated with the direct functions are generally the ones to receive attention, for two reasons. First, the direct functions are often expected to have some important effect on participant outcomes. They may even characterize the intent of the program, as the inspection function characterizes the orientation of an allowance program to the quality of participants' housing. Second, the direct functions frequently offer clear-cut alternatives, such as the choice between having an inspector examine participants' housing and allowing participants to do so themselves, which are generally lacking in the indirect functions.

From the perspective of administrative costs, however, the indirect functions can be extremely important. In the AAE they accounted for more than half of all administrative expenditures. This section examines the nature of those indirect costs.

Categories of Indirect Cost

Indirect costs were incurred for six administrative functions that do not involve providing specific services or assistance to any participant family: (1) phase-in, (2) audit and control, (3) management support, (4) maintenance of records, (5) relations with suppliers, and (6) office and equipment.

Most costs occurred in management support, maintenance of records, and office and equipment. Table 6-10 shows the proportion of total indirect costs represented by these three functions. The medians across sites show that these functions accounted for 88 percent of total indirect costs for the enrollment and transition periods and only slightly less (86 percent) for the second year. Although not shown in the table, the indirect cost share for each of these functions remained fairly constant over all three time periods. From the enrollment period to the second year, management support increased slightly (from 37 percent to 42 percent) while maintenance of records showed a small decline (from 22 percent to 18 percent) and office and equipment also declined (from 30 percent to 22 percent).

Table 6-10. Management Support, Maintenance of Records, and Office Equipment as a Fraction of Total Indirect Costs, by Time Period

Site	Enrollment	Transition	Second Year
Salem	0.90	0.95	0.91
Springfield	0.74	0.66	0.67
Peoria	0.85	0.88	0.87
San Bernardino	0.92	0.89	0.84
Bismarck	0.94	0.96	0.97
Jacksonville	0.95	0.88	0.84
Durham	0.85	0.83	0.80
Tulsa	0.72	0.78	0.87
Median	0.88	0.88	0.86

The cost of maintaining records was significant at all sites except Springfield, where all expenditures for record keeping associated with participant forms were charged to the direct-cost function that utilized the form. This practice understated the indirect cost for maintaining records (only 7 percent of total indirect costs) and slightly increased the reported cost of direct functions at Springfield relative to other agencies. In addition, this agency had the largest costs for relations with suppliers. These two factors combined to produce the relatively smaller share of indirect costs attributed to the three functions at Springfield (74 percent in the enrollment period, 67 percent in the second year).

Indirect Cost Rate

The conventional means for estimating indirect costs involves the relationship between indirect costs and either direct costs or total costs. This widely used and simple approach is employed here; indirect costs are presented relative to direct costs. The indirect cost rate r is the ratio of indirect to direct costs. It is used as a loading factor $(L_r=1+r)$; total administrative costs (TAC) can be calculated by multiplying direct costs (DC) by the loading factor $(TAC=L_r \cdot DC)$. Table 6–11 shows the ratio of total indirect costs to total direct costs for all agencies by time period.

Table 6-11.   Indirect Cost Rates:
Ratio of Indirect Cost to Direct Cost, by Site and by Time Period

| | First Year | | | | |
Site	Enrollment	Transition	Total	Second Year	Two-year Total
Salem	1.18	4.28	1.46	2.26	1.67
Springfield	0.89	1.12	0.95	1.22	1.06
Peoria	1.35	2.95	1.58	3.00	2.01
San Bernardino	1.11	3.09	1.47	3.79	1.91
Bismarck	1.87	2.25	1.97	2.04	2.00
Jacksonville	1.32	1.67	1.39	1.98	1.53
Durham	1.25	1.59	1.35	2.06	1.59
Tulsa	0.42	1.44	0.57	2.15	0.82
Median	1.22	1.96	1.43	2.11	1.63

Indirect costs for the two-year period of the AAE varied around a median of 163 percent of direct costs. Six of the eight agencies ranged between 153 percent and 201 percent.[37]

Of all the indirect cost rates during the enrollment period, the Tulsa agency's rate (42 percent) is the lowest. This low rate resulted from the large amount of subcontracting of direct functions during the enrollment period. Subcontracting reduced costs for several indirect functions (such as management support and overhead) that were incurred as part of indirect costs at the other seven sites. These charges were still incurred (by the subcontractor), but they appear as direct cost items for the agency. The result is that the large subcontracting effort at Tulsa inflates direct costs while reducing indirect cost charges.

The transition period indirect cost rates ranged from 112 percent of direct costs (at Springfield) to 428 percent (at Salem). At four sites the transition period rates were considerably higher than enrollment period figures. This abrupt increase is the result of major changes in agency activities and the subsequent changes in staffing levels. Table 6–12, which shows the staffing changes during the three periods, measures total agency staff in units of full-time equivalent positions during each period. The table clearly illustrates the shift from intake to maintenance activities. All agencies except Tulsa required staff reductions at some point; Tulsa was not required to discharge staff because most intake activities during the enrollment period were subcontracted.

Table 6–12. Agency Staff Levels, in Full-Time Staff Equivalents

Site	Enrollment	Transition	Second Year
Salem	18.2	12.3	7.9
Springfield	18.2	19.8	14.9
Peoria	13.9	11.6	8.4
San Bernardino	18.3	17.1	8.2
Bismarck	8.7	6.7	6.2
Jacksonville	15.5	9.9	5.7
Durham	13.4	10.8	7.7
Tulsa	8.2[a]	9.7	10.2

[a]Excludes a substantial amount of subcontract labor.

Springfield used by far the largest staff for second-year maintenance activities: 14.9 full-time person equivalents. This is consistent with the agency's high second-year costs relative to other sites, resulting especially from the agency policy of providing high levels of services to recipients. Apparently because of its relatively large staff for direct maintenance costs, Springfield had a substantially lower indirect cost rate in the second year than any other agency—122 percent of direct costs.

Scale Effects in Indirect Costs

The general purpose of indirect functions is to provide the services and materials necessary to operate the direct functions. For most of indirect functions, the services and materials are provided to and for agency staff members. Management support includes organizing and allocating staff among administrative tasks; maintenance of records alleviates the burden of all record keeping for staff working on other administrative functions; the office and equipment function provides work space, utilities, office equipment, and general office supplies for agency staff. Because agency staff members are the most direct beneficiaries, it is reasonable to suspect that staff size influences the indirect cost rate. Economies of scale would be expected for the indirect functions if the rate at which indirect costs are incurred declines for "larger" agencies (that is, those agencies with larger staffs).

The indirect cost data and agency staff levels can be combined to provide a crude indication of economies of scale within the AAE. Figure 6–9 displays the indirect cost rates and full-time staff equivalents during the enrollment period and the second year.[38] The median indirect cost rate over both periods was $1.63 per dollar of direct costs; the median full-time staff equivalent was 9.45 staff members. The graph shows that whenever agencies required less than the median full-time staff, the observed indirect cost rate was above the median. For agencies larger than the median, the observed indirect cost rate was generally below the median. The graph implies that as agency size increases, indirect costs increase less rapidly and the indirect cost rate declines. Conversely, as agency size decreases, indirect costs decrease more slowly, so the indirect cost rate increases.

Figure 6–9 is considered suggestive rather than conclusive evidence of the existence of economies of scale within the indirect functions. Various other factors might counter the apparent implications of the graph. For example, if wages and costs increased more for indirect than for direct cost functions in the second year, this alone could cause the indirect cost rate to be relatively higher during the second year. Experimental conditions could also influence the results. The AAE required a full-time director for the program. Because the salary of the director was charged principally to management support, these charges (indirect costs) were distributed over a smaller staff in the second year compared with the enrollment period. In this example, the apparent economies of scale would result from the regulations imposed in the experiment.

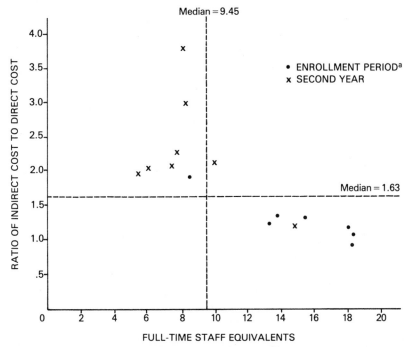

Figure 6-9. Indirect Cost Rate Versus Agency Staff

[a]One data point is omitted. Tulsa's indirect cost rate during the enrollment period was 0.42 for 8.2 full-time staff equivalents. This point is not comparable to other agencies because of the large amount of subcontracting done during the enrollment period.

These alternative explanations of the data notwithstanding, regression equations estimated for use in the administrative cost simulation model express the same general relationship. In these equations costs for the management support function are estimated as a function of the staff required for the direct functions. Office and equipment costs are estimated as a function of the total number of staff. Record maintenance costs are estimated as a function of the number of households in various stages of participation. (The equations are presented in appendix F.)

Projections from the simulation model therefore describe some economies associated with agency size. Although discussions elsewhere have used a constant indirect cost rate of 116 percent,[39] the rate estimated by the model varies in response to any factors that affect total direct cost levels, such as the number of participants or the particular procedures chosen for the direct functions. Table 6–13 illustrates the latter relationship; it shows three simulations with a constant number of participants but substantial variation in the direct costs of the administrative procedures chosen. As the direct costs increase, the indirect costs increase more slowly. Thus the simulation of high-cost procedures has an indirect cost rate about one-third lower than that for the low-cost procedures.

Table 6–13. Direct and Indirect Costs

	Least-Cost Procedures	Benchmark	Highest-Cost Procedures
Direct cost per recipient-year	$ 68	$110	$131
Indirect cost per recipient-year	$110	$128	$137
Total cost per recipient-year	$177	$238	$268
Ratio of indirect to direct costs	1.62	1.16	1.05

Source: Administrative Cost Simulation Model

In the example the average indirect cost per recipient-year increases with agency size. In simulations varying the number of participants, however, the average indirect cost declines. In the model the unit cost of the direct functions remains constant regardless of the number of participants.[40] Thus as the number of participants increases, the slower increase in direct costs results in a declining average cost per recipient-year.

Given the limitations of the AAE design and the alternative explanations advanced earlier, the AAE data cannot support a conclusion that scale economies exist for indirect costs. The evidence is sufficiently suggestive, however, to warrant caution in the application of fixed indirect cost rates across programs or agencies, particularly as the scale of local operations in any national program is likely to vary well beyond the range observed in the experiment.

ADDITIONAL DIMENSIONS OF ADMINISTRATIVE COST

The ten direct and six indirect functions described thus far provide the framework for describing total administrative costs. Aggregating costs for the individual functions allows two additional factors to come into play in determining average costs per household. The first is attrition and the consequent need to expend administrative effort on families that do not become full program participants. The second is the relative proportion of new applicants and continuing recipients in the program.

Attrition Costs for Intake Functions

Attrition occurred at each intermediate stage of participation. Only about half of the families who applied to the AAE were actually enrolled in the program. The rest, 7,305 families, made up the applicant dropouts. In addition, more than one-fourth of the enrollees, enrollee dropouts, failed to become recipients of a housing allowance. The agencies incurred substantial intake costs in dealing with the dropouts.

Administrative costs attributable to those who dropped out before becoming recipients, including both applicant and enrollee dropouts, are termed "intake attrition costs." Attrition costs at a given site depend on the number of dropouts at each stage of intake and the unit costs of the administrative functions performed for those families before they dropped out.[41] Any dropout household incurs administrative costs for each stage of participation it passes through.

A family that applied and was selected for possible participation in the AAE, if it dropped out before enrolling, typically incurred direct administrative costs of $11.04—$5.67 for outreach and $5.37 for screening and selection at the median AAE rates. A family that passed through all stages short of becoming a recipient incurred direct administrative costs of $61.49. Including indirect costs (at 116 percent), this dropout household would cause total expenditures of $133 without ever receiving an allowance payment.

The eight agencies together spent about $214,000 (direct costs only) to deal with people who never became recipients. This total amounts to 36 percent of total direct costs for intake, or a median of $37 for each recipient slot that was actually filled. These figures are presented by agency in table 6–14. Attrition costs ranged from 21 percent to 44 percent of total intake costs for all agencies except Jacksonville.

Total attrition costs are affected both by the level of unit costs and by the dropout rate. A striking illustration of the importance of dropout rates is that Jacksonville spent over 70 percent of its intake expenditures on families who did not become recipients. Although the median expen-

Table 6–14.   Direct Costs Attributable to Attrition

Site	Number of Recipients	Attrition Cost Per recipient	Attrition Cost Total	Ratio of Attrition Cost to Total Intake Cost
Jacksonville	339	$159.20	$ 53,969	0.71
Peoria	935	30.51	28,527	0.44
Springfield	851	50.73	43,171	0.40
Durham	516	41.48	21,404	0.38
Tulsa	915	63.17	57,801	0.33
Salem	948	24.19	22,932	0.32
San Bernardino	822	32.71	26,888	0.30
Bismarck	430	12.94	5,564	0.21
Total	5,756	$ 37.10[a]	$213,548	0.36[a]

[a]Median value

diture on dropouts for all sites was $37 per recipient, the Jacksonville agency spent $159, more than twice the next highest amount.

This high attrition expenditure rate occurred even though Jacksonville's unit costs for individual intake functions were not inordinately high. For example, the *unit* cost of outreach at Jacksonville ($2.91) was much less than the median (\$5.67 per applicant), as shown in table 6–15. But because so many of Jacksonville's applicants dropped out before becoming recipients,[42] the attrition cost for outreach ($12.57) was somewhat higher than the median ($8.94).

Table 6–15.
Comparison of AAE Eight-Site Median versus Intake Attrition Costs: Jacksonville

	Unit Costs Median	Unit Costs Jacksonville	Dropout Rates Median	Dropout Rates Jacksonville	Attrition Costs per Recipient Median	Attrition Costs per Recipient Jacksonville
Outreach	$5.67[a]	$2.91[a]	1.51	4.33	$ 8.94	$ 12.57
Screening	5.37[a]	8.92[a]	1.51	4.33	7.98	38.58
Certification	5.62[b]	10.07[b]	0.32	2.05	1.82	20.64
Enrollment	11.99[b]	13.26[b]	0.32	2.05	3.82	27.18
Services	23.04[b]	19.48[b]	0.32	2.05	6.01	39.93
Inspection	9.80[b]	9.83[b]	0.32	2.05	3.52	20.15
Totals	—	—	—	—	$37.10	$159.05

[a]Cost per applicant
[b]Cost per enrollee

Although attrition costs in Jacksonville were affected primarily by the dropout rate, total attrition costs at other sites are equally affected by unit cost levels. Springfield, whose unit cost for enrollee services was $45.04 (nearly double the median), illustrates this point. Even though the enrollee dropout rate was not especially high, Springfield's attrition cost per recipient for the enrollee services function was nearly $19 per recipient, compared with the median of $6.01.

These results indicate that attrition represented a major AAE cost factor, equivalent to more than one-third of direct expenditures for intake, and may therefore represent a significant opportunity for management or policy to have an impact on costs in a national housing allowance program.

It is unrealistic to expect that any program can eliminate attrition—not every applicant can become a recipient. Nonetheless, most attrition in the AAE occurred at two points on which some influence might be exercised. Nearly one-fourth of the applicants initially found eligible were not selected for further participation; nearly one-third of the households that enrolled did not meet the housing quality requirement.

The attrition from selection reflects the limited participation opportunities in the AAE. Although a universal entitlement program would not have such limits, the most likely versions of a housing allowance program would involve participation limits. Thus unless outreach procedures can be controlled so carefully that they attract only the exact number of participants needed to fill the available recipient slots, selection will be a continuing source of attrition.

Enrollee attrition was generally attributed to enrollees' inability to find housing that would meet the program's housing quality requirement.[43] Two policy alternatives might be expected to influence this dropout rate: altering the housing quality standard to make the enrollees' task easier, or providing additional services to help enrollees find units that meet the standard. AAE data do not support an estimate of the effect of altering the housing standard, but the effect of providing intensive services had a substantial effect on reducing attrition and attrition costs in some circumstances.

Although the effect of altering policies cannot be estimated precisely, the AAE data can provide a perspective on the importance of policy control of attrition. Table 6-16 presents several hypothetical illustrations; total administrative costs for intake are calculated as a function of the median unit costs for the intake functions and the attrition rates associated with selection and the housing quality requirement. If the AAE had been able to offer enrollment to all eligible applicants and if there were no attrition between enrollment and receipt of allowance payments (no quality requirement), average intake costs might have been one-third lower. Controlling enrollee attrition rate would have a higher payoff than eliminating selection: eliminating selection reduces the estimated intake costs by about 7 percent, while simply holding enrollee attrition to the lowest level observed in the AAE causes an 18 percent decline in the estimated total.

Table 6-16.   Effect of Alternative Attrition Assumptions

Alternatives	Direct Intake Cost per Recipient[a]	Loaded Intake Cost per Recipient[b]
AAE average attrition factors[c]	$101	$220
Lowest AAE enrollee attrition rate[d]	83	184
No enrollee attrition	71	159
No selection attrition[e]	94	209
No selection or enrollee attrition	66	147

[a]Based on median reported costs for each intake function.
[b]Based on an indirect cost rate of 122 percent of direct costs, the overall reported rate for the enrollment period.
[c]Ratio of eligible applicants to enrollees = 1.75; ratio of enrollees to recipients = 1.41.
[d]Ratio of enrollees to recipients = 1.16.
[e]Ratio of eligible applicants to enrollees = 1.33.

One interesting implication of these figures is that the administrative costs of a housing allowance or similarly earmarked income transfer program are likely to appear higher than those of a nonearmarked program such as welfare. Even if the two programs carried out identical administrative functions with identical efficiency, the average costs per recipient would be higher in the earmarked program; if benefit levels were the same, the earmarked program would have the higher ratio of administrative costs to total program costs. This finding argues for caution in cross-program comparisons of administrative costs, especially in the use of figures such as the ratio of administrative costs to program costs as the basis for judgments about differing programs' relative efficiencies.

Program Phase and Turnover

A program's growth or turnover rate can also cause average administrative costs to vary. A program that is just beginning, like the AAE in its first year, incurs high intake costs relative to the number of recipient-years of service it delivers. A program in a steady-state phase may incur intake costs only to replace dropouts and thus have a lower average cost per recipient-year. Terminating programs would incur only maintenance costs because they would accept no new recipients. Such programs have the lowest average cost per recipient-year.

These principles are dramatically visible in the comparison in table 6–17 of first- and second-year figures from the AAE.

Table 6–17. First- and Second-Year Administrative Costs

	First Year	Second Year
Total administrative costs	$1,830,818	$1,028,813
Total recipient-years	2,754	4,577
Total payment costs	$2,535,211	$4,569,091
Administrative cost per recipient-year	$665	$224
Ratio of administrative cost to total cost	0.42	0.18

By such standard rules of thumb as the average administrative cost per recipient-year or the percentage of total costs, the AAE agencies would appear to be much more efficient in their second year than in their first. In fact, it is quite possible that the reverse is true. Observational evidence suggests that several agencies in the second year did not cut back staff levels as far as they might have and that if efficiency were judged in terms of work load or outputs per level of input, the heavy intake period in the first year would be deemed most efficient. The contrary indication in the figures in table 6–17 simply results from the fact that the agencies were doing different jobs in the two periods.

A nonexperimental program would, of course, be unlikely to follow an intensive start-up year with a complete cessation of intake, but the same general administrative cost patterns could be expected. Such patterns are illustrated in table 6–18, which uses the administrative cost simulation model to project administrative costs for a five-year period. The simulated agency, beginning with no recipients, takes in 1,000 in the first year and provides 500 recipient-years of payments and services. The administrative cost per recipient-year in this first year is more than double that for the subsequent years, during which the turnover rate is 250 recipients and the agency provides 1,000 recipient-years of payments and services. Table 6–18 also shows that the longer the period over which costs are averaged, the lower the average cost.

Table 6–18.   Agency Costs (Benchmark Estimate) by Program Phase

Year	Average Cost per Family per Year in That Year	Cumulative Average Cost per Family per Year
1 (build-up)	$555	$555
2 (steady-state)	198	317
3 (steady-state)	198	269
4 (steady-state)	198	249
5 (steady-state)	198	238

Source: Administrative Cost Simulation Model

It is also clear from the example that the average duration of a participant's stay in the program, as reflected in the turnover rate, can alter administrative costs. If the turnover rate in this example had been 0.1 instead of 0.25, the average cost per recipient-year in years 2–4 would have been reduced by 16 percent, to $167; the five-year cumulative average would have dropped 12 percent, to $210. Conversely, a turnover rate of 0.5 would imply average steady-state costs of $257 (up 30 percent from the example) and a cumulative average of $290 (up 22 percent).

Like the findings on attrition, the results of these analyses argue for caution in using some of the common measures of administrative costs either for cross-program comparison or for comparisons (or budgeting) of different local agencies operating the same program. Any income transfer program has both one-time intake costs and repetitive costs for case maintenance. For any such program, therefore, the administrative costs in start-up periods or growth situations (for example, in areas in which the local economy is declining) can be expected to be higher than those observed in steady-state operations. Programs with high turnover rates, for example, in areas with much seasonal employment, where individuals are likely to be eligible for assistance for only part of the year, are likely to have higher administrative costs than those in more stable, low-turnover situations.

CONSIDERATIONS FOR POLICY AND FUTURE RESEARCH

It is traditional in cost analyses to focus on the bottom line—in this case, the estimated administrative cost per recipient-year of a housing allowance program. The absence of a continuing, nonexperimental housing allowance program means that the AAE estimates hold less than the usual amount of interest, but they do provide some perspective on the overall level of administrative effort implied by such a program.

Estimates from the individual agencies' cost reports ranged from $165 to $429 per recipient-year, with a median of $256. Analytic estimates from the reported cost data and from the administrative cost simulation model tended to range between $200 and $300. These figures suggest that the costs of administering a housing allowance program are roughly comparable to those of welfare administration: an analysis of welfare costs in fiscal year 1976 showed state administrative costs per case ranging from $77 to $561 per year, with a national average of $287.[44] Because the housing allowance program involves some functions not performed by welfare agencies (housing inspection, for example), one would expect housing allowance costs to be slightly higher, and the wide ranges may in fact mask such a difference. Any such difference would not appear to be large, however.

It is also interesting to compare the AAE estimates to the costs of administering HUD's Section 8 program for existing housing, which resembles a housing allowance program in many respects. The available estimates for Section 8 indicate direct costs of $131 for bringing a housing unit into the program,[45] roughly comparable to the AAE overall average of $116 in intake costs per recipient. The estimated ongoing costs per leased unit per month are $16, or $192 per year, compared with AAE average direct maintenance costs of $69 per recipient-year. The data available on Section 8 are not sufficient to clarify this latter divergence, although it appears that it might result from recipient turnover within leased units. Although the different measurement orientations (housing unit in Section 8 and recipient in the AAE) make precise comparison impossible, a housing allowance appears somewhat less expensive to administer than the Section 8 program.

Choice of Procedures

In many respects the most interesting findings from the AAE cost analysis are not the bottom-line estimates, but the factors that influence total administrative costs. The choice of administrative procedures is a good example.

It is not surprising to find that there are alternative ways of carrying out administrative functions or that some ways are more expensive than others. The impact of such choices has not previously been measured in the context of income transfer programs, however. The AAE results suggest that policy control of administrative procedures could have a major impact on the costs of such programs. Simulation estimates, for example, ranged from $177 to $268 per recipient-year within the feasible range of administrative alternatives (excluding procedures found in other analyses to have substantial shortcomings in effectiveness). If roughly the same relationship were observed in the AFDC program, with more than 3.5 million recipients, it would imply that the choice of administrative procedures could cause national administrative expenditures to vary by more than $300 million—a strong argument for research to attempt to identify opportunities for savings.

Intake and Maintenance Costs

The distinction between intake and maintenance costs in the AAE analysis also has some important implications for policy efforts to control administrative costs. A calculation of average administrative costs must amortize intake costs over the expected length of a family's (continuous) participation in the program. This means that the relative importance of controlling costs in particular administrative functions depends directly on turnover, or the average participation period. The longer the average family receives benefits, the greater the importance of the maintenance functions relative to the intake functions. In the AAE analysis major differences in administrative costs per recipient were found for the intake functions, but when intake costs were amortized over the assumed five-year period of participation, these differences seemed unimportant beside the apparently smaller cost differences observed for the maintenance functions. When turnover is high, of course, cost control of the intake functions could become the major issue.

Attrition Costs

The concept of attrition costs is a particularly interesting product of the AAE analysis, because it has not been included in previous examinations of assistance programs. Dropout rates have sometimes been considered an obstacle to appropriate levels of program participation but not an administrative cost problem. The AAE analysis shows that the cost of dealing with applicants who do not become recipients can be substantial. Attrition costs can be especially heavy in an earmarked program in which full participation is contingent on meeting some requirement *after* the usual kinds of application and eligibility determination procedures have been completed.

Unlike the cost factors, attrition costs do not seem to merit much attention in long-standing nonearmarked programs such as AFDC. But for new programs in which applicants are likely to be uninformed about benefits and procedures, and for programs that involve a long or complicated process between the individual's first contact with the agency and the attainment of beneficiary status, analysis of attrition costs might yield substantial benefits to program management.

Indirect Costs

Indirect costs in the AAE were not analyzed in the same depth as direct costs, a pattern that appears typical of much of the existing literature on administrative costs; indeed, indirect costs are not infrequently omitted in such analyses. Yet, the AAE findings suggest that this could be a fruitful area for further research.

Indirect costs amount to a substantial proportion of total administrative costs. In the AAE, in fact, very few situations were observed in which indirect costs did not exceed direct costs, sometimes by a multiple of two or more. If policy mechanisms could be found to influence indirect costs, their impact on total costs could be substantial. The AAE analysis did not identify any clear alternative procedures for performing the indirect functions that would allow such control to be exercised. This suggests that identifying policy mechanisms may be difficult, although it probably also reflects the fact that only limited analyses of the indirect functions were performed.

Rules of Thumb

The AAE analysis produced a number of reminders about the limitations of some of the rule-of-thumb measures commonly used for budgeting or for discussing administrative efficiency. The ratio of administrative costs to payment costs or total program costs, for example, is particularly sensitive to a program's phase of operations. A program in a start-up year or a period of heavy growth necessarily has a higher administrative total cost ratio than an equally efficient program in steady-state operations. Moreover, the ratio is sensitive to benefit levels, which may be a function of participant characteristics. Thus if two agencies have identical administrative procedures and costs, but applicants to one agency have lower average incomes (and therefore higher average payments), that agency will appear to be more efficient.

A single average administrative cost per recipient-year has some of the same weaknesses. Unless the cost is calculated in a way that standardizes the ratio of intake to maintenance costs, programs with a high growth or turnover rate will have higher average costs and hence appear less efficient. Unless the ratio of indirect to direct costs is standardized, AAE findings suggest that smaller program agencies (perhaps agencies serving rural areas) will seem more costly and inefficient. And earmarked programs—or agencies within earmarked programs that apply the earmark more rigorously or whose client populations are particularly subject to exclusion by the earmark—will similarly appear to have high costs and low efficiency because of attrition. For budgeting and efficiency analyses, then, the AAE analysis suggests the need for a framework that separates intake, maintenance, and indirect costs, and incorporates explicit assumptions about program growth, turnover, attrition, and agency size.

The Approach

Retrospectively, one can think of a number of improvements to the approach. The level of detail with which actual cost data were recorded and at which the simulation model was constructed were insufficient for some of the analyses that would have been desirable. The specification of alternative procedures occurred in parallel with data collection, as on-site observers' accounts were analyzed, and the observers were not used in the second year of agency operations. The data base for the simulation model was weaker than one would wish.

Despite these hindsights, the basic elements of the cost analyses approach appear to have been extremely useful. Particularly important were the conceptual framework of administrative functions, the emphasis on measuring staff time rather than accounted costs, and the dual approach to analysis (reported costs and simulation). The AAE findings suggest that administrative costs offer a rich topic for future policy research in income assistance programs, and the approach used here seems to offer a strong foundation for such future efforts.

NOTES

1. See, for example, Frederick C. Cue, *Evaluation of AFDC-QC Corrective Action* (Washington, D.C.: Touche Ross & Co., 1977); and John D. Newman et al., *Comprehensive Study of AFDC Administration and Management* (Washington, D.C.: Booz, Allen & Hamilton, 1977).

2. Congressional Research Service, *Administration of the AFDC Program* (Washington, D.C.: U.S. Government Printing Office, 1977), p. 126.

3. At approximately the same time that the AAE was being designed, effort was under way to develop a system for measuring work load and productivity in the Unemployment Insurance Service. That system as it has developed has shown a number of parallels with the AAE system, particularly in its work measurement approach. Major differences are that the UI system operates for a shorter period of time, at a much greater level of detail, and without the AAE orientation toward measuring the relative cost of alternative ways to perform an administrative task.

4. For further description of the data collection methodology, see Maloy et al., *Two-Year Costs.*

5. For more description and documentation, see Charles M. Maloy et al., *The Administrative Cost Simulation Model: A Methodology for Projecting Administrative Costs of a Housing Allowance Agency* (Cambridge, Mass.: Abt Associates, 1977).

6. All cost figures in this chapter reflect expenditures in the 1973–1974 time period, unadjusted for inflation.

7. The reasons for Jacksonville's high attrition rate are analyzed in W. L. Holshouser, *Report on Selected Aspects of the Jacksonville Housing Allowance Experiment* (Cambridge, Mass.: Abt Associates, 1976), and in Marian F. Wolfe and W. L. Hamilton, *Jacksonville: Administering a Housing Allowance Program in a Difficult Environment* (Cambridge, Mass.: Abt Associates, 1976).

8. Neither year is typical of a steady-state operation in an ongoing program. The first year of the AAE had a much greater emphasis on intake than would be expected in a steady state; the second year, with no intake at all, is also atypical.

9. All direct costs in the second year were for maintenance activities. Jacksonville, which had the fewest recipients from first-year intake activities, was in effect the smallest agency during the second year.

10. The number of recipient-years of service provided by an agency is analytically defined as the agency's total number of monthly payments to all recipient families divided by twelve.

11. The relationship between length of tenure and annual recipient dropout rate is developed in appendix F.

12. Annual average payments are calculated by dividing the total value of payments by the total number of recipient years of payments (the sum of the number of participants receiving payments in each month, divided by twelve) for the first two years at each agency. Administrative cost equals total (direct and indirect) maintenance cost divided by total recipient years, and one-fifth of intake costs divided by the total number of recipients.

13. Participants in Jacksonville had lower average incomes than at other sites. Since payments were larger for families (of the same size) with lower incomes, the average payment in Jacksonville was notably higher than elsewhere.

14. Generating enrollees, helping enrollees become recipients, processing payments, and other maintenance services.

15. See Maloy et al., *Two-Year Costs*, chap. 7.

16. To standardize for agency size differences, an agency's total direct costs for each function are divided by the number of participants affected by that function. Note that the denominator in the unit cost calculation therefore varies from function to function.

17. The simulation model somewhat arbitrarily defined "routine" and "expanded" outreach procedures, where the former was estimated on the basis of outreach costs for agencies relying mainly on referrals from other organizations, and the latter was the average for agencies making substantial use of the public media. The estimates were $4.37 and $5.90 per applicant, respectively. Because these estimates reflect the central tendency of the two groups of agencies, it is likely that they substantially understate the potential cost variation associated with alternative procedures.

18. Jean MacMillan and William L. Hamilton, *Outreach: Generating Applications in the Administrative Agency Experiment* (Cambridge, Mass.: Abt Associates, 1977), appendix D.

19. Multivariate analysis of reported costs yields similar results, although not all procedural combinations could be estimated from agency reports because not all were observed in the AAE. See Abt Associates, *Administrative Costs of Alternative Procedures: A Compendium of Analyses of Direct Costs in the Administrative Agency Experiment* (Cambridge, Mass.: 1977), attachment V.

20. Direct costs per enrolled household were estimated at $3.09 for self-declaration, $5.31 for documentary verification, and $6.58 for third-party verifica-

tion. These figures are slightly higher than those reported in chapter 5; the earlier figures represented the estimate for certifying a single household, while these take into account the fact that households dropped out after certification but before enrollment.

21. See Donald E. Dickson, *Certification: Determining Eligibility and Setting Payment Levels in the Administrative Agency Experiment* (Cambridge, Mass.: Abt Associates, 1977), appendix F.

22. Because the agencies conducted a large proportion of their third-party verifications with a few organizations (most commonly welfare agencies), local variations in the attitude or ability of those organizations might affect agency costs, but this would not be expected to be a major factor and could not be tested in the AAE data. Regional wage variations are, of course, important and influence the averages in figure 6–7, but both the multivariate analysis and the simulation model are adjusted for these variations.

23. Both procedures involved an individual session to complete the enrollment forms. In the group procedure, the individual sessions were used only for signing forms and followed a group discussion of the program and explanation of rights and responsibilities.

24. The average reported cost for agencies using the group method was about $4 per household lower than the average for agencies using individual sessions only. However, substantial variation in the averages within each group meant that the differences did not prove significant in multivariate analysis. See Abt Associates, *Administrative Costs,* 1977, appendix VI.

25. William L. Holshouser, Jr., *Supportive Services in the Administrative Agency Experiment* (Cambridge, Mass.: Abt Associates, 1977), appendix F.

26. David W. Budding, *Inspection: Implementing Housing Quality Requirements in the Administrative Agency Experiment* (Cambridge, Mass.: Abt Associates, 1977), appendix C.

27. In addition, both Tulsa and Jacksonville had subcontract arrangements that appear to have influenced the reported costs. Tulsa's costs included management time spent in dealing with the subcontractor; Jacksonville's reflect the fact that the subcontractor (the city code enforcement department) had a fixed-rate contract that reportedly understated the actual cost of doing the work.

28. The index is defined and discussed in Maloy et al., *Two-Year Costs,* appendix B.

29. The nature of the outreach function makes such estimation of unit costs more difficult. In most cases, the output unit (for example, screened applicants in the screening function, certifications performed in the certification function) does not depend on the way the function is performed. But out-

reach efforts, in combination with the size and characteristics of the eligible population and other, imperfectly understood behavioral factors, determine the number of applications. As a result, the analysis of reported costs was unable to produce stable estimates of procedural costs, and the simulation analysis was forced to use an averaging procedure that tends to understate cost variation.

30. The number of recipient years is computed as the sum of the number of participants receiving payments in each month, divided by twelve.

31. Second-year costs are believed to be more representative than first-year or two-year combined levels. The first year includes only a very small fraction of the costs of maintenance functions. Further, for functions that operate mainly on an annual cycle (such as certification and inspection), the first year is considerably less than a full cycle. The unit maintenance costs for all time periods are available from table A-18 in appendix A of Maloy et al., *Two-Year Costs.*

32. Jacksonville is an exception, with a cost nearly 50 percent above the next highest agency. This figure probably reflects the unexpectedly small number of recipients in the agency, which provides a smaller base in the denominator than elsewhere.

33. AAE guidelines required participants to pay at least that portion of their rent equal to the amount of the subsidy in order to continue receiving payments.

34. Abt Associates, *Administrative Costs,* 1977, attachment VII.

35. The marginal direct cost of an additional recipient in a given month was estimated at $0.76. The estimated marginal cost of a change in payment amounts was $3.34.

36. Both explanations are plausible. Agencies reacted differently to the generally lower work load in their second year of operations, some trimming staff to the bare minimum and some maintaining staff with an eye to future operations. Such variations probably introduce some "noise" into the average cost figures. Moreover, because the on-site observers were present only for the first year of operations, it is likely that procedural variations in the second year were less precisely defined for analysis.

37. For accounting reasons noted earlier, Springfield's indirect costs are somewhat understated but probably not enough to put them within the 153–201 range.

38. The transition period is not considered representative because of the rapid changes in staffing levels and the shifts in emphasis regarding agency activities.

39. This rate results from a benchmark simulation involving 1,000 participants and a selection from among alternative procedures that emphasizes those

found most effective or, in the absence of important effectiveness differential, the least-cost procedure (see table 6-13).

40. This is an assumption in the model that appears valid within the range of participant numbers observed in the AAE (approximately 300 to 1,000 participants). Numerous situations can be hypothesized in which the assumption would not stand up, however.

41. This relationship is derived systematically in appendix E of Maloy et al., *Two-Year Costs.*

42. For every family that became a recipient in Jacksonville, 4.33 applicants dropped out. The AAE median was 1.51.

43. Conceivably, an agency could enroll many more families than would be required to meet the recipient slots available. In such a case enrollee dropouts would reflect limited participation opportunities as well as the housing quality requirement. This did not happen to any measurable degree in the AAE sites covered in this report, although it did occur in the second enrollment period at Jacksonville.

44. Alan M. Hershey et al., *Colorado Monthly Reporting Experiment and Pre-Test: Preliminary Research Results* (Denver: Mathematica Policy Research, 1977), pp. 89–90.

45. Office of Policy Development and Research, *Lower Income Housing Assistance (Section 8): Interim Findings of Evaluation Research* (Washington, D.C.: Department of Housing and Urban Development, 1978). Note that these data are for a later period than the AAE data.

7

Reflections on the Administrative Agency Experiment

The Administrative Agency Experiment was a multifaceted research project from which it would be difficult to draw a single, unified conclusion. Rather than attempt such a feat, this chapter presents some reflections on the experiment as a whole. It considers first some general patterns in the AAE findings and then some important characteristics of the research design, in each case looking at the possible implications of the AAE for future research on social program administration.

AAE FINDINGS

If there is a central theme in the findings of the AAE, it is that definable alternative methods exist for carrying out administrative functions and that the choice among alternatives makes a difference.

For some administrative functions, the analysis identified two or more procedures or methods by which the function could be performed. No two agencies carried out identical procedures, even when they were judged to be using the same method. But classifying agencies by method produced workable groups with smaller differences within than across groups. Moreover, because the methods resulted from the natural development of local administrative strategies rather than from external direction, the stability of the groupings gives reason to believe that a national funding agency could require local agencies to carry out particular methods and achieve reasonable cross-agency conformity of procedures.

The AAE analysis considered ten direct functions (involving contact with clients) and six indirect functions (providing direction and resources for conducting the direct functions). All the direct functions had discernible alternative methods. For some functions two or more method dimensions could vary independently: supportive services, for example, could be provided in an individual or a group format, and it might or might not involve a substantial emphasis on ad hoc responses to individuals' problems. In the case of outreach and some other functions, methods could be described in terms of a continuum of intensity without clear dividing lines, making the methods less susceptible to national regulation. In general, however, at least the direct functions seem to offer usable handles for policy. And because many of these functions have close analogies in other housing and general assistance programs, particularly Section 8 and welfare, it seems likely that similar examples of feasible alternatives could be found in those situations as well.

AAE analysis did not reveal clear alternative methods for the indirect functions, however. Agency procedures seemed to represent eight variations on a common theme rather than two or more distinct alternatives. This result may stem partly from limitations of the research, for the direct functions received much more intensive analytic effort than the indirect functions. But the analysis was curtailed largely because it appeared unlikely to identify important alternative methods. It will therefore be the task of future research to investigate the indirect functions more closely, perhaps using a different approach, in order to determine whether distinct policy options exist.

To find clear alternative methods is useful only if the choice among them makes a difference. The AAE findings show that the choice often does make a difference, not only in efficiency but frequently in a program's ability to meet its overall goals.

The least surprising of the AAE findings is that the choice of procedures can affect administrative cost levels. Even so, the size and nature of the effects might not have been anticipated. The simulation analysis in table 6–13, for example, indicated that an agency's choice of methods for the direct functions could cause direct costs to vary between $68 and $131 per recipient-year. If we assume that agencies, in the absence of specific instructions, would choose methods throughout this range, then the average agency's direct costs might be $100 per recipient-year. A directive specifying that agencies must use the least costly methods could then be expected to reduce administrative costs by 32 percent,[1] a substantial proportion in any program context.

Perhaps the most interesting aspect of the cost analysis, however, is the finding that the policymaker can influence administrative expenditures by means other than choosing the methods with the lowest unit cost. For example, the apparent economies of size in indirect costs suggest that allocating local service responsibility to a few large agencies would entail lower administrative costs than serving the same clientele through more, smaller agencies. Other analyses show that, because intake costs are amortized over length of individuals' participation in the program, any policy decisions that lengthen the average participation period will reduce the average cost per recipient-year. A particularly intriguing example is the idea that choosing a more expensive method can sometimes reduce average costs: simulation analysis suggested that providing intensive supportive services could, in some situations, reduce attrition costs enough to yield a lower total cost per recipient than would result from less intensive (and expensive) services. These findings mean that an analysis of administrative costs cannot stop with an identification of alternative methods and the average cost of performing each; information on the other effects of alternative methods is necessary for a meaningful determination of costs.

Apart from costs, the choice among alternative procedures can also determine the effectiveness with which program rules are enforced. Three sets of rules in the AAE required enforcement mechanisms: the household eligibility criteria; the housing quality requirement; and the requirement that allowance recipients pay their rent (or at least that portion of the rent equal to the value of the allowance) in order to continue receiving benefits. In two of those three cases (certification and housing inspection) the choice among alternative methods was found to influence the effectiveness of enforcement and thus the extent to which program benefits were applied to the intended kinds of households and housing situations.

The enforcement of program rules is often equated with cost containment—particularly with the exclusion of ineligible persons from the benefit rolls. The AAE analysis did not find that the differential effectiveness of alternative methods meant that some methods saved more money than others. Rather, the analysis of certification methods found substantial differences in the ability to avoid both positive and negative error, but no significant effect on the total benefits provided. Thus, while the AAE suggests that research can identify differentially effective enforcement mechanisms, it also suggests that more effective enforcement does not always reduce program costs.

Participation is another area in which the choice among alternative methods makes a substantial difference. Outreach had the most obvious importance in the AAE; it could be expected to have equivalent salience for any new program but probably less for a well-established program. The choice of supportive services procedures had strong effects in some situations, with the more intensive services enhancing the probability that families would be able to participate. Some analyses indicated that the stringency with which the housing quality requirement was enforced also influenced participation, greater stringency leading to lower participation rates. The service and inspection effects are specific to a housing allowance program, but they suggest that participation in assistance programs may be influenced by a number of administrative decisions, not all of them obvious.

The choice of administrative methods can alter the composition as well as the level of participation. The AAE evidence suggests, for example, that reliance on referral and word-of-mouth communications can result in low application rates from some groups, such as the elderly and working poor. Similarly AAE agencies offering limited responsive services to enrollees saw high dropout rates for black households and households planning to move to new dwelling units. In effect, the choice among administrative procedures could provide or deny certain population groups an equal opportunity to receive program benefits.

The effects on costs, enforcement, and participation are likely to find analogies across a broad spectrum of social programs. In addition, it is possible for the choice among administrative methods to influence the achievement of program-specific goals. In the AAE the choice of procedures had some effect on the extent to which participants improved their housing circumstances (although this was mainly the indirect effect of responsive services in enhancing participation for families planning to move). Other programs might seek other effects. But even without turning to program-specific effects, the AAE's examples of alternative methods that seem susceptible to policy manipulation and show strong effects on costs, enforcement, and participation argue that program administration offers a fruitful area for future policy research.

ON THE RESEARCH APPROACH

The AAE also offers some insights about the utility of the nonexperimental "natural variation" research design for studying program administration.

A major advantage of the natural variation approach is that it can be used when theory or past experience are insufficient to allow confident specification of hypotheses. The analysis of supportive services illustrates the point. In the policy debate of the late 1960s and early 1970s, both advocates and critics of the housing allowance concept argued that many low-income people—especially minority group members in segregated markets—would be unable to obtain decent housing without help. But opinions varied widely on what kind of help and how much help would be needed. Some argued for legal assistance in overcoming discrimination, others for the availability of child care or transportation services to help people look for housing, and still others for teaching people what constitutes good housing and how to find it.

The suggestions were much too diverse and contradictory for the researcher to define a small set of alternative treatments with any confidence of capturing the most important effects, and a controlled variation design that provided a rigorous test of all major alternatives would have required funding a prohibitively large number of agencies. Instead, the agencies were allowed to formulate their own service strategies, and the detailed records kept by the on-site observers were used to identify the dimensions along which the agencies varied and to hypothesize about the possible effects of variation. This analysis was no small task: several months of effort and countless dead ends preceded the simple dichotomous classification of agencies according to whether they provided extensive responsive services. That classification did not correspond exactly to any of the suggestions in the policy literature. In other words, a research design built on systematic variation would probably not have tested the one variation that proved to be strongly associated with outcomes in the AAE.

For a natural variation design to produce persuasive findings in this kind of exploratory situation, it is important to have data measuring the phenomenon from multiple perspectives. In the supportive services analysis, for example, the open-ended nature of the observers' materials could leave some doubt about the validity of the classification scheme. But because the classification was defined in terms of the intensity of the services offered, its validity could be checked by examining the administrative cost data; and in fact, the agencies for which observational data indicated a heavy emphasis on responsive services proved to have used uniformly higher amounts of staff time per enrollee. Similarly, although the cross-agency analysis seemed to show clear effects, the effects attributed to services could have resulted from other influences operating at the agency level. But because the Springfield agency had kept detailed records of which participants received help, it was possible to replicate the cross-agency analysis within a single site and bolster confidence in the general finding.

The use of multiple measurement perspectives pervades the AAE. The administrative cost analysis is probably the most striking example, as the agency cost reports and the administrative cost simulation model were used in parallel for every major analysis. More generally, the AAE's three independent lines of longitudinal measurement—direct observation, agency records, and participant surveys—allowed nearly every important question to be investigated by two or more analytic approaches. This triangulation[2] of measurement approaches does not allow the precise estimation that can come from controlled variation, but it substantially reduces the uncertainty of interpretation inherent in a natural variation design.

Another important strength of the natural variation design for the AAE's purposes was that it allowed a reasonably confident analysis of administrative costs. A controlled variation design would almost certainly have required some agencies to carry out two or more alternative procedures in parallel, which might be expected to produce costs that differed from normal program operations (particularly for management). Even if the design avoided within-agency variation, controlled variation might result in unnatural combinations of procedures and biased estimates.

The contribution of the administrative cost analysis in the AAE went well beyond the cost estimates. In some respects the cost analysis provided, or at least strengthened, the basic framework of the research. All agency functions resulted in administrative expenditures, and expenditures were measured in the same terms (mainly dollars and personnel time) for all functions. No other outcome measure had these characteristics. As a result, it was the measurement and analysis of costs that tended to define the boundaries between functions and the linkages among them. Often it was the cost analysis that defined alternative methods, particularly because the simulation model required procedural distinctions that were more simplistic and clear-cut than those evident in the on-site observers' narrative records.

The natural variation design was important for cost analysis because it allowed the agency to be the unit of analysis. Similarly, the design allowed analysis of other aspects of agency behavior; it was possible to ask why agencies chose particular procedures as well as what effects the procedures had. The discussion in this book has generally concentrated on the effects of the procedures, but an interesting example of the focus on agency behavior occurred in a special study of the program in Jacksonville.

The fundamental issue was institutional behavior in the face of conflicting goals. The agency administering the program in Jacksonville was also responsible for enforcing the city's housing code, and it strictly enforced the city code as the standard for housing allowance participants. Much of the housing stock, however, was substandard according to the code, and the vacancy rate for low-priced standard units was very low. Further, the agency philosophy favored a "lean" housing allowance program, so supportive services were held to a minimum. As a result, only 33 percent of the enrolled households were able to qualify for payments, and the Jacksonville agency became the only one to fall seriously short of its targeted number of allowance recipients.

HUD allowed the agency to reopen enrollment, and encouraged any changes in administrative procedures that the agency felt were necessary to improve its performance. The results were apparently good. The agency met its recipient target with a much higher qualifying rate for enrollees. But analysis showed that the agency had recruited mainly white households with incomes in the upper end of the eligible range. In effect, the agency had satisfied the explicit performance measures by trading off a less explicitly measured program goal rather than by altering the agency's philosophy.

The Jacksonville experience is useful both for understanding the possibility of conflicting goals inherent in the housing allowance program and for gaining insights into the kinds of performance measures such a program might require. That experience could occur only with a natural variation design. Also critical was a flexible, opportunistic, research approach, in which a special substudy could be commissioned to pursue an issue that arose, unanticipated, in the course of the research.

Although the Jacksonville study was an unusual case, involving a substantial addition to the research effort, the flexibility to pursue imperfectly anticipated issues seems to be an essential ingredient of the natural variation approach. Three elements of the AAE design proved critical to flexibility (and sometimes to the absence of flexibility). First, the initial data collection design was both broad and deep, attempting to cover all aspects of agency and participant behavior that seemed potentially relevant even in the absence of specific hypotheses about administrative effects. Second, the fact that data collection was longitudinal and continued over a two-year period meant that the later efforts could be modified to obtain additional information about issues raised in the early efforts.

A third and particularly strong contribution to flexibility was made by the on-site observers. They accumulated information through a fundamentally open-ended process, and even though the observations were structured by the logs in which they were recorded, the data could be examined and interpreted from a variety of perspectives. This was especially true when the observers themselves were asked to do the interpretation: many questions that arose well after the observation period were answered by observers examining their own notes and reconstructing unrecorded bits of information. Extended on-site observation is not common in policy research, but it seems to be a useful component of a natural variation approach.

Although the preceding paragraphs have attempted to point out some of the strengths of the AAE's approach, they certainly are not intended to argue that the project was ideally designed. The reader will have noticed constraints on the analyses presented in earlier chapters, such as the limits to generalization posed by eight sites, the absence of precise estimates of the strength of relationships, and the reliance on inference where direct measurement might have been possible. Those who worked on the project are even more acutely aware, with the power of hindsight, of things that could have been done differently, of data that might have been collected if their utility had been foreseen. Often we yearned for the power of the classic experimental design and for the ability to present stronger conclusions and fewer caveats.

But the administration of assistance programs is not a field with a highly developed history of empirical research. The AAE was of necessity an exploratory research effort, and related research for at least the next few years will also tend to be exploratory. There is much to be learned about social program administration, and some of the learning process should be able to build and improve on the experience of the Administrative Agency Experiment.

NOTES

1. Assuming constant indirect cost rates.
2. Eugene J. Webb et al., *Unobtrusive Measures: Nonreactive Research in the Social Sciences* (Chicago: Rand, 1966).

Appendix A

Analysis of Word-of-Mouth Applications

When applicants to the AAE agencies were asked where they first heard about the housing allowance program, a consistently high proportion said that they had learned of it through friends or relatives. It was hypothesized that this word-of-mouth communication resulted both from the agencies' outreach efforts—people who heard a television announcement told their neighbors, for example—and from the first-hand experience of people who had already been in direct contact with the agency.

To test the hypotheses, the number of word-of-mouth applications at each agency in each month was regressed on the number of applicants in the same month who said they heard of the program from sources other than friends and relatives and on the cumulative number of people who had previously applied to the program. Table A–1 presents the results of this analysis.[1]

Table A-1. Factors Determining Word-of-Mouth Application:
Regression Analysis of the Number of Word-of-Mouth Applications per Month

Independent Variables[a]	Mean Value	Zero-Order Correlation with Number of Word-of-Mouth Applicants per Month	Regression Coefficient	F-Value	Change in R^2
Cumulative total number of applications in previous months	755	0.33	0.032	23.24**	0.11[b]
Number of applications per month from all sources other than word of mouth	162	0.81	0.472	139.10**	0.65[b]
Constant			−2.064		
Statistics: Adjusted R^2 = 0.75; standard error of estimate: 29.85; number of cases = 54					

Source: Application forms
Data base: Eligible applicants by program month
Note: The equation shown was also estimated separately for the elderly, the working poor, and welfare groups (elderly word-of-mouth applicants per month as a function of the cumulative number of elderly applicants and the number of elderly applicants from all other sources in the month). The magnitude and direction of the relationships were similar for all three groups. The major difference was that the adjusted R^2 for the elderly was only 0.53, compared with 0.71 and 0.74 for the working poor and welfare recipients, respectively; this indicates that word-of-mouth application is not as strongly related to application from other sources for the elderly as it is for the working poor and welfare recipients.
[a]Dependent variable is number of word-of-mouth applicants per month at a given agency.
[b]Change in R^2 resulting from entering the variable last in the equation; the adjusted R^2 therefore is not equal to the sum of changes in R^2.
**Probability less than 0.01.

NOTES

1. A full description and discussion can be found in Jean Macmillan and William L. Hamilton, *Outreach: Generating Applications in the Administrative Agency Experiment* (Cambridge, Mass.: Abt Associates, 1977), appendix A.

Appendix B

Analysis of Hearing of and Applying to the Program

For a multivariate analysis of hearing about the program and deciding to apply, a logit model was chosen as appropriate. For binary dependent variables, procedures such as linear regression may yield values outside the zero to 1 range. The logistic response function is more appropriate, because it has asymptotes at 0 and 1, so the constraints on predicted values of the dependent variables are automatically met. The predicted probabilities were derived as follows.

The formula for estimating logit coefficients β_i is given by

$$\text{Probability } (Y=1) = \frac{1}{1+e^{-\alpha-\sum_{i=1}^{n}\beta_i X_i}}$$

The predicted probability that $Y=1$ if all independent variables are set at their mean values is:

$$\text{Pr}(Y=1) = \frac{1}{1+e^{-\hat{\alpha}-\sum_{i=1}^{n}\hat{\beta}_i \overline{X}_i}}$$

where α and β_i are the maximum likelihood estimates of α and β_i. The predicted probability that $Y=1$ for any value of a particular variable X_j with all other independent variables set at their mean values is

$$\text{Pr}(Y=1) = \frac{1}{1+e^{-\alpha-\sum_{i\neq j}\hat{\beta}_i \overline{X}_i - \hat{\beta}_j X_j}}$$

Table B-1. The Probability of Hearing about the Housing Allowance Program for Selected Subgroups of the Eligible Population

Group Characteristic	Number in Group	Probability of Hearing [Pr (H)= Number Hearing/ Number Eligible]	Logit Prediction of Probability of Hearing[a]
Total	1,417	.21	.19[b]
Elderly	417	.11**[c]	.13**[d]
Nonelderly	978	.25	.22
White	644	.25**	.25
Black	773	.17	.15
Elementary education	411	.10**	.11
Some high school	516	.23	.22**
Completed high school	320	.28	.24**
Some college	140	.31	.29**
Welfare recipient[e]	673	.23*	.23**
Does not receive welfare	744	.18	.16
Male-headed household[f]	744	.20	.18
Female-headed household	672	.22	.20
Male respondent	340	.15**	.16
Female respondent	1,076	.23	.20
Public housing waiting list	195	.26**	.24*
Has lived in public housing	324	.27	.25**
No experience with public housing	809	.17	.16
Household income			
$0–1,999	367	.13**	.18[g]
$2,000–3,999	384	.24	.18
$4,000–5,999	257	.26	.20
$6,000+	241	.26	.21
Rent paid per month			
Less than $50	205	.09**	.18[g]
$50–74	557	.18	.18
$75–100	205	.24	.19
$100+	404	.29	.20

Source: Jacksonville outreach survey
Data base: All respondents (missing cases indicated by valid number in group)
[a]Value of the logit function evaluated at the indicated values of each independent variable with all other independent variables at their mean values.
[b]Logit function evaluated at the mean of all independent variables.
[c]Significance level based on a chi-square statistic using the categories indicated in the table.
[d]Significance level based on a t-test for the logit coefficient of each independent variable. All household characteristics except income and rent, which are continuous, have been entered in the logit equation using a separate dummy variable for each possible category. (The total number of dummy variables for a characteristic is one less than the total number of categories.)
[e]Includes Food Stamps. Aid to Families with Dependent Children, Aid to the Blind and Disabled, and General Assistance. Does not include Social Security.
[f]All other individual characteristics refer to the respondent rather than the head of household. However, the age, education, and race of respondents was similar to that of household heads. (The respondent was required to be the head or the head's spouse.)
[g]Based on the median value for the interval.
*Probability less than 0.05.
**Probability less than 0.01.

Table B-2. The Probability of Applying to the Housing Allowance Program among Respondents Hearing about the Program for Selected Subgroups of the Eligible Population

Group Characteristics	Number Hearing in Group	Probability of Deciding to Apply among Those Hearing [Pr (A/H) = Number Applying/ Number Hearing]	Logit Prediction of Probability of Deciding to Apply among Those Hearing[a]
Total	295	.32	.28[b]
Elderly	45	.18*	.10**
Nonelderly	248	.34	.33
White	163	.31	.33
Black	132	.33	.22
Elementary education	40	.42	.40
Some high school	121	.34	.26
Completed high school	89	.29	.30
Some college	43	.21	.23
Welfare recipient[c]	158	.43**	.39**
Does not receive welfare	137	.19	.18
Male-headed household[d]	149	.26*	.28
Female-headed household	146	.38	.28
Male respondent	52	.23	.23
Female respondent	243	.34	.29
Public housing waiting list	51	.55**	.46*
Has lived in public housing	86	.27	.23
No experience with public housing	140	.26	.26
Household income			
$0–1,999	49	.29*	.33[e]
$2,000–3,999	91	.43	.30
$4,000–5,999	68	.32	.27
$6,000+	62	.19	.24
Rent paid per month			
Less than $50	19	.42	.25[e]
$50–74	103	.31	.26
$75–100	50	.22	.28
$100+	116	.35	.30

Source: Jacksonville outreach survey
Data base: Respondents who had heard about the program (missing cases indicated by valid number in group)
[a]Value of the logit function evaluated at the indicated values of each independent variable with all other independent variables at their mean values.
[b]Logit function evaluated at the mean of all independent variables.
[c]Includes Food Stamps, Aid to Families with Dependent Children, Aid to the Blind and Disabled, and General Assistance. Does not include Social Security.
[d]All other individual characteristics refer to the respondent rather than the head of household. However, the age, education, and race of respondents was similar to that of household heads. (The respondent was required to be the head or the head's spouse.)
[e]Based on the median value for the interval.
*Probability less than 0.05
**Probability less than 0.01

Table B-3. The Probability of Applying to the Housing Allowance Program for Selected Subgroups of the Eligible Population

Group Characteristic	Number in Group	Probability of Hearing [Pr(H)]	×	Probability of Deciding to Apply among Those Hearing [Pr(A/H)]	=	Probability of Applying [Pr(A)]	Logit Prediction of Probability of Applying[a]
Total	1,417	.21		.32		.07	.04[b]
Elderly	417	.11		.18		.02	.01**
Nonelderly	978	.25		.34		.09	.06
White	644	.25		.31		.08	.07
Black	733	.17		.33		.06	.03**
Elementary education	411	.10		.42		.04	.03
Some high school	516	.23		.34		.08	.04
Completed high school	320	.28		.29		.08	.05
Some college	140	.31		.21		.07	.05
Welfare recipient[c]	673	.23		.43		.10**	.07**
Does not receive welfare	744	.18		.19		.04	.02
Male-headed household[d]	744	.20		.26		.05*	.04
Female-headed household	672	.22		.38		.08	.05
Male respondent	340	.15		.23		.04**	.03
Female respondent	1,076	.23		.34		.08	.05

Public housing waiting list	195	.26	.55	.14**	.09**
Has lived in public housing	324	.27	.27	.07	.05
No experience with public housing	809	.17	.26	.05	.03
Household income					
$0–1,999	367	.13	.29	.04*	.04^e
$2,000–3,999	384	.24	.43	.10	.04
$4,000–5,999	257	.26	.32	.09	.04
$6,000+	241	.26	.19	.05	.04
Rent paid per month					
Less than $50	205	.09	.42	.04*	.04^e
$50–74	557	.18	.31	.06	.04
$75–100	205	.24	.22	.05	.04
$100+	404	.29	.35	.10	.05

Source: Jacksonville outreach survey

Data base: All respondents (missing cases indicated by valid number in group)

[a]Value of the logit function evaluated at the indicated values of each independent variable with all other independent variables at their mean values.

[b]Logit function evaluated at the mean of all independent variables.

[c]Includes Food Stamps, Aid to Families with Dependent Children, Aid to the Blind and Disabled, and General Assistance. Does not include Social Security.

[d]All other individual characteristics refer to the respondent rather than the head of household. However, the age, education, and race of respondents was similar to that of household heads. (The respondent was required to be the head or the head's spouse.)

[e]Evaluated at the median of the interval.

*Probability less than 0.05

**Probability less than 0.01

So, for example, for a dummy variable X_j there will be two predicted probabilities, one for $X_j=0$ and one for $X_j=1$, with other independent variables set at their mean values. If $X_j=0$

$$\Pr(Y=1)= \frac{1}{1+e^{-\hat{\alpha}-\sum_{i \neq j}\hat{\beta}_i\overline{X}_i}}$$

If $X_j=1$

$$\Pr(Y=1)= \frac{1}{1+e^{-\alpha-\sum_{i \neq j}\hat{\beta}_i\overline{X}_i-\hat{\beta}_j}}$$

For continuous variables, the probability that $Y=1$ can be computed for any value of X_j. In tables B–1 to B–2, where predicted probabilities are being compared with actual probabilities computed from categorized data, X_i is set at the median for the category.

Tables B–1, B–2, and B–3 summarize the results of three analyses using the special survey of the eligible population conducted in Jacksonville.[1] Table B–1 focuses on the probability that a member of the eligible population had heard about the experimental program. Table B–2 examines the probability that an individual who had heard about the program would apply for benefits. Table B–3 combines the first two tables, investigating the probability that a given member of the eligible population applies to the program. All three tables show for selected population subgroups the simple proportion that was aware of or applied to the program as well as the logit prediction.

NOTES

1. These analyses are described and discussed in full in Jean MacMillan and William L. Hamilton, *Outreach: Generating Applications in the Administrative Agency Experiment* (Cambridge, Mass.: Abt Associates, 1977), Appendix C.

Appendix C

Analysis of Enrollees' Plans to Move and Success in Becoming Recipients

As part of the investigation of the effect of supportive services, considerable analysis was undertaken of the factors influencing the likelihood that a household enrolling in the housing allowance program would qualify for and receive payments. Whether an enrollee's preprogram dwelling unit could meet program standards was expected to be the critical factor. A direct measure of this condition was not available, but enrollees' stated plans to stay in their preprogram units or to move to different units were taken to represent much the same phenomenon: those who planned to stay, particularly if they were acting on reasonable expectations that their units would meet the standards, would have an easier time becoming recipients than those who planned to move.

Tables C–1 to C–4 therefore summarize a series of analyses that first explored the factors associated with enrollees' plans to move (table C–2) and then examine separately the probability of becoming a recipient for those who planned to move (table C–3) and those who planned to stay (table C–4).[1] Table C–1 presents definitions and properties of the variables used in the analysis.

Table C-1. The Enrollee Sample Analysis File

Variable Name and Description	Source	Number of Valid Cases	Values, Coding, and Distribution (%)	
Demographic variables				
Black: Black head of household	Application form	1,199	0 = Head not black	72
			1 = Black head	28
Age of head	First participant survey	1,193	Mean = 40.9	
			s.d. = 18.0	
Household size	Certification form	1,199	Mean = 3 2	
			s.d. = 2.0	
Total income per capita: Gross household income divided by household size	Certification form	1,199	Mean = 1452.47	
			s.d. = 757.25	
PCT income limit: Net income as a percentage of the site eligibility limit for households of relevant size	Certification form and C* values	1,199	Mean = .42	
			s.d. = .20	
Handicapped head: Households headed by handicapped individuals	Application form	1,199	0 = Head not handicapped	88
			1 = Handicapped head	12
AFDC: AFDC recipient households	First participant survey	1,177	0 = Not AFDC recipient	61
			1 = AFDC recipient	39
Female-headed, several children: Female-headed households with three or more children	Application form and first participant survey	1,199	0 = Others	83
			1 = Female-headed, three or more children	17
Several adults: Households with more than one adult who do not constitute a couple	First participant survey	1,199	0 = Couple or single-adult household	86
			1 = Several adults but not couple	14

Variable	Source	N	Values	%
Single adult with children: Single-adult households with one or more children	First participant survey	1,199	0 = Others 1 = Single-adult household with children	65 35
Access to automobile: Whether household owns or has use of a car	First participant survey	1,199	0 = No access 1 = Access to car	11 89
Past moves: Number of moves during past three years	First participant survey	1,191	Mean = 1.9 s.d. = 2.1	
Subsidized housing: Whether household was living in subsidized housing	Information supplied by agencies	1,197	0 = Not in subsidized housing 1 = In subsidized housing	92 8

Housing variables

Variable	Source	N	Values	%
Deviation from C^* rent: Proportionate deviation of household's rent from C^* for families of its size at its site	Enrollment and certification forms and C^* values	1,199	Mean = -0.22 s.d. = 0.38	
People per room: Number of rooms (excluding bathrooms) divided by household size	Enrollment and certification forms	1,198	Mean = 0.74 s.d. = 0.42	
Housing deficiencies: Number of seven major housing deficiencies	First participant survey and housing evaluation form	1,135	0 = 1 = 2 = 3 = 4 = 5 = 6 = 7 =	45 24 15 8 4 3 1 0
Bad heating: Enrollee's assessment of how well heating system works	First participant survey	1,083	1 = Good 2 = Fair	72 16

Table C-1. continued

Variable Name and Description	Source	Number of Valid Cases	Values, Coding, and Distribution(%)	
			3 = Poor	11
			4 = No system or not working	1
Inadequate plumbing: Whether plumbing facilities are shared or incomplete	First participant survey	1,197	0 = Complete and not shared	89
			1 = Shared or incomplete	11
Inadequate kitchen: Whether kitchen facilities are shared or incomplete	First participant survey	1,199	0 = Complete and not shared	91
			1 = Shared or incomplete	9
Unit satisfaction: The household's degree of satisfaction with its unit	First participant survey	1,195	−2 = Very dissatisfied	23
			−1 = Somewhat dissatisfied	16
			0 = Neither	4
			1 = Somewhat satisfied	21
			2 = Very satisfied	36
Neighborhood variables				
Street litter: Dirtiness of streets	Housing evaluation form	1,145	0 = Clean streets and/or sidewalks	53
			1 = Some litter	35
			2 = Considerable amount of litter	10
			3 = Accumulations of litter, trash, broken glass	2

Variable	Source	N	Coding	%
No sidewalks: Absence of sidewalks	Housing evaluation form	1,143	0=Sidewalks 1=No sidewalks	67 33
Abandoned cars: Presence of abandoned cars	Housing evaluation form	1,141	0=No abandoned cars 1=Abandoned cars	86 14
Abandoned buildings: Presence of abandoned buildings	Housing evaluation form	1,141	0=No abandoned buildings 1=Abandoned buildings	89 11
Bad street maintenance: Extent of deterioration in streets	Housing evaluation form	1,145	0=Well-paved and maintained streets 1=Paved street with minor deterioration 2=Paved street with numerous chuck holes 3=Unpaved or severe incidence of chuck holes on paved street	59 29 5 7
Safe residential factor	First participant survey	1,199	Mean=0.00, s.d.=0.84	
Schools factor	First participant survey	1,199	Mean=0.00, s.d.=0.91	
Safe and clean factor	First participant survey	1,199	Mean=0.00, s.d.=0.80	
Children's facilities factor	First participant survey	1,199	Mean=0.00, s.d.=0.79	
Convenience factor	First participant survey	1,199	Mean=0.00, s.d.=0.73	
Social cohesiveness factor	First participant survey	1,199	Mean=0.00, s.d.=0.64	
Neighborhood satisfaction: The household's degree of satisfaction with its neighborhood	First participant survey	1,193	−2=Very dissatisfied −1=Somewhat dissatisfied	16 9

Table C-1. continued

Variable Name and Description	Source	Number of Valid Cases	Values, Coding, and Distribution(%)	
			0 = Neither	5
			1 = Somewhat satisfied	21
			2 = Very satisfied	50
Program incentive variable				
Subsidy per capita: Monthly housing allowance for which household qualified divided by household size	Enrollment and certification forms and C* values	1,199	Mean = 32.73 s.d. = 17.80	
Dependent variables				
Moving intention scale: Moving plans expressed at enrollment and in survey	Enrollment form and first participant survey	1,198	1 = Stay twice	33
			2 = Mixed, inconsistent, undecided	22
			3 = Move twice	45
Survey moving plans: Moving plans expressed in survey	First participant survey	1,199	1 = Stay	40
			2 = Don't know	8
			3 = Move	52
Becoming a recipient	Payments initiation and termination forms	1,199	0 = Prepayment terminee	24
			1 = Recipient	76
Moving behavior for recipients only	Payments initiation form	916	0 = Stayer	55
			1 = Mover	45

Source: AAE application, certification, enrollment, payments initiation, housing evaluation forms; first participant survey; C* values; agency-supplied information
Data base: Enrollee sample (N = 1,199)

Table C-2. Analysis of Moving Plans

Variable	Equation 1 [a]			Equation 2 [a]		
	Regression Coefficient	(Standard Error)	Standardized Coefficient	Regression Coefficient	(Standard Error)	Standardized Coefficient
Bad heating	0.06	(0.03)*	0.05	0.07	(0.03)	0.06
Inadequate plumbing	0.19	(0.06)**	0.07	0.18	(0.06)**	0.07
Deviation from C* rent	-0.60	(0.06)***	-0.26	-0.58	(0.06)***	-0.25
People per room	0.04	(0.07)	0.02	0.06	(0.07)	0.03
Street litter	-0.00	(0.03)	-0.00	-0.00	(0.03)	-0.00
No sidewalks	0.08	(0.04)	0.04	0.05	(0.04)	0.03
Black	0.14	(0.05)**	0.07	0.14	(0.05)**	0.07
Age of head	-0.00	(0.00)	-0.03	-0.00	(0.00)	-0.02
Household size	-0.00	(0.01)	-0.01	-0.01	(0.00)	-0.02
PCT income limit	-0.10	(0.09)	-0.02	-0.10	(0.09)	-0.02
Several adults	0.22	(0.05)***	0.09	0.24	(0.05)***	0.09
Subsidized housing	0.18	(0.07)*	0.06	0.15	(0.07)*	0.05
Past moves	0.02	(0.01)*	0.05	0.02	(0.01)*	0.05
Safe residential	-0.09	(0.02)***	-0.08			
Schools	-0.02	(0.02)	-0.02			
Safe and clean	-0.05	(0.03)	-0.04			
Social cohesiveness	-0.07	(0.03)*	-0.05			
Unit satisfaction	-0.25	(0.01)***	-0.46	-0.24	(0.01)***	-0.45
Neighborhood satisfaction				-0.07	(0.02)***	-0.12
Constant	1.89			1.93		
N:						
Dependent variable	1,198			1,198		
Independent variables	1,083–1,199			1,083–1,199		

Source: First participant survey, first housing evaluation form, agency operating forms, agency-supplied information on subsidized housing

Data base: Enrollee sample ($N = 1,199$)

[a] Multiple $R = 0.76$; adjusted $R^2 = 0.58$.

*Probability less than 0.05.
**Probability less than 0.01.
***Probability less than 0.001.

Table C-3. Analysis of the Probability
of Becoming a Recipient for Enrollees Who Planned to Move

Variable	Regression Coefficient	(Standard Error)	Standardized Coefficient
Black	−0.09	(0.04)*	−0.10
Age of head	−0.00	(0.00)	−0.07
Household size	0.01	(0.01)	0.05
AFDC recipient	−0.09	(0.04)*	−0.09
Female-headed with several children	−0.04	(0.05)	−0.04
Single adult with children	0.02	(0.05)	0.02
Handicapped head	−0.00	(0.06)	−0.00
Access to automobile	0.05	(0.05)	0.03
Past moves	0.01	(0.01)	0.03
Subsidized housing	−0.12	(0.05)*	−0.09
Subsidy per capita	0.00	(0.00)**	0.16
Vacancy rate	2.96	(0.60)***	0.20
Inspection	−0.43	(0.08)***	−0.23
Services	0.04	(0.01)***	0.14
Constant		0.48	
N			
Dependent variable		620	
Independent variables		611–620	

Source: AAE second annual report, first participant survey, first housing evaluation
form, agency operating forms, agency labor hour forms, agency-supplied information on
subsidized housing
Data base: Enrollee sample ($N=1,199$)
Note: Multiple $R=0.48$, adjusted $R^2=0.21$.
   *Probability less than 0.05
  **Probability less than 0.01
***Probability less than 0.001

Table C-4. Analysis of the Probability
of Becoming a Recipient for Enrollees Who Planned to Stay

Variable	Regression Coefficient	(Standard Error)	Standardized Coefficient	Reduction in R^2 When Variable Is Excluded
Housing deficiencies	−0.04	(0.01)**	−0.14	0.01
Bad heating	−0.08	(0.03)*	−0.11	0.02
Inadequate plumbing	−0.20	(0.08)*	−0.13	0.01
Inadequate kitchen	−0.04	(0.10)	−0.02	0.00
Deviation from C* rent	0.03	(0.05)	0.03	0.00
Black	0.03	(0.05)	0.03	0.00
AFDC recipient	0.06	(0.03)	0.09	0.01
Subsidy per capita	0.00	(0.00)*	0.12	0.01
Vacancy rate	2.19	(0.51)***	0.24	0.03
Inspection	−0.19	(0.08)*	−0.13	0.00
Services	0.01	(0.01)	0.06	0.00
Constant		0.80		
N				
Dependent variable		484		
Independent variables		424–484		

Source: AAE second annual report, first participant survey, first housing evaluation form, agency operating forms, agency labor hour forms, agency-supplied information on subsidized housing
Data base: Enrollee sample ($N=1,199$)
Note: Multiple $R=0.30$; adjusted $R^2=0.07$.
  *Probability less than 0.05
 **Probability less than 0.01
***Probability less than 0.001

NOTES

1. A number of additional and alternative analyses were also performed, including a series of logit analyses (the dependent variables are categorical). The analyses are described and discussed in full in William L. Holshouser, Jr., *Supportive Services in the Administrative Agency Experiment* (Cambridge, Mass.: Abt Associates, 1977), appendix B.

Appendix D

Analysis of Effect of Responsive Services

LOG-LINEAR ANALYSIS OF INTERACTION

The analysis of service effects on success in becoming a recipient primarily uses the class of procedures discussed by Goodman and Bishop, Feinberg, and Holland for analyzing multivariate contingency data using log-linear models.[1]

The basic research question is, To what degree does service affect success in becoming a recipient of a housing subsidy for suspected high-risk groups? As such, the question is basically conditional or "interactive;" that is, does service make more difference for the high-risk category of the special-interest variable (for example on race, blacks) than for the low-risk category (whites)? The data for this analysis are categorized or made categorical by collapsing some continuous variables. Most variables were easily dichotomized. The objective of the analysis is to search for and evaluate the relative effects on the dependent variable (success in becoming a recipient) of the main and interaction effects of service and the special-interest group variables, while controlling for market condition and move plans (which could provide competing explanations to service effects).

The procedures outlined by Goodman and others examine the effects of a set of categorical predictors on the log odds of a binary dependent variable similar to the way in which predictor effects are evaluated in traditional ANOVA designs.[2] Recall that in ANOVA designs, a dependent variable is partitioned into a set of main effects and interaction terms as follows:

$$\mu_{ij} = \mu + \alpha_1 + \gamma_{ij} \tag{1}$$

where

μ_{ij} = mean on the dependent variable for level i of variable A and level j of variable B

μ = the grand mean on the dependent variable

α_i, β_j, γ_{ij} = main and interaction effects for the two predictor variables A and B on the dependent variable

In the log-linear models, the partition is in terms of the natural logarithm of the ratio of success to failure (log odds) for each ij level of the two predictor variables, rather than the mean as in expression 1. If we further assume that all variables are binary, expression 1 for the log-linear model is expressed as follows using Goodman's notation:[3]

$$\frac{P_{ij}}{(1-p_{ij})} = \alpha^c + \beta_j^{AC} + \beta_j^{BC} + \beta_i^{ABC} \tag{2}$$

where

$$\beta_1^{AC} = -\beta_2^{AC}$$
$$\beta_1^{BC} = -\beta_2^{BC}$$
$$\beta_{11}^{ABC} = \beta_{22}^{ABC} = -\beta_{21}^{ABC} = -\beta_{12}^{ABC}$$

A, B = independent variables

C = a binary dependent variable

α = a constant effect of the general effect of the marginal distribution of the dependent variable

β = effect of main and interaction terms on the natural logarithm of the odds of success at the appropriate levels of the predictor variable

From expression 2 any reduced parameter model can be evaluated using a likelihood chi-squared statistic defined for the two-predictor variable case of expression 2 as

$$\chi^2 = 2 \sum_{ij} f_{ij}^0 \ln \frac{f_{ij}^0}{f_{ij}^E}$$

where

f_{ij}^O = observed frequencies

f_{ij}^E = frequencies generated by the model of expression 2

In addition, chi-squared effects can be computed for every parameter in the model, a useful procedure in evaluating the importance of any given parameter of expression 3 for predicting the odds on the dependent variable. These chi-square values for each parameter are found using a step-forward procedure that begins with the no-effect model and successively adds one term at a time, noting the drop in the chi-squared statistic at each step in the procedure until all parameters have been included.[4] The larger the chi-squared reduction with the addition of any given parameter, the more important that parameter in explaining the odds on the dependent variable. The difference between chi-square values given by expression 3 with and without the parameter of interest included in the expression is itself distributed as χ^2 and can be evaluated with one degree of freedom. Hence in the two predictor variable examples one would begin by examining expression 3 for the no-effects model (that is, prediction of the odds based only on knowledge of the marginal distribution of the dependent variable) relative to the value of expression 3 with each main effect added separately. These two differences would provide estimates of chi-squared effects for each of the two main effects. The chi-squared effect for the interaction term can then be easily found by comparing the expression 3 value computed with the two main effects included to the value for the fully saturated model (zero).[5]

Another heuristic aid in helping to identify potentially important interaction effects is to plot these effects on the log scale.

The interpretation of these plots is very similar to the interpretation of similar plots in ANOVA.[6] The calibration in the ordinate is based on the natural logarithm of the odds of success to failure on the dependent variable. The abscissa takes two values, one for each level of the service variable. A separate line is then drawn for each level of the other variables of interest, such as race. Roughly interpreted, the steeper the slope of the lines, the greater the effect of the service variable. In addition, the greater the distance between the two lines, the greater the effect of the race or other variable. If no interaction is present, the two lines are parallel. The degree to which the lines are not parallel is a measure of the degree of interaction.

ENTROPY AS A MEASURE OF OVERALL FIT

An overall measure of the predictive ability of a nominal or ordinal dependent variable by a set of continuous predictor variables has been proposed by Theil based on the information theoretic concept of entropy.[7] The main use of entropy in information theory is to measure predictive uncertainty associated with a probability distribution. For any given binominal probability distribution, the entropy of that distribution can be defined as

$$H(D) = -\sum_{i=1}^{2} P_i \ln P_i \qquad (4)$$

where P_i = probability of being in the ith level of the dependent variable D. As a statistic by itself, $H(D)$ is relatively meaningless. However, in the binomial case the maximum value of $H(D)$ is equal to ln 2 when the probability of success is maximally *uncertain*, ($p = 0.50$), and the minimum value of $H(D)$ is 0 when the probability of success is maximally *certain*, ($p = 1.00$). Hence if $H(D)$ is compared with these maximum and minimum values, a meaningful interpretation is possible; that is, $H(D)$ can be expressed as a percentage reduction in uncertainty, given a particular marginal distribution in a binary variable, relative to maximal uncertainty.

The same principle can be extended to the multivariate case, with one or more predictors and a dependent variable. Consider the one-predictor case, because the multiple predictor case is a simple extension. If the object is to evaluate the reduction in uncertainty of predicting a dependent variable (D) relative to a given predictor variable (A), the maximum uncertainty must be evaluated in terms of the marginal distribution of the dependent variable, that is, what would be predicted if only the marginal distribution on the dependent variable were known. This is precisely $H(D)$, which is maximum at $p = 0.50$. If variable A is also binary, the conditional entropy of variable D, given variable A, is

$$H_A(D) = \sum_{i=1}^{2} \sum_{j=1}^{2} P_{ij} \ln P\text{\textbullet}j / P_{ij} \qquad (5)$$

where

i = levels of the dependent variable

j = levels of the independent variable

$H_A(D)$ must always be less than $H(D)$ because adding information about another variable in predicting the conditional distribution should never increase uncertainty in prediction. At worst, uncertainty reduction should be zero. Hence the measure

$$\frac{H(D)-H_A(D)}{H(D)} \tag{6}$$

can be thought of as the degree to which uncertainty is reduced by having knowledge of the conditional distribution of variable D, given variable A, relative to knowing only the marginal distribution of variable D.

Theil points out that in regression theory we measure uncertainty reduction in terms of the statistic $1-R^2$, or in terms of squared error about an idealized regression line.[8] Hence, if $1-R^2$ is interpreted as the average degree of uncertainty of the dependent variable when the distribution of the predictor variables is known, relative to the uncertainty that prevailed prior to knowledge of these predictors, then it would appear that[9]

$$1-R^2 \approx 1-\frac{H_A(D)}{H(D)} \approx \frac{H(D)-H_A(D)}{H(D)} \tag{7}$$

Such a statistic provides a useful adjunct to the log-linear approach.

The analyses summarized here follow generally from the analyses in appendix C.[10] Factors that appeared important in the regression analyses or seemed salient from a policy point of view were examined to determine, first, whether supportive services did affect enrollees' chances of becoming recipients and, second, whether the effect occurred differentially for different policy-important groups.

Table D-1 presents the results of analyses in the Springfield site only. That agency kept logs of the frequency with which individual enrollees used the available services, so it is possible to define a service utilization variable that categorizes individuals according to high or low usage of services. Most analyses shown include only those enrollees planning to move to new units.

Tables D-2 through D-8 present analyses carried out for enrollees at all eight sites. In these tables each analysis is carried out for the full enrollee population, for enrollees at the four sites judged to have relatively tighter housing markets, and for enrollees planning to move in the tight-market sites. The service variable used in this analysis concerns the availability of reponsive services and is measured at the level of the site rather than the individual; that is, the variable distinguishes enrollees at the four sites offering relatively high levels of responsive services from enrollees at the four relatively low-service sites.

Table D-1. Factors Influencing Enrollee Success Rates in Springfield

Effects of Service Utilization and Plans to Move on Enrollee Success Rates in Springfield

		Plan to Move	Plan to Stay	Totals
High service	P_s	0.804	0.904	0.836
	P_s/P_f	4.097	9.171	5.112
	$\ln P_s/P_f$	1.410	2.216	1.632
Low service	P_s	0.515	0.756	0.600
	P_s/P_f	1.039	3.103	1.498
	$\ln P_s/P_f$	0.038	1.132	0.404
Totals	P_s	0.648	0.819	0.707
	P_s/P_f	1.840	4.533	2.417
	$\ln P_s/P_f$	0.610	1.511	0.883

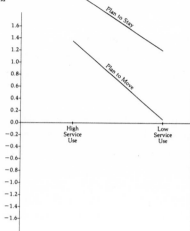

Overall reduction in uncertainty $u(Y/X) = 0.0916$

Parameter	X^2 Effect	$P_A - P_B$	$\ln P_A - \ln P_B$
A (Plans by service)	39.99	0.171	0.901
B (Service)	82.86	0.236	1.228
A × B (Plans by service)	1.67	0.141	0.288

Effects of Service Utilization and Race on Enrollee Success Rates in Springfield (Enrollees Planning to Move Only)

		Black	White	Totals
High service	P_s	0.819	0.736	0.756
	P_s/P_f	4.419	2.782	3.091
	$\ln P_s/P_f$	1.486	1.023	1.128
Low service	P_s	0.524	0.551	0.542
	P_s/P_f	1.101	1.227	1.185
	$\ln P_s/P_f$	0.096	0.205	0.170
Totals	P_s	0.643	0.648	0.646
	P_s/P_f	1.797	1.840	1.828
	$\ln P_s/P_f$	0.586	0.610	0.603

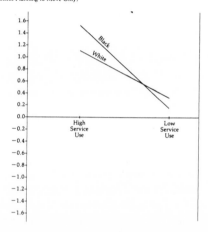

Overall reduction in uncertainty $u(Y/X) = 0.0266$

Parameter	X^2 Effect	$P_A - P_B$	$\ln P_A - \ln P_B$
A (Race)	0.02	0.005	0.024
B (Service)	36.93	0.214	0.958
A × B (Race by service)	2.31	0.110	0.572

Effects of Service Utilization and Sex of Head of Household on Enrollee Success Rates in Springfield (Enrollees Planning to Move Only)

		Female Head	Male Head	Totals
High service	P_s	0.780	0.683	0.751
	P_s/P_f	3.529	2.143	3.010
	$\ln P_s/P_f$	1.261	0.762	1.102
Low service	P_s	0.573	0.497	0.544
	P_s/P_f	1.338	0.987	1.192
	$\ln P_s/P_f$	0.291	−0.041	0.176
Totals	P_s	0.683	0.581	0.648
	P_s/P_f	2.153	1.384	1.840
	$\ln P_s/P_f$	0.767	0.325	0.610

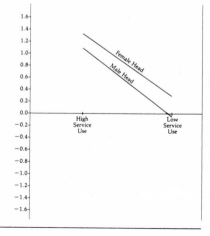

Overall reduction in uncertainty $u(Y/X) = 0.0246$

Parameter	X^2 Effect	$P_A - P_B$	$\ln P_A - \ln P_B$
A (Sex of head)	8.01	0.102	0.442
B (Service)	36.77	0.207	0.956
A × B (Sex by service)	0.36	0.021	0.194

Effects of Service Utilization and Family Size on Enrollee Success Rates in Springfield (Enrollees Planning to Move Only)

		Family Size < 4	Family Size ≥ 4	Totals
High service	P_s	0.740	0.761	0.751
	P_s/P_f	2.825	3.168	3.010
	$\ln P_s/P_f$	1.039	1.153	1.102
Low service	P_s	0.598	0.480	0.544
	P_s/P_f	1.485	0.925	1.192
	$\ln P_s/P_f$	0.396	−0.078	0.176
Totals	P_s	0.667	0.628	0.648
	P_s/P_f	2.000	1.686	1.840
	$\ln P_s/P_f$	0.693	0.522	0.610

Overall reduction in uncertainty $u(Y/X) = 0.0273$

Parameter	X^2 Effect	$P_A - P_B$	$\ln P_A - \ln P_B$
A (Family size)	1.29	0.039	0.171
B (Service)	36.77	0.207	0.926
A × B (Family size by service)	3.61	0.139	0.428

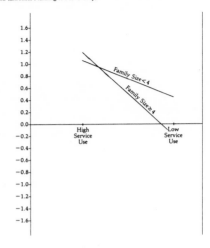

Effects of Service Utilization and Age of Head of Household on Enrollee Success Rates in Springfield (Enrollees Planning to Move Only)

		Age ≥ 62 years	Age < 62 years	Totals
High service	P_s	0.576	0.767	0.751
	P_s/P_f	1.345	3.272	3.010
	$\ln P_s/P_f$	0.296	1.185	1.102
Low service	P_s	0.478	0.549	0.544
	P_s/P_f	0.852	1.219	1.192
	$\ln P_s/P_f$	0.160	0.198	0.176
Totals	P_s	0.526	0.657	0.648
	P_s/P_f	1.111	1.919	1.840
	$\ln P_s/P_f$	0.105	0.652	0.610

Overall reduction in uncertainty $u(Y/X) = 0.0244$

Parameter	X^2 Effect	$P_A - P_B$	$\ln P_A - \ln P_B$
A (Age)	3.99	0.131	0.808
B (Service)	36.77	0.207	0.926
A × B (Age by service)	0.91	0.120	0.531

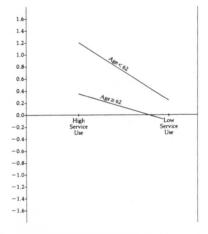

Effects of Service Utilization and Receipt of Welfare Income on Enrollee Success Rates in Springfield (Enrollees Planning to Move Only)

		Some Welfare	No Welfare	Totals
High service	P_s	0.757	0.721	0.751
	P_s/P_f	3.101	2.538	3.010
	$\ln P_s/P_f$	1.132	0.932	1.102
Low service	P_s	0.566	0.486	0.544
	P_s/P_f	1.305	0.947	1.192
	$\ln P_s/P_f$	0.266	−0.055	0.176
Totals	P_s	0.669	0.576	0.648
	P_s/P_f	2.020	1.360	1.840
	$\ln P_s/P_f$	0.703	0.307	0.610

Overall reduction in uncertainty $u(Y/X) = 0.0264$

Parameter	X^2 Effect	$P_A - P_B$	$\ln P_A - \ln P_B$
A (Welfare status)	5.13	0.093	0.660
B (Service)	36.77	0.207	0.926
A × B (Welfare by service)	0.10	0.044	0.121

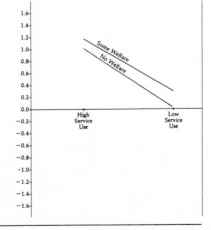

Source: AAE application, enrollment, and payments initiation forms, and site background data

Table D–2. Effects of Services, Plans to Move, and Market Tightness on Enrollee Success Rates

Effects of Services and Plans to Move on Enrollee Success Rates

		Plan to Move	Plan to Stay	Totals
High service	P_s	0.699	0.812	0.757
	P_s/P_f	2.324	4.306	3.122
	$\ln P_s/P_f$	0.843	1.460	1.138
Low service	P_s	0.550	0.819	0.676
	P_s/P_f	1.220	4.514	2.083
	$\ln P_s/P_f$	0.199	1.507	0.734
Totals	P_s	0.607	0.816	0.707
	P_s/P_f	1.546	4.427	2.407
	$\ln P_s/P_f$	0.436	1.488	0.878

Overall reduction in uncertainty $u(Y/X)=0.0525$

Parameter	X² Effect	P_A-P_B	$\ln P_A - \ln P_B$
A (Plans)	407.28	0.207	1.502
B (Service)	58.55	0.081	0.404
A×B (Plans by service)	34.19	0.156	0.691

Effects of Services and Market Tightness on Enrollee Success Rates

		Tight Markets	Loose Markets	Totals
High service	P_s	0.703	0.859	0.757
	P_s/P_f	2.368	6.099	3.122
	$\ln P_s/P_f$	0.862	1.808	1.138
Low service	P_s	0.512	0.850	0.676
	P_s/P_f	1.049	5.682	2.083
	$\ln P_s/P_f$	0.048	1.737	0.734
Totals	P_s	0.595	0.853	0.707
	P_s/P_f	1.468	5.804	2.407
	$\ln P_s/P_f$	0.384	1.758	0.878

Overall reduction in uncertainty $u(Y/X)=0.1086$

Parameter	X² Effect	P_A-P_B	$\ln P_A - \ln P_B$
A (Market)	633.09	0.258	1.374
B (Service)	58.56	0.081	0.404
A×B (Plans by service)	33.54	0.182	0.743

Effects of Plans to Move and Market Tightness on Enrollee Success Rates

		Plan to Move	Plan to Stay	Totals
Tight markets	P_s	0.489	0.744	0.595
	P_s/P_f	0.956	2.907	1.468
	$\ln P_s/P_f$	−0.045	1.067	0.384
Loose markets	P_s	0.812	0.886	0.853
	P_s/P_f	4.308	7.788	5.804
	$\ln P_s/P_f$	1.460	−2.053	1.758
Totals	P_s	0.607	0.816	0.707
	P_s/P_f	1.546	4.427	2.407
	$\ln P_s/P_f$	0.436	1.488	0.878

Overall reduction in uncertainty $u(Y/X)=0.1042$

Parameter	X² Effect	P_A-P_B	$\ln P_A - \ln P_B$
A (Plans)	407.28	0.209	1.052
B (Market)	633.09	0.258	1.374
A×B (Market by plans)	18.66	0.181	0.519

Source: AAE application, enrollment, and payments initiation forms, and site background data

Table D-3. Effects of Services and Race on Enrollee Success Rates

Full Population

		Black	White	Totals
High service	P_s	0.727	0.772	0.757
	P_s/P_f	2.665	3.382	3.122
	$\ln P_s/P_f$	0.980	1.218	1.138
Low service	P_s	0.368	0.772	0.678
	P_s/P_f	0.583	3.392	2.083
	$\ln P_s/P_f$	−0.539	1.222	0.734
Totals	P_s	0.531	0.772	0.707
	P_s/P_f	1.132	3.391	2.407
	$\ln P_s/P_f$	0.124	1.221	0.878

Overall reduction in uncertainty $u(Y/X) = 0.0730$

Parameter	X^2 Effect	$P_A - P_B$	$\ln P_A - \ln P_B$
A (Plans)	404.79	0.241	1.091
B (Service)	58.55	0.079	0.404
$A \times B$ (Plans by service)	174.10	0.359	1.523

Tight Market Sites Only

		Black	White	Totals
High service	P_s	0.711	0.708	0.709
	P_s/P_f	2.457	2.427	2.441
	$\ln P_s/P_f$	0.899	0.887	0.893
Low service	P_s	0.315	0.654	0.515
	P_s/P_f	0.460	1.889	1.062
	$\ln P_s/P_f$	−0.776	0.636	0.060
Totals	P_s	0.476	0.677	0.596
	P_s/P_f	0.909	2.095	1.475
	$\ln P_s/P_f$	−0.085	0.740	0.389

Overall reduction in uncertainty $u(Y/X) = 0.0782$

Parameter	X^2 Effect	$P_A - P_B$	$\ln P_A - \ln P_B$
A (Race)	161.55	0.201	0.835
B (Service)	155.82	0.194	0.833
$A \times B$ (Race by service)	103.02	0.342	1.424

Enrollees Planning to Move in Tight Market Sites Only

		Black	White	Totals
High service	P_s	0.653	0.634	0.643
	P_s/P_f	1.880	1.730	1.799
	$\ln P_s/P_f$	0.631	0.548	0.587
Low service	P_s	0.265	0.537	0.392
	P_s/P_f	0.361	1.161	0.645
	$\ln P_s/P_f$	−1.020	0.149	−0.439
Totals	P_s	0.400	0.578	0.489
	P_s/P_f	0.668	1.371	0.956
	$\ln P_s/P_f$	−0.403	0.315	−0.045

Overall reduction in uncertainty $u(Y/X) = 0.0786$

Parameter	X^2 Effect	$P_A - P_B$	$\ln P_A - \ln P_B$
A (Race)	80.05	0.178	0.718
B (Service)	151.84	0.251	1.026
$A \times B$ (Race by service)	53.17	0.291	1.252

Source: AAE application, enrollment, and payments initiation forms, and site background data

Table D-4. Effects of Services and Sex of Head of Household on Enrollee Success Rates

Full Population

		Female Head	Male Head	Totals
High service	P_s	0.773	0.735	0.759
	P_s/P_f	3.402	2.767	3.156
	$\ln P_s/P_f$	1.224	1.018	1.149
Low service	P_s	0.661	0.723	0.683
	P_s/P_f	1.953	2.614	2.150
	$\ln P_s/P_f$	0.669	0.961	0.765
Totals	P_s	0.702	0.728	0.711
	P_s/P_f	2.358	2.673	2.461
	$\ln P_s/P_f$	0.858	0.983	0.901

Overall reduction in uncertainty $u(Y/X) = 0.0086$

Parameter	X^2 Effect	$P_A - P_B$	$\ln P_A - \ln P_B$
A (Sex of head)	5.80	0.026	0.125
B (Service)	55.13	0.076	0.384
$A \times B$ (Sex by service)	20.65	0.100	0.498

Tight Market Sites Only

		Female Head	Male Head	Totals
High service	P_s	0.722	0.687	0.709
	P_s/P_f	2.593	2.194	2.441
	$\ln P_s/P_f$	0.953	0.786	0.893
Low service	P_s	0.508	0.535	0.515
	P_s/P_f	1.032	1.153	1.062
	$\ln P_s/P_f$	0.031	0.142	0.060
Totals	P_s	0.590	0.611	0.596
	P_s/P_f	1.438	1.569	1.475
	$\ln P_s/P_f$	0.363	0.451	0.389

Overall reduction in uncertainty $u(Y/X) = 0.0300$

Parameter	X^2 Effect	$P_A - P_B$	$\ln P_A - \ln P_B$
A (Sex of head)	1.45	0.021	0.088
B (Service)	155.83	0.194	0.833
$A \times B$ (Sex by service)	3.65	0.062	0.278

Enrollees Planning to Move in Tight Market Sites Only

		Female Head	Male Head	Totals
High service	P_s	0.669	0.592	0.643
	P_s/P_f	2.016	1.450	1.800
	$\ln P_s/P_f$	0.701	0.372	0.587
Low service	P_s	0.380	0.431	0.3922
	P_s/P_f	0.614	0.758	0.645
	$\ln P_s/P_f$	−0.488	−0.277	−0.438
Totals	P_s	0.481	0.508	0.489
	P_s/P_f	0.928	1.032	0.956
	$\ln P_s/P_f$	−0.074	0.032	−0.045

Overall reduction in uncertainty $u(Y/X) = 0.0463$

Parameter	X^2 Effect	$P_A - P_B$	$\ln P_A - \ln P_B$
A (Sex of head)	1.41	0.027	0.106
B (Service)	151.84	0.251	1.025
$A \times B$ (Sex by service)	8.49	0.128	0.540

Source: AAE application, enrollment, and payments initiation forms, and site background data

Table D-5. Effects of Services and Family Size on Enrollee Success Rates

Full Population

		Family Size ≥ 4	Family Size < 4	Totals
High service	P_s	0.721	0.767	0.758
	P_s/P_f	2.578	3.281	3.126
	$\ln P_s/P_f$	0.947	1.188	1.140
Low service	P_s	0.596	0.696	0.676
	P_s/P_f	1.474	2.292	2.083
	$\ln P_s/P_f$	0.388	0.829	0.734
Totals	P_s	0.641	0.723	0.707
	P_s/P_f	1.789	2.610	2.408
	$\ln P_s/P_f$	0.582	0.960	0.879

Overall reduction in uncertainty $u(Y/X) = 0.0107$

Parameter	X^2 Effect	$P_A - P_B$	$\ln P_A - \ln P_B$
A (Family size)	38.35	0.082	0.378
B (Service)	58.93	0.082	0.406
A × B (Family size by service)	2.41	0.054	0.201

Tight Market Sites Only

		Family Size ≥ 4	Family Size < 4	Totals
High service	P_s	0.653	0.741	0.711
	P_s/P_f	1.878	2.862	2.457
	$\ln P_s/P_f$	0.630	1.052	0.899
Low service	P_s	0.434	0.571	0.515
	P_s/P_f	0.766	1.330	1.063
	$\ln P_s/P_f$	−0.267	0.285	0.061
Totals	P_s	0.517	0.646	0.597
	P_s/P_f	1.069	1.822	1.479
	$\ln P_s/P_f$	0.0667	0.600	0.391

Overall reduction in uncertainty $u(Y/X) = 0.0418$

Parameter	X^2 Effect	$P_A - P_B$	$\ln P_A - \ln P_B$
A (Family size)	65.18	0.129	0.533
B (Service)	157.44	0.196	0.838
A × B (Family size by service)	0.87	0.049	0.130

Enrollees Planning to Move in Tight Market Sites Only

		Family Size ≥ 4	Family Size < 4	Totals
High service	P_s	0.584	0.685	0.644
	P_s/P_f	1.405	2.174	1.809
	$\ln P_s/P_f$	0.340	0.776	0.593
Low service	P_s	0.360	0.421	0.392
	P_s/P_f	0.564	0.728	0.645
	$\ln P_s/P_f$	−0.573	−0.318	−0.438
Totals	P_s	0.437	0.531	0.489
	P_s/P_f	0.777	1.131	0.958
	$\ln P_s/P_f$	−0.252	0.123	−0.043

Overall reduction in uncertainty $u(Y/X) = 0.0490$

Parameter	X^2 Effect	$P_A - P_B$	$\ln P_A - \ln P_B$
A (Family size)	21.08	0.094	0.375
B (Service)	152.93	0.252	1.031
A × B (Family size by service)	1.12	0.040	0.181

Source: AAE application, enrollment, and payments initiation forms, and site background data

Table D-6. Effects of Services and Age of Head of Household on Enrollee Success Rates

Full Population

		Age ≥ 62 years	Age < 62 years	Totals
High service	P_s	0.806	0.746	0.757
	P_s/P_f	4.142	2.926	3.122
	ln P_s/P_f	1.421	1.075	1.138
Low service	P_s	0.767	0.650	0.676
	P_s/P_f	3.294	1.875	2.083
	ln P_s/P_f	1.192	0.628	0.734
Totals	P_s	0.782	0.688	0.707
	P_s/P_f	3.580	2.202	2.407
	ln P_s/P_f	1.275	0.789	0.878

Overall reduction in uncertainty $u(Y/X) = 0.0115$

Parameter	X^2 Effect	$P_A - P_B$	ln P_A – ln P_B
A (Age)	53.95	0.094	0.486
B (Service)	58.55	0.081	0.404
A × B (Age by service)	2.26	0.057	0.218

Tight Market Sites Only

		Age ≥ 62 years	Age < 62 years	Totals
High service	P_s	0.768	0.697	0.709
	P_s/P_f	3.296	2.301	2.441
	ln P_s/P_f	1.193	0.833	0.893
Low service	P_s	0.712	0.476	0.515
	P_s/P_f	2.471	0.910	1.062
	ln P_s/P_f	0.905	−0.095	0.060
Totals	P_s	0.736	0.568	0.596
	P_s/P_f	2.792	1.314	1.475
	ln P_s/P_f	1.027	0.273	0.389

Overall reduction in uncertainty $u(Y/X) = 0.0441$

Parameter	X^2 Effect	$P_A - P_B$	ln P_A – ln P_B
A (Age)	68.89	0.168	0.754
B (Service)	155.83	0.194	0.833
A × B (Age by service)	10.70	0.165	0.640

Enrollees Planning to Move in Tight Market Sites Only

		Age ≥ 62 years	Age < 62 years	Totals
High service	P_s	0.650	0.642	0.643
	P_s/P_f	1.849	1.792	1.799
	ln P_s/P_f	0.615	0.583	0.587
Low service	P_s	0.519	0.380	0.392
	P_s/P_f	1.079	0.614	0.645
	ln P_s/P_f	0.076	−0.488	−0.439
Totals	P_s	0.577	0.488	0.489
	P_s/P_f	1.364	0.954	0.956
	ln P_s/P_f	0.310	−0.047	−0.045

Overall reduction in uncertainty $u(Y/X) = 0.0519$

Parameter	X^2 Effect	$P_A - P_B$	ln P_A – ln P_B
A (Age)	8.00	0.089	0.348
B (Service)	151.84	0.251	1.026
A × B (Age by service)	3.45	0.131	0.107

Source: AAE application, enrollment, and payments initiation forms, and site background data

Table D-7. Effects of Services and Receipt of Welfare Income on Enrollee Success Rates

Full Population

		Some Welfare	No Welfare	Totals
High service	P_s	0.772	0.735	0.759
	P_s/P_f	3.383	2.773	3.156
	$\ln P_s/P_f$	1.219	1.020	1.149
Low service	P_s	0.688	0.672	0.6825
	P_s/P_f	2.202	2.049	2.150
	$\ln P_s/P_f$	0.789	0.717	0.765
Totals	P_s	0.719	0.696	0.707
	P_s/P_f	2.555	2.287	2.407
	$\ln P_s/P_f$	0.938	0.827	0.878

Overall reduction in uncertainty $u(Y/X) = 0.0067$

Parameter	X^2 Effect	$P_A - P_B$	$\ln P_A - \ln P_B$
A (Welfare)	4.62	0.023	0.111
B (Service)	55.00	0.076	0.384
$A \times B$ (Welfare by service)	1.61	0.021	0.127

Tight Market Sites Only

		Some Welfare	No Welfare	Totals
High service	P_s	0.726	0.651	0.705
	P_s/P_f	2.646	1.867	2.390
	$\ln P_s/P_f$	0.973	0.624	0.971
Low service	P_s	0.512	0.518	0.514
	P_s/P_f	1.047	1.074	1.056
	$\ln P_s/P_f$	0.046	0.071	0.055
Totals	P_s	0.610	0.570	0.598
	P_s/P_f	1.565	1.325	1.485
	$\ln P_s/P_f$	0.448	0.282	0.396

Overall reduction in uncertainty $u(Y/X) = 0.0304$

Parameter	X^2 Effect	$P_A - P_B$	$\ln P_A - \ln P_B$
A (Welfare)	6.37	0.040	0.240
B (Service)	167.78	0.191	0.816
$A \times B$ (Welfare by service)	7.35	0.081	0.374

Enrollees Planning to Move in Tight Market Sites Only

		Some Welfare	No Welfare	Totals
High service	P_s	0.672	0.570	0.644
	P_s/P_f	2.045	1.325	1.811
	$\ln P_s/P_f$	0.716	0.281	0.594
Low service	P_s	0.392	0.378	0.394
	P_s/P_f	0.645	0.662	0.650
	$\ln P_s/P_f$	−0.439	−0.412	−0.431
Totals	P_s	0.505	0.460	0.492
	P_s/P_f	1.020	0.853	0.968
	$\ln P_s/P_f$	0.020	−0.159	−0.032

Overall reduction in uncertainty $u(Y/X) = 0.0464$

Parameter	X^2 Effect	$P_A - P_B$	$\ln P_A - \ln P_B$
A (Welfare)	4.26	0.045	0.179
B (Service)	155.93	0.250	1.025
$A \times B$ (Welfare by service)	6.32	0.108	0.462

Source: AAE application, enrollment, and payments initiation forms, and site background data

Table D-8. Chi-Square Summary Table for
Predicting Success in Becoming a Recipient for All Eight Predictor Variables

Mean Effects		Selected[a] Two-way Interactions	
Parameter	χ^2 effects	Parameter	χ^2 effects
Welfare status	3.59	Age × Market	28.74***
Age of head	43.15***	Race × Service	102.72***
Race of head	378.99***	Sex × Service	18.07***
Service type	51.81***	Market × Service	29.03***
Sex of head	4.20*	Plans × Service	25.06***
Market condition	543.61***	Family size × Sex	10.31**
Family size	80.45***	Family size × Market	12.19***
Move plans	424.07***	Plans × Market	15.69

Overall reduction in uncertainty $u(Y/X) = 0.1835$

Source: AAE application, enrollment, and payments initiation forms and site background data

[a]Only terms greater than 10.00 are reported here.
χ^2 (no-effects model) = 1473.67; df = 134
χ^2 (main-effects model) = 364.99; df = 127
χ^2 (two-way interaction model) = 172.53; df = 98
*$0.01 \leq p \leq 0.01$
**$0.01 \leq p \leq 0.05$, df = 1
***$0.01 \leq p \leq 0.001$

NOTES

1. Leo A. Goodman, "The Multivariate Analysis of Qualitative Data: Inter-actions among Multiple Classifications," *Journal of the American Statistical Association* 65 (1970): 226–256; Leo A. Goodman, "The Analysis of Multidi-mensional Contingency Tables: Stepwise Procedures and Direct Estimation Methods for Building Models for Multiple Classifications," *Technometrics* 13 (1971): 33–61; Leo A. Goodman, "A Modified Multiple Regression Approach to the Analysis of Dichotomous Variables," *American Sociolo-gical Review* 37 (1972): 28–46; Yvonne Bishop, Stephen Feinberg, and Paul Holland, *Discrete Multivariate Analysis: Theory and Practice* (Cambridge, Mass.: MIT Press, 1975).

2. Goodman, "Analysis of Multidimensional Contingency Tables;" "Modified Multiple Regression Approach." See Bishop, Feinberg, and Holland, *Dis-crete Multivariate Analysis;* Ruth A. Killian and Douglas A. Zahn, "A Bib-liography of Contingency Table Literature: 1900 to 1974," *International Sta-tistics Review* 44: 71–112, for recent reviews.

3. Notation used in this paper is consistent with that used by Goodman, "Modified Multiple Regression Approach." The β_1^{AC} term refers to the weighting constant for the first category of predictor variable A for the natural logarithm of the odds of success to failure on dependent variable C. The β_{11}^{ABC} term refers to the weighting constant for the first category of variable A and the first category of variable B relative to the natural logarithm of the odds for dependent variable C. When the appropriate terms are added to the weighting constant α, the result equals the natural logarithm of the odds on dependent variable C for the appropriate cell (i,j) of the multiway contingency table.

4. Goodman, "Analysis of Multidimensional Contingency Tables," pp. 43 ff.

5. The various chi-squared terms are defined algebraically as follows:

    $\chi^2(A) = \chi^2(C) - \chi^2(C|A)$ where $\chi^2(C)$ is the chi-squared effect when only the distribution of the dependent variable is known, and $\chi^2(C|A)$ is the effect on predicting the dependent variable (C) given the independent variable (A).

    $\chi^2(B) = \chi^2(C) - \chi^2(C|B)$
    $\chi^2(A \times B) = \chi^2(C|A,B) - 0.0$

6. See Allen L. Edwards, *Experimental Design in Psychological Research* (New York: Holt, Rinehart and Winston, 1968).

7. Henri Theil, "On the Estimation of Relationships Involving Qualitative Variables," *American Journal of Sociology* 76 (1970): 103–154.

8. *Ibid.*

9. *Ibid.*, pp. 133–134.

10. For a complete discussion, see Holshouser, *Supportive Services*, appendix D.

Appendix E

Analysis of Eligibility Status and Adjustments to Reported Income

A series of multivariate analyses was carried out in the investigation of certification procedures. Results of some of those analyses are reproduced here.[1]

Table E-1 presents the results of a logit analysis of elgibility status (defined by an agency decision, based either on initial screening or on subsequent certification, that an applicant was eligible or ineligible). The three models shown in the table consider the hypotheses that the probability of being found ineligible is related to outreach (the means by which the applicant heard of the program), to individual characteristics, to the length of time the program had been in operation, or to unique characteristics of the various agencies.

Tables E-2 and E-3 report on logit analyses of the probability that certification activities would result in a change in the income that an applicant reported on the application form (excluding changes of less than $50 per year). The analyses consider household characteristics, certification procedures, the passage of time between application and certification, and a few other factors (the local unemployment rate, length of time since program operations began) as possible determinants of the probability of a change.

Table E-1. Determinants of Eligibility Status

Model I

Variable[a]	β	t-Statistic
Referral	-0.738	-8.06*
Media	0.064	0.94
Other outreach	-0.228	-1.05
Program month	-0.142	-10.02*
Salem	-2.789	-22.04*
Springfield	-2.300	-17.63*
Peoria	-2.147	-16.77*
San Bernardino	-2.204	-21.23*
Tulsa	-1.053	-11.10
Jacksonville	-1.972	-16.25*
Durham	-1.767	-14.84*
Chi square	13,740	

Model II

Variable[a]	β	t-Statistic
Sex	-0.582	-8.55*
Race	0.029	0.35
Age	-1.259	-12.06*
Income	0.001	32.29*
Household size	-0.601	-19.39*
Salem	-2.040	-12.93*
Springfield	-2.107	-12.92*
Peoria	-2.106	-12.88*
San Bernardino	-1.007	-6.54*
Tulsa	-0.428	-3.30*
Jacksonville	-1.052	-6.38*
Durham	-1.131	-6.49*
Chi square	15,577	

Model III

Variable[a]	β	t-Statistic
Sex	-0.520	-7.51*
Race	0.048	0.56
Referral	-0.022	-0.20
Media	0.010	0.12
Other outreach	0.014	0.59
Age	-1.125	-10.47*
Program month	-0.110	-5.48*
Income	0.001	31.98*
Household size	-0.591	-19.06*
Salem	-1.970	-12.35*
Springfield	-1.885	-11.09*
Peoria	-1.880	-10.99*
San Bernardino	-1.099	-7.01*
Tulsa	-.250	-1.82
Jacksonville	-.897	-5.31*
Durham	-1.066	-6.04*
Chi square	15,607	

Source: AAE application forms

Data base: Applicants ($N = 15,087$; missing cases, 312)

[a]Dichotomous variables coded as follows: Race is calibrated as 1 for minority, 2 for nonminority; Sex as 1 for male, 2 for female. The outreach variables are 0_1, calibrated as 1 for referral, 0 otherwise; 0_2, as 1 for media, 0 otherwise, and 0_3, as 1 for other, 0 otherwise. The default value ($0_1 = 0_2 = 0_3 = 0$) is word of mouth. Each site variable is calibrated as 1 for that site, 0 otherwise. The default case (Salem = Springfield = . . . = Tulsa = 0) is Bismarck.

*Probability less than 0.05.

Roughly the same factors are included in subsequent analysis, which examined the magnitude of adjustments to reported income (table E-4), whether adjustments increased or decreased reported income (table E-6). Table E-5 considers the "allocation effect" of certification—that is, the absolute difference between the benefits for which an applicant would qualify on the basis of income and household size reported at application and the benefits after adjustment by certification. Table E-7 examines the extent to which the agencies' choice of certification procedures in individual cases was related to household and programmatic characteristics.

Table E-2.   Logit Analysis of Incidence
of Nontrivial Income Change in Seven AAE Sites

Independent Variables	Beta	t-Value
Age	−0.131	−6.201*
Female	−0.250	−4.441*
Black	0.043	0.743
Spanish	−0.347	−2.829*
Income (thousands)	−0.086	−5.385*
Percentage grant income	0.020	5.847*
(Percentage grant^2)	−0.0003	−8.159*
Household size change	0.713	8.014*
Unemployment rate	0.038	4.213*
Elapsed time (ten-day units)	0.151	9.006*
(Elapsed time^2)	−0.003	−3.347*
Program month	0.088	6.585*
Complete third party[a]	1.339	19.845*
Complete documentation[a]	1.127	13.117*
Complete mixture[a]	1.843	11.161*
Partial third party[a]	1.182	8.566*
Partial documentation[a]	0.718	7.651*
Constant	−1.120	

Source: AAE application and certification forms
Data base: Certified applicants in all sites except Bismarck ($N = 7,724$, excluding 247 ineligible applicants; missing cases, 151)
Note: Chi-square value, 177.8; chi-square statistics with 18 df; $N = 7,724$.
[a]The excluded category is self-declaration. The partial-mixture method includes only eleven cases and is therefore omitted from the analysis.
*Probability less than 0.05.

Table E-3. Logit Analysis of Incidence
of Nontrivial Income Change in Seven AAE Sites

Independent Variables	Beta	t-Value	X² Value	Number of Cases
Part A: Documentary verification excluded			1162.6[a]	7,734
Age	−0.129	−6.106*		
Female	−0.266	−4.744*		
Black	0.044	0.756		
Spanish	−0.356	−2.912*		
Income (thousands)	−0.117	−2.772*		
Percentage grant income	0.018	5.336*		
(Percentage grant²)	−0.0002	−7.657*		
Household size change	0.713	7.995*		
Unemployment rate	0.030	3.376*		
Elapsed time (ten-day units)	0.150	8.995*		
(Elapsed time²)	−0.003	−3.280*		
Program month	0.084	6.625*		
Third party verification	0.351	5.314*		
Mixture	0.891	5.540*		
Self-declaration	−0.951	−12.965*		
Constant	−0.043			
Part B: Partial verification excluded			1148.2[b]	7,734
Age	−0.127	−6.049*		
Female	−0.243	−4.325*		
Black	0.039	0.669		
Spanish	−0.319	−2.609*		
Income (thousands)	−0.111	−2.631*		
Percentage grant	0.025	7.294*		
(Percentage grant²)	−0.0003	−9.603*		
Household size change	0.705	7.949*		
Unemployment rate	0.034	3.765*		
Elapsed time (ten-day units)	0.159	9.527*		
(Elapsed time²)	−0.004	−3.741*		
Program month	0.090	6.738*		
Complete verification	0.458	5.835*		
Self-declaration	−0.858	−10.215*		
Constant	−0.271			

Source: AAE application and certification forms
Data Base: Certified applicants in all sites excluding Bismarck (N=7,734, excluding 247
ineligible applicants; missing cases, 141)
[a]Chi-square statistics with 17 df
[b]Chi-square statistics with 16 df
*Probability less than 0.05

Table E-4. Regression Analysis of the
Magnitude of Income Changes in Seven AAE Sites

Independent Variables	Regression Coefficient	Standardized Coefficient	F
Age	−105.8	−0.132	68.681*
Female	−233.9	−0.017	48.369*
Black	17.4	0.007	0.238
Spanish	18.4	0.003	0.054
Income (thousands)	−245.3	−0.456	72.795*
(Income²)	26.4	0.453	77.349*
Percentage grant income	−4.0	−0.176	94.338*
Household size change	299.9	0.145	101.254*
Unemployment rate	16.7	0.047	8.640*
Elapsed time (ten-day units)	59.0	0.255	40.483*
(Elapsed time²)	−2.2	−0.178	20.496*
Program month	1.3	0.002	0.026
Complete third party[a]	−199.4	−0.094	20.443*
Complete documentation[a]	−245.1	−0.085	20.489*
Complete mixture[a]	13.4	0.003	0.027
Partial third party[a]	−93.6	−0.018	1.356
Partial documentation[a]	3.0	0.001	0.002
Constant	1754.7		

Source: AAE application and certification forms
Data Base: Certified applicants with income changes in all sites except Bismarck ($N=4{,}207$, excluding 247 ineligible applicants; missing cases, 116)
Note: $R^2=0.15$; $N=4{,}207$.
[a]Excluded category: Self-declaration.
*Probability less than 0.05

Table E-5.   Regression Analysis of Allocation Effect of Certification

	Actual Allocation Effect (With Special Deductions)	
Independent Variables	Regression coefficient	F-statistic
Age of head of household	−11.714	28.36*
Female head of household	−29.743	28.16*
Black head of household	−9.020	2.33
Spanish-speaking head of household	−32.547	6.52*
Total income reported at application	−0.013	50.41*
Percent of income from grants	−0.936	180.92*
Number of persons in household at application	17.885	114.38*
Local unemployment rate	3.154	10.37*
Elapsed time	7.591	150.78*
Program month	2.134	2.59
Income certification method		
Complete third party	34.208	31.24*
Complete documentation	28.126	10.99*
Partial third party	24.568	5.75
Constant	131.295	
R^2 (adjusted)	0.109	

Source: AAE application and certification forms
Note: Certification methods that represent 5 percent or less of the cases are excluded.
*Probability less than 0.05

Table E-6. Logit Analysis of Direction of Income Changes in Seven AAE Sites

Independent Variables	Beta	t-Value
Age	−0.021	−0.719
Female	−0.279	−3.632*
Black	0.206	2.532*
Spanish	−0.119	−0.679
Income (thousands)	−0.277	−12.472*
Percentage grant	−0.030	−6.859*
(Percentage grant²)	0.0003	7.125*
Household size change	−0.089	−1.335
Unemployment rate	0.025	1.910
Elapsed time (ten-day units)	−0.033	−1.587
(Elapsed time²)	0.002	1.769
Program month	−0.057	−3.021*
Complete third party	0.298	3.038*
Complete documentation	0.067	0.559
Complete mixture	0.697	3.765*
Partial third party	0.873	4.591*
Partial documentation	0.607	4.436*
Constant	1.997	

Source: AAE application and certification forms
Data base: Certified applicants with income changes in all sites except Bismarck ($N=$ 4,207, excluding 247 ineligible applicants; missing cases, 116)
Note: Chi-square value, 751.2; chi-square statistics with 18 df; N=4,207.
*Probability less than 0.05

Table E-7. Logit Analysis of Likelihood of Verification

Independent Variables	Beta	t-Value	X² Value	Number of Cases
Peoria			1074.4ᵃ	1,449
Age	−0.039	−0.636		
Female	−0.030	−0.148		
Nonwhite	0.055	0.231		
Income (thousands)	0.435	6.814*		
Percentage grant	0.010	4.985*		
Household size change	0.336	0.980		
Elapsed time (ten-day units)	0.023	0.473		
Program month	−0.204	−3.239*		
Constant	1.368			
San Bernardino			53.8ᵇ	1,000
Age	−0.073	−1.289		
Female	−0.038	−0.256		
Black	−0.432	−1.925		
Spanish	0.617	3.576*		
Income (thousands)	−0.019	−0.456		
Percentage grant	0.001	0.737		
Household size change	0.279	1.695		
Elapsed time (ten-day units)	0.014	0.565		
Program month	−0.214	−3.613*		
Constant	1.230			
Jacksonville			147.3ᵃ	1,143
Age	−0.078	−1.242		
Female	0.528	3.088*		
Nonwhite	−0.367	−2.489*		
Income (thousands)	0.283	5.869*		
Percentage grant	−0.001	−0.590		
Household size change	−0.461	−2.212*		
Elapsed time (ten-day units)	0.006	0.275		
Program month	−0.200	−6.363*		
Constant	0.821			

Source: AAE application and certification forms
Data base: Certified applicants ($N=3,592$, excluding 13 ineligible applicants; missing cases, 22)
ᵃChi-square statistics with 9 df
ᵇChi-square statistics with 10 df
*Probability less than 0.05

NOTES

1. A full description and discussion of these analyses is presented in Donald E. Dickson, *Certification: Determining Eligibility and Setting Payment Levels in the Administrative Agency Experiment* (Cambridge, Mass. Abt Associates, 1977), appendices B, C, D, and E.

Appendix F

Indirect Cost Relationships in the Administrative Cost Simulation Model

MANAGEMENT SUPPORT

For the equation

$$Y = ax^b$$

where

Y = the number of staff required for the management support function excluding the director

x = the number of staff from all other functions

the value of a and b were obtained by regressing the natural log of the number of full-time equivalent staff for the function management support and relations with suppliers on the natural log of the number of full-time equivalent staff in all nonmanagement functions.[1] Each site provided two data points for the regression: one from the enrollment period, the other from the second program year.

For analysis, the number of full-time equivalent staff was calculated as follows. The yearly average paid leave rate (vacation, holidays, and sick time as a fraction of total time) at each site, based on the first twenty-four program months, was computed. The number of hours that represent one full-time equivalent staff member at each site for each period (enrollment and maintenance) was determined by dividing the total number of work hours in the time period by one plus the paid leave rate. The resulting number is referred to as the average FTE hours.

For each site and time period the number of staff hours charged to the management support function was computed and divided by the average FTE hours to obtain the number of full-time equivalents for that site and time period. The number of full-time equivalents in the nonmanagement functions was obtained by summing hours charged to screening, enrollment, certification, inspection, associated services, payment operations, and audit and control, and dividing this total by the average FTE hours.

Data from Tulsa for the enrollment period were excluded because of the large amount of subcontracting at that time. San Bernardino was not included at either time period because the proportion of management support staff there was out of range of the proportion of that staff at any other site. The resulting coefficients were

$$\ln Y = -0.18081 + 0.6197 \ln X \quad R^2 = 0.69$$
$$Y = 0.8346x^{0.6197} \quad\quad\quad F = 24.66$$

where

Y = number of full-time equivalent staff in management support and relations with suppliers

x = number of nonmanagement full-time equivalent staff

MAINTENANCE OF RECORDS FUNCTION

This function has two components: maintenance of records for recipients and the maintenance of records for enrollees and applicants.

The equation estimating requirements for recipients was

$$Y = ax^b$$

where

Y = number of management staff required for maintaining recipient records

x = the average number of recipients in the second program year

The value of a and b were obtained by regressing the natural log of the number of full-time equivalent staff in maintenance of records at each site during the maintenance period (program year 2, when no new recipients were entering the program) on the average number of recipients at each site during that year. The number of full-time equivalents at each site was adjusted by the following multiplicative factor before being entered as data for the regression:

Salem	0.6
Peoria	0.95
San Bernardino	0.875
Bismarck	0.5
Jacksonville	0.82
Durham	0.85

These adjustment factors were obtained from the sites as estimates of the portion of their maintenance-of-records work load that was devoted to nonexperimental record keeping (excluding record keeping done solely for data needed by Abt Associates). Tulsa was excluded from the regression because the amount of subcontracting there inflated the proportion of total staff time spent on maintenance of records. Springfield was excluded because maintenance-of-records time was charged to individual services functions, and it was impossible to isolate the actual amount of time devoted to record keeping.

The regression yielded the following results:

$$\ln Y = -2.51804 + 0.43987 \ln x \qquad R^2 = 0.66$$
$$F = 7.6$$

where

Y = number of full-time staff in maintenance of records
x = number of recipient years

For the maintenance of records for applicants and enrollees, the basic equation is again $Y = ax^b$, where Y is the number of management staff required for maintaining applicant and enrollee records and x is the number of applicants and enrollees in the program during the enrollment period. The values of a and b were obtained by regressing the natural log of the number of full-time equivalent staff in maintenance of records at each site during the enrollment period on the number of applicants plus new enrollees. The number of full-time equivalents at each site was adjusted by the same multiplicative factors used in determining the coefficients for maintenance of records for recipients.

The coefficients obtained from the regression were

$$\ln Y = -7.3219 + 0.99134 \ln x \qquad R^2 = 0.8786$$
$$Y = 0.00065 \, x^{0.99134} \qquad\qquad F = 28.95$$

SPACE AND UTILITY COSTS

Annual costs for space and utilities at the agencies are expected to depend principally on the number of staff required for administering the program. AAE data on numbers of staff used in this analysis come from the enrollment period and are used in units of full-time equivalents (FTE). It is believed that agencies planned their first-year space requirements in accordance with the expected staff size during the enrollment period, purchasing sufficient space for the enrollment period even though staff size would be reduced during the last few months of the year. The Salem agency, which shared space with the housing authority of the city of Salem, was omitted from the analysis.

After the number of staff, the most influential factor expected to affect space and utility costs was rental market conditions. As a proxy measure of commercial rental market conditions, the housing vacancy rate was used. The total vacancy rate was corrected for the estimated percentage of substandard housing units. It is expected that space and utility costs would vary with the tightness of the housing rental market: as vacancy rates decrease, space and utility costs should increase. In the analysis, conditions were measured relative to the average vacancy rate observed across the eight agency sites. Letting VR denote housing market vacancy rate and PS denote the percentage of substandard, then the proxy measure for housing market tightness is defined as MKT $=1/(\text{VR}(1-\text{PS}))$.

The resultant model used to explain space and utility costs is

$$\text{SU} = a + b \bullet \text{FTE} + c \bullet [\text{MKT} - \overline{\text{MKT}}] + u \qquad (1)$$

where

$\text{SU} =$ annual space and utility costs

$\text{FTE} =$ average number of full time equivalent staff

$[\text{MKT} - \overline{\text{MKT}}] =$ deviation of rental market conditions from the average

$u =$ random disturbance term

$a, b, c =$ regression coefficients to be estimated

The parameter estimates for the space and utility cost equations were estimated using multiple regression. The equation estimated was

$$SU = -551 + 983 \, FTE + 459 \, [MKT - 17.24] \qquad (2)$$
$$(218) + (123)$$

$$R^2 = 0.91$$
$$F = 21.4$$
$$n = 7$$

NOTES

1. The relations-with-suppliers function, which accounted for a very small proportion of indirect costs, was combined with the management support function for this analysis.

Index

applicant characteristics,
155–58
eligibility and income, 135–75
interacts with application and
enrollment, 160–63
process of, table, 136
recertification, 163–70
Certification methods, 233
and changes in income data,
149
cost of, 153–55
Changes in
circumstances, 138
household size, 156
income, 164
location patterns, 71
projected income and
certification, 148–50
Collection of data, 185–86
on dwelling units, 90–99,
124–26
Controlling inspection costs,
103–05
Cost
administration, 181–225
analyses, 77
attracting special groups, 34
attrition, 215–18
certification procedure, 166,
168
family, 194–97
future research, 122–126
implications, 62–65
initial certification, 152–55
inspections, 99–105
intake and maintenance,
190–92, 203–08
policy considerations, 221–25
program phase, 220
savings, 96

variation importance (intake
functions), 202
Cost per enrollee of mixed-
method inspection
strategies, table, 104
Cost of intake functions by site,
198
Cost per participant, by level
and method of services
offered, table, 62
Crowding, reduction of, 114,
120–21, 122
Counseling, 50, 74, 77

Data
AAE, 9–11
Data collection, 237
and analysis strategy, 185–86
on dwelling units, 124–26
Demand experiment, 3, 4, 5
Department of Housing and
Urban Development
(HUD), 3, 4–5, 7–8, 11,
12, 53, 66, 105, 111, 139,
221, 237
Detailed elicitation and avoid-
ance of error, 162–63
Direct costs, 182, 183, 187,
197–208, 214, 215, 232
attributable to attrition, 216
vs. indirect costs, 194
Disaggregating housing allow-
ance program costs, 183
Discretionary decisions of
choice of procedures, 158
housing standards, 112
Discrimination, 56, 57
Dissatisfaction, 70
Dropout rates. *See* Attrition